WIT...WN

VALUE
CLARIFICATION

As Learning Process

A SOURCEBOOK

Dedicated to my wife and children for
their patience in the process

VALUE
CLARIFICATION

as Learning Process

A SOURCEBOOK

by
BRIAN P. HALL

Consultant Authors:
MICHAEL KENNEY
MAURY SMITH

EDUCATOR FORMATION SERIES DIRECTOR:
Richard J. Payne

Design Consultant: Marion Faller
Design Mechanicals: Joanne Cossa
Cover Drawing: Rita Corbin
Photography © 1973 Dale Strohl

Library of Congress Catalogue Card Number: 73-81108
ISBN -0-8091-1773-8

Published by Paulist Press
Editorial Office: 1865 Broadway
            New York, New York 10023
Business Office: 400 Sette Drive
            Paramus, New Jersey 07652

Printed and bound in the United States of America

ACKNOWLEDGMENTS

Roberto Assagioli, M. D., *PSYCHOSYNTHESIS*. Hobbs, Dorman and Company, Inc., New York, 2nd ptg., 1969. With permission of the publishers.

Ludwig Binswanger, Excerpt from "Extravagance" in *BEING-IN-THE-WORLD: SELECTED PAPERS OF LUDWIG BINSWANGER*, translated by Jacob Needleman. Copyright © 1963 by Basic Books, Inc., Publishers, New York. Used with permission.

THE CAMBRIDGE ANCIENT HISTORY, Volume V, (1927) "Athens 478-401 B.C.," Reprinted by permission of Cambridge University Press.

Lewis Carroll, *ALICE IN WONDERLAND AND THROUGH THE LOOKING GLASS*. New York: Grosset & Dunlap, Inc., Companion Library Edition.

Miguel Cervantes, *DON QUIXOTE,* Translated by Walter Starkie. Used by permission of Macmillan, London and Basingstoke.

Kenneth Clark, *CIVILISATION*. New York: Harper & Row, 1969. Used with permission.

Harvey Cox, Excerpts from *THE FEAST OF FOOLS* reprinted by permission of the publishers, Harvard University Press, Cambridge, Mass., Copyright © 1969 by Harvey Cox.

Sebastian de Grazia, *OF TIME, WORK AND LEISURE*. Copyright © 1962 by The Twentieth Century Fund, New York. Used with permission.

Miguel de Unamuno, *THE TRAGIC SENSE OF LIFE,* translated by Crawford Flitch. Used by permission of Macmillan, London and Basingstoke.

Jacques Ellul, *THE TECHNOLOGICAL SOCIETY,* translated by John Wilkinson. Copyright © 1964 Alfred A. Knopf, Inc., New York. Used with permission.

Richard I. Evans, *DIALOGUE WITH ERIC FROMM*. New York, Harper & Row, 1968. Used with permission.

Viktor E. Frankl, *THE DOCTOR AND THE SOUL: FROM PSYCHOTHERAPY TO LOGOTHERAPY.* Copyright © 1965, rev. ed., Alfred A. Knopf, Inc., New York. Used with permission.

Viktor Frankl, *PSYCHOTHERAPY AND EXISTENTIALISM.* Copyright © 1967 by Viktor Frankl. Reprinted by permission of Washington Square Press. Division of Simon & Schuster, Inc., New York.

Erich Fromm, *THE SANE SOCIETY*. New York: Holt, Rinehart and Winston, 1955, London, Routledge and Kegan Paul, 1956. Used with permission.

William Glasser, *REALITY THERAPY: A NEW APPROACH TO PSYCHIATRY*. New York: Harper & Row, 1965. Used with permission.

Harold Greenwald, Excerpt from "Play and Self-Development" in *WAYS OF GROWTH* edited by Herbert Otto and John Mann. Copyright © 1968 by Herbert Otto and John Mann. Reprinted by permission of Grossman Publishers.

Daniel Henninger and Nancy Esposito, "Regimented Non-Education: Indian Schools" in *THE NEW REPUBLIC*, February 15, 1969. Reprinted by permission of *THE NEW REPUBLIC,* Copyright © 1969, Harrison-Blaine of New Jersey, Inc.

Seymour Hersh, "Germ Warfare: For Alma Mater, God and Country" in *DIVIDED WE STAND*. New York: Harper & Row, 1970.

Table of Contents

Introduction

To raise the issue of values is to raise an issue with a myriad of implications, because the topic of values is really the topic of discovering why human beings act in the manner which they do. Psychological insights, anthropological studies, sociological observation, educational techniques, and more than a touch of instinct and guessing all combine whenever someone wishes to thoughtfully pursue this subject. Therefore, it might be wise to start this book with a few warnings about it.

1. The approach of the book combines a number of disciplines. Experts in any one specific discipline will probably question the adequacy of the descriptions and the depth of the studies, and yet it is not the goal of this book to produce yet another study in psychology or sociology, etc. It is meant to produce some insights into the character, impact, formation and clarification of the values which men possess and live by. That means borrowing from various disciplines and allowing the reader—participant in the book—to explore those opening insights on their own.

2. The approach of the book not only combines disciplines, it seeks to combine persons. No one can approach the topic of values without bringing to that effort his own values, his own approaches. The author has been conscious of this, not only in writing this book, but in consulting with others on the production of the book and working with numerous groups who have attempted their own value clarifying efforts. There is only one really safe method to avoid imposing one's own value priorities and approaches on another. It is by inviting the other to work things out with you. So even the reader is part of the combination of persons in this book. That is the reason why certain exercises are incorporated in the text and why the reader is strongly urged to work out those exercises while reading the book. In that way, the book becomes a catalyst for your own search, a tool for your own clarifying. In that way also, the views of the author can be tested, expanded, played with by you —as they should.

3. Since the subject is so complicated—because human beings are complicated—the book attempts to be a montage of experiences, thoughts, approaches, insights rather than a narrowly defined microscopic examination of any one aspect of the question of values. Some portions of the montage will seem self-evident to you; some will be too obscure or remote to be useful to your own approach to values. All that is to be expected. The book is merely intended to give you a number of "handles" with which to come to grips with the central problem. Its value, hopefully, comes from the number of handles and their availability. It is the reader's task to find the comfortable ones for him.

*   **4.** *The book is primarily directed to educators. Yet even that word should be defined as broadly as possible. There are educators in classrooms; but there are also educators on the streets, in clinics, in homes. There are educators with a multitude of skills and a fund of teaching tools; there are educators whose only skill and only tool are their own personhood and life experience. This book, very simply, is directed to all those "educators"; so, if the word is used, the non-professional teacher should not feel that what is being said is not directed to him.*

*   **5.** *The book has a pattern which, at first glance, might not be too evident. Maybe a brief "roadmap" might be of value. Values come from the inside and from the outside—from the culture of a specific man or from the history of that man, as well as from those intensely personal pains and joys which each of us experiences and sometimes can even share and make sense of. All of those elements are part of this book; all of them are part of the search. If we can remember these varied sources— this raw material of a value system, if you will—the pattern of the book becomes more understandable.*

Basically, the book raises questions about values and then tries to suggest approaches to answers:

*   **1.** *Who is reading the book? Twentieth-century man in the midst of a cultural transition which is affecting his values in the midst of his reflection on values. If he is to do this reflecting with some objectivity, he must be "in the mood" (Chapter One).*

*   **2.** *What is a value? It doesn't do much good to write a book about "something" if everyone is using "something" differently. In addition, a significant proportion of man's learning (as well as communication) comes from making more precise what he means by the words he bandies about (Chapter Two).*

*   **3.** *There are as many kinds of values as there are kinds of apples. Can we sort them out? That is a good question. Generally people would think that when we approach the subject of values, we would approach it somewhat like the amateur apple eater, who simply wants to know the difference between good and bad apples. If that were true, then this book would be about "good" and "bad" values and would be another treatise in ethics, or moral guidance, or character development.* **It isn't!** *When apple growers get together, they talk about different kinds of apples—all good or bad, depending on how they have been grown and what people are looking for. This book is a conversation between author and reader on different kinds of values —all good or bad—depending on how they were obtained and what people are looking for (Chapter Three).*

*   **4.** *Finally, man is complicated and fits things together in varied ways. How does he fit values together? How does he put wife and self together? Privacy and companionship? Money and leisure? Work and play? That's the issue of ranking priorities and values (Chapter Four).*

*   **5.** *Now it is time to come down from the ivory tower of theory and mental constructs and walk into that morass of anguish and joy, triumphs and failure which are part and parcel*

of a single human being's experience. What in the past of a man's experience is indicative of his values? The negative experiences of the past which indicate "warring" values are normally described in terms of **guilt** (Chapter Five).

6. The future also encroaches on man and his decisions. It is the future which stands as either a threat or an opportunity for man. If it is a threat, he is anxious; if it is an opportunity, he dreams and fantasizes. In either case, he is grappling with his values (Chapter Six).

7. Finally, all of this is resolved in the present. The present incorporates the past and the future in the midst of a man being and doing. It is the arena in which values are acted out, lived, affirmed. It is the arena of work and of play (Chapter Seven).

That is the roadmap of this book. It is also an invitation to an adventure. (Caution: adventures are sometimes frightening for "educators," but usually freeing and exciting for "students.") The adventure here is knowing more about me; knowing more about others; allowing others to know more about me and themselves. With that in mind, try Chapter 1 and see if it makes sense!

Preface

As has been noted in the Introduction to this book, it has been written generally for all those people who might call themselves "educators." A little more specifically, my intention was originally to provide a book on value clarification for use in adult education. The book could be used with high school students, but is more appropriately used with adults at the college level, and more specifically for teachers in training. For two years now, the contents of this book have been used as the curriculum for a graduate course in values and meaning for students preparing for social ministry. That is to say, it has been used for students preparing themselves to be educators, counselors, and social workers. It has been specifically used in adult group education.

The question has often been raised: Does not this kind of theory negate the idea of mystery in life? I would just like to say: Certainly not from the point of view of the author. Value clarification is a methodology, not a philosophy. It is a method to help people to reflect and discover their own methodologies and a way of helping people to explore life and discover meaning for themselves. Quite simply, if I clarified all of my values, this would not explain my life simply because those values would have particular meaning to me and may have no new meaning to other persons. If, for example, my first value in life was faith in other human beings, the mystery would not be gone out of things because what that would mean would be very particular to me. As such I could probably write a whole volume on faith. In other words, we are talking about a methodology which helps to show a person where he is in life. It does not seek to explain his mystery but simply acts as a guide in his journey.

This becomes abundantly clear when we begin to think of those values which are so central to civilization—art, for example. What art is for me no doubt relates deeply to the culture that I come from. To say that my first value in life is art explains nothing about the mystery of art or how that value is integral to meaning in my life or to the nature of the culture from which I come. The only way I would discover those things would be to discover, investigate and do research on that value which is particular to myself and my culture. In other words, value clarification is not an answer to all of life. There is a greater complexity. I say this simply to answer those persons who might think that I'm trying to say that value clarification is the "new thing" or is a new answer. No indeed. It is simply another tool, another way of looking at things which hopefully might be helpful to the reader, the teacher and the counselor in their investigation and discovery of their own methodology and way of doing things.

Several years ago I spent a year studying under Ivan Illich in Cuernavaca, Mexico. At the introductory meeting of the students to the center, Illich had the following to say: "You know, it has always interested me that the first crucifix of Christ to be discovered in Western art showed Christ on the cross with a donkey's head." The point here is that Christ, indeed life itself, laughs at us. The more I meditate and do research on values, the more I am aware of the complexity and the magnitude of the questions. Probably the value that has become most important to me and the one that I feel is most important to the mental health and the spiritual development of man, and yet least understood, is the value that man is "limited." We can never know all the answers. The only saving grace I think that I have sometimes in this insane world we live in is the image of the world as a circus. All the people in the circus appear as clowns. We are all fools and really see the totality of knowledge in very diminished portions that are distorted much of the time. That person who can see a unity in things and express it is a genius indeed. We need to laugh at ourselves. As I write this book, I would offer it to you, the reader, as a fragment of reality to be placed with your own reality to form a greater unity. I do not claim the answers or even a better way of viewing things but simply another view whereby we may try to discover our limitations and our values as each one of us seeks to find truth and make sense out of the world in which we live.

Value clarification is art. It is a method of play. It is a way of laughing at the world. It is a window through which we look. It is another construct. I hope that you find it helpful.

I would particularly like to thank various people who have helped me with the book, and in particular my family—my wife Diane, Tina and Martin—who have been so patient during these months. I give special thanks to Maury Smith and Michael Kenney who have patiently worked with me. Michael in particular has been helpful, since we have been working on this kind of material over a number of years. In addition I would like to thank Joe Osborne, Jim Dorsey and our relentless typist Bucky Profeta. Finally special thanks go to Dick Payne, John Kirvin and Kevin Lynch, without whose interest this book would not have been possible.

Brian P. Hall

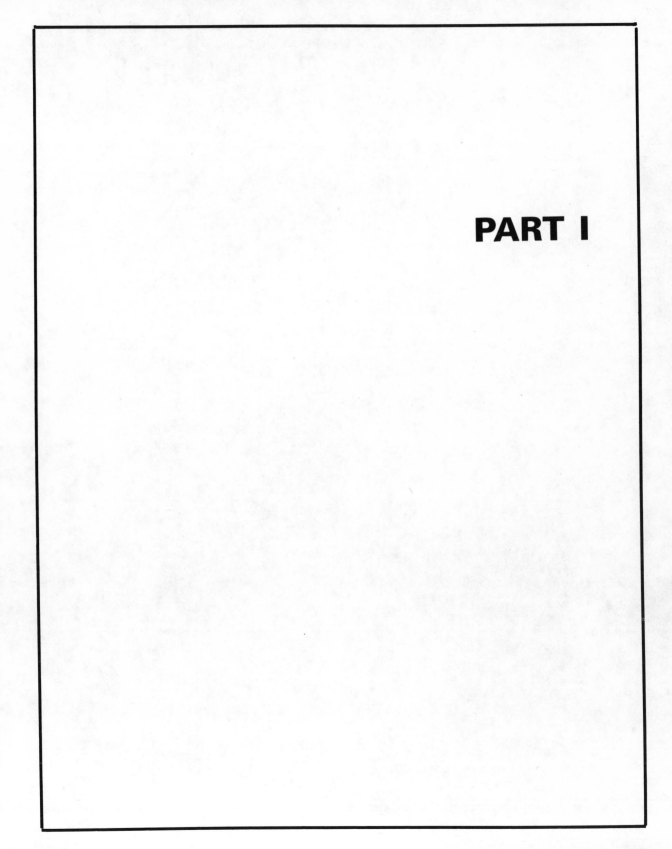

PART I

1.
The Press of Time

Suddenly a white rabbit with pink eyes ran close by her. There was nothing so very remarkable in that; nor did Alice think it so very much out of the way to hear the Rabbit say to itself, "Oh, dear! Oh, dear! I shall be too late!" . . . The Rabbit actually took a watch out of his waistcoat pocket, and looked at it, and then hurried on.

Lewis Carroll, Alice in Wonderland

INTRODUCTION

As we begin to look at the subject of values clarification, the question of time becomes an important indicator of what is important to us, of what our values are. Time is a good place to begin, because it is an excellent vehicle to get at the cultural aspects as well as the more personal side of value clarification. Time and space are always interconnected. This chapter is therefore going to look at man and society in relationship to the time man has and space he occupies and to perceive both time and space as value indicators.

TIME

As we view Time, I would suggest the following diagram as a guide:

PAST	PRESENT	FUTURE
memory	act choice behavior	imagination
history	change	possibility

Time, as we see, consists of past, present and future. Naturally there is a sense, a very important sense, in which everything is in the present. My consciousness is present. As I think in the now, I remember the past and I imagine about the future. In the present I act or I am acting.

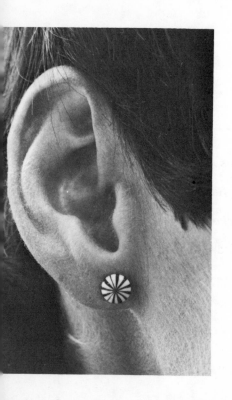

We speak of the past as memory: the past of both our cultural or social history and our own personal or individual history. They are both interwoven, and do a great deal to dictate and form the beliefs, aspirations and values that run our lives. Let us look a little closer. You might ask yourself: What kind of day did I have yesterday? It could have been a bad day or a good day. Perhaps it was the kind of day you will never forget. Maybe you did something you would rather forget. On the other hand maybe it was one of those days where you came to a great insight about yourself, so that you feel differently about life and people, today.

There is a sense that the past is present, in that I have been affected by it. So it is that guilt resides in the past as a part of my memory. Celebrations and parties have to do with the past. I feel good about my past and I celebrate it, by having a birthday party, or a graduation party for my daughter. Farewell parties are to celebrate the goodness of past relationships which have to end. These things are important to us; the past influences us day by day.

Current Analyses of Time

The cultural, social, and personal effects of time—past, present, and future—have been the subject of many current analyses.

Our cultural past is very much present and having a decided effect on the day-to-day lives of many people in the United States. There are two states of mind that many people live by, which are present states of consciousness, and they relate directly to our history as a nation.

The Common Ideal

The first consciousness is that of man as pioneer. It has to do with the aspirations, beliefs and attitudes toward life that the early pioneer immigrants had when they came to this country. America was a new beginning to the early immigrant, a new community in which human dignity was based on a kind of rugged individualism.

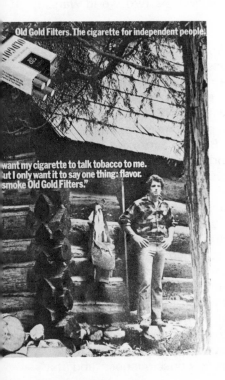

The place where this image is most obvious is in its popularity through the media. For example this is the theme of many cigarette advertisements. The country freshness of Salem. Why if you smoke Marlboro you can almost feel the branding iron in your hand. "Old Gold Filters are for independent people." The slogans are usually accompanied by a man's man doing some independent thing, the image being he is single and his wife is home cooking the vitals and looking after the kids! Another place is in popular television programs like *Gunsmoke* or *Mannix.* The heroes are almost always too task orientated to have time for marriage. They are moral, hard working images of pioneer man.

Their popular appeal simply indicates that a great many people are attracted by this imagery. And why not? After all it is very appealing. In the first place it gives one a sense of self-worth. The independent man that we see in *Bonanza* or *Batman* is also a savior. "He is really somebody." In other words, inherent in the appeal of such images is the acceptance or acknowledgment of some value or need of which the person may or may not be aware.

Another rationale for investment in an image from the past is that, for many, the past is more secure. It contains certainty in an uncertain world. But here again the investment is not so much in history as in the value of security. The problem with this attitude is that it represents a loss of reality, since we do not in fact live in that kind of society.

The Common Un-Ideal

The second state of mind has to do with an image of man as consumer and producer. The point is that along with the pioneer came the Industrial Revolution, and with it an increasingly mechanized society. As Jacques Ellul states:

> "The term industrial revolution is applied exclusively to the development of machinery, but that is to see only one side of it. In actual fact, the industrial revolution was merely one aspect of the technical revolution. . . . The technical revolution meant the emergence of a state that was truly conscious of itself and was autonomous in relation to anything that did not serve its interests—a product of the French Revolution. It entailed the creation of a precise military technique (Frederick the

Great and Napoleon) in the field of strategy and in the fields of organization, logistics and recruitment; the beginning of economic technique with the physiocrats, and the later liberals. In administration and police power, it was the period of rationalized systems, unified hierarchies, card indices, and regular reports" (The Technological Society, pp. 42-43).

With the rise of industrialism there was a natural movement from the field to the factory. Man became industrialized. Power became corporate, and the masses grew in their feelings of powerlessness. There is a predominance of the organization, and success means being an organization man. In such a set-up the individual is always working and being directed by others. Rapid industrialization, the depression years as well as two world wars, ushered in a new consciousness.

Many of the creature features such as the Dracula and Frankenstein series symbolize the feelings of a large segment of the society as it relates more to mindless efficiency than it does to people. The struggle with this concept was illuminatingly portrayed in the movie *2001* where two astronauts battle for their lives in an almost human relationship with a computer named Hal. Hal, having killed all the crew of the space ship, locks the last man out from the ship to die in space. But the astronaut manages to get in through an escape hatch and starts to disconnect the computer. Hal then goes through successive stages of anxiety and fear, pleading not to be disconnected.

Pioneer consciousness is cynical about human motives, and tends to distrust feelings and intuition. Reason is the highest faculty, and function is a supreme virtue. Reality is for the most part the observable; it is the manufactured goods, the laws we live by and the progress of science. Institutions, organizations and society take priority over the individual. Progress, for example, tends to be measured in terms of my place in the institution or society, rather than the kind of person I am. I am what I do.

The second consciousness is that of man as consumer. It is well summarized in terms of its relationship to the work ethic. Sebastian de Grazia describes this work consciousness and its implications:

"It is outside our limits to trace the spread of this work ethic or gospel of work, as it much later came to be called, over Germany, Scandinavia, England, and elsewhere in Europe. We are chiefly interested in the fact that it eventually reached the United States, there to obtain the fullest expression. Perhaps the linking of work to God is no longer so clear as it once was, yet we can certainly see that the shadows of the great reformers fell over the idea of work in America. Here, all who can must work, and idleness is bad; too many holidays means nothing gets done, and by steady methodical work alone can we build a great and prosperous nation. Here, too, work is good for you, a remedy for pain, loneliness, the death of a dear one, disappointment in love, or doubts about the purpose of life" (Of Time, Work and Leisure, p. 41).

Man: "What's My Marketability?"

The second consciousness is that of man as consumer. Erich Fromm calls him "marketed man" and has this to say.

> "The person with a marketing orientation is neither productive nor exploitive nor hoarding nor receptive. His whole idea is that the only way to create is to exchange. The market becomes really the judge of values. The market refers not to the local market, but to the market in which things, labor, and personality are for sale. The market is a central feature of our economy. In feudal times, labor was not a commodity, but something to be bought. It was a traditional thing which the Lord found wherever it was. Today labor is a commodity. And among our middle-class white collar workers, in the whole hierarchy of bureaucrats up through the vice president, not only labor but also personality is a commodity. People are traded and used on the basis of the kind of personality required by a given situation" (Dialogue with Erich Fromm, p. 6).

The above as an attitude is much more present and operative in our society than the influence of pioneer man. Our original excursion into this cultural journey was in order to see how time and values are related. When man sees his primary value in terms of how he functions, what then is his marketability? Time becomes understood in this sense. "By the time I am twenty-six I am going to have my master's degree and start my own business. If I can make twenty-three, or maybe twenty-two thousand a year by the time I am thirty-four, I think I will have made it." "Marge and I are going to make sure we have plenty of insurance, money in the bank and a half decent house before we think about kids. I mean, you've only got one lifetime—right?" "I've got thirteen years behind me at the plant. You don't think I can afford to switch jobs now, do you? I don't have time—I mean it would mess up our pension." "In my type of work you don't have time to really meet people. I know the guys at work better than my own wife—at least it seems that way at times—you know what I mean? It seems every time we get settled I get moved to another part of the country. You get to know people and you have to leave again, so why bother?" The message: Work and my function as a worker is of higher value than family and friends.

Living in the Rat Race

Emphasis is on function as career, on succeeding, on buying a better car, a bigger house and more insurance. This is the time press. We use the expression: "Life is a rat race." Racing means competition, winning or losing. Winning against whom or what? Winning against time. I must build sufficient security before the bottom falls out, because, if it does, no one will be around to help me. This is a pessimism often supported by religion. It is not unusual to walk into a church and hear sermons on the sinfulness of man with such statements as: "Trust in God, not in man." Yes, one could support such a statement biblically and theologically. But when it becomes the constant theme of a priest or minister, with the emphasis on the mistrustful nature of people rather than the constancy of God, one should ask if this is not the values of

THIS IS LOVE IN 1971

Rat Race Maintenance

Stretch your time-out. With richer, longer L&M Super Kings. Relax. Right now. This... is the L&M moment.

L&M SUPER KINGS

Consumer Consciousness speaking rather than religious conviction.

Advertising is always an interesting guide of what the society is thinking. In relationship to this question of time and function, feminine hygiene ads are to the point. Wear Tampax tampons so that you won't have to make excuses. This way, says the advertisement, you will be free to enjoy yourself more—anytime. Message: If you buy our brand of tampons, ladies, you will function better and have more of that time to yourself. Buy our cosmetics; they'll make all of you look like you've been out in the fresh air. THIS IS AN ACT OF LOVE. Message: It is an act of love when we help you function better—give you more time.

A recent television advertisement for a national speed reading course showed a very handsome, aggressive looking bachelor in his late twenties (plus pretty secretary) climbing aboard his own personal jet plane. Sitting at an executive looking desk, with a very executive looking black attaché case, he states: "In this modern cosmopolitan world of ours there simply is not enough time to keep up with all the material you personally must read to remain successful, unless you can read faster." His plane lands, the secretary takes his case, and he walks briskly off the plane—stops a moment—and recommends that you and I take the speed reading course before it is too late. Message: If you want to succeed, function well, you have to beat time!

As man has become more function orientated with more and more value being placed on what he does, he needs more and more things with which to maintain himself. Better transportation, air conditioning to keep him cool for the next interview, a swimming pool to keep him in shape, an instant breakfast to give more time in the morning. To quote Charles Reynolds Brown, "We have too many people who live without working, and we have altogether too many people who work without living."

To come closer to the point, Staffen Linder in his book *The Harried Leisure Class* has the following to say:

"People and goods need maintenance, and maintenance needs time. We need time to maintain our bodies. We have to sleep, eat, and clean our teeth. We need time to look after the young, the old, and the sick, i.e., to maintain others. We need time to look after various goods and put them in order. We have to cook, wash clothes, clean the house, and do the garden. We need time also to discharge various financial obligations. We must manage our capital (if we have any), keep books, file income tax returns, and make decisions on what to buy and not to buy. In practice it may be difficult to draw a line between consumption time and maintenance time. Eating can be a pleasure, or a form of personal work. In spite of this difficulty, there is a difference between time devoted to enjoying consumption goods and, on the other hand, time devoted to looking after the people who are to enjoy them, and time devoted to maintaining the goods themselves" (p. 38).

Experience I

In order to experience some of the things we have been talking about, try the following exercise. First put down on a piece of paper the amount of hours your employer officially requires you to work. If you are self-employed, or regulate your own work time, put down eight hours. Next, fill in the following timetable for *time beyond* the normal work time you marked down:

Approximate hours per week

a. *Time I worry or think about my work.*

b. *Time I put in beyond what is required (what I wrote down).*

c. *Time I spend traveling and maintaining car.*

d. *Time I need to rest or recuperate from work.*

e. *Time I use studying for work (if applicable).*

Total

Add up all the hours and consider them to be a unit of ten. Then look at the following list of arbitrary values and pick out those that apply to you. Add one or two more values if you wish. "Work" on the following list represents work as defined on the list above. It is work beyond the normal work day. It is therefore represented by the unit ten. Look the list over.

Work __10__
Wife _____
Husband _____
Children _____
Close friend or family _____
Religion _____
Home _____
Finances _____
Recreation with family or friends _____
Recreation alone _____

Now if the unit "work" represents ten, try to figure out what each of the others would be in terms of how much time you spend with each of them. When you have done this, rewrite the list as above, putting the value with the highest number first, and one with the second highest number next, and so on. Finally, reflect on what your use of time says your priorities are. You might try this as a family exercise to stimulate discussion. You might consider answering some of the following questions:

1. Am I satisfied with the priorities (ranking) that I have indicated by my use of time?

2. If I were to change my ranking, what would it be, and what would I have to do with my time priorities?

3. Can I guess at the ranking of some people I see in society who seem to feel their whole life value is their work?

TIME as Future Shock

So far we have been talking about time—past with its inherent value system being very much present. We have talked about present time and consciousness as being rooted in functionary and consumer man. Where does the future fit in? The past represents memory; the present, behavior; the future, imagination. It is in the future that we find all our anxiety and fears. It is in the future that we also find hope. It is the future that is man's greatest threat, the reason being that it is the least predictable and as such uncontrollable. In the present I can act. I can act now if I so wish. The past is history, and as such can be examined and looked at like a fine painting or tragedy. It is finished and static, and as such offers a kind of security to many. It is tradition and identity; it is my heritage and contains some certainty. The future, on the other hand, is never so certain.

Culturally, time is upon us, and is moving so rapidly that we have no chance of "beating it" in the sense of consuming it like a speed reading course. It is impossible to keep up with the facts, because the knowledge explosion is too great. Computers can, in fact, absorb more data than a human being can.

"Irving Kaplan, a psychologist who has been much concerned with the impact of computers, has expressed the new situation in the following terms:

" 'The accelerating rate of technical progress . . . implies three interesting alternatives for the future, each of these alternatives being of a very radical nature.

" 'The first alternative . . . is that the rate of progress in the technological world of the near future is beyond the comprehension of minds utilizing the contemporary frame of reference. Under this alternative we would not be far from the truth if we predicted that the next twenty years will see far more technological progress than has the previous 2,000,000.

" 'The second alternative would be a deceleration of technical progress. Such a decline could be due either to the exhaustion of technological potential or to the attainment of such a high level of technology that the culture would be satiated with the technological product and society would shift its values.

" 'The third alternative would be a catastrophic event such as a disease epidemic of tremendous proportions, a destructive astronomical event, or a war of sufficient destructive force to destroy the nation's or the world's industry and technology.

" 'Each of these alternatives is so far removed from contemporary experience as to present the individual with a problem of credibility. Whatever direction progress takes from this point on will be a dramatic one' " (An Alternative Future for America II, pp. 3-4).

Where Do Values Fit?

The fascinating reality is that as we view time in pioneer and consumer man, we realize that along with the image goes a value orientation. What happens to our values in a rapidly changing world?

The hierarchy and bureaucracy that most people over 35 are familiar with may be well on its way to collapse. It was the ideal of the organization man that has been misplaced in time by the 800th lifetime. Alvin Toffler speaks of the ad-hocracy. Whereas at one time, when a machine broke down in a plant, the operator would tell the foreman, who would in turn inform management, who would phone the engineering department to tell them to send a mechanic over to the machine, now there is no time. Time is money. Production cannot wait that long. Hence the operator is expected to get the mechanic to fix the machine as quickly as possible. The result is that people in large plants are more and more short circuiting distant management and being forced to learn new levels of working together. This is more personal and demands another set of values.

The problem of family is another example of how the rapidity of time demands special coping values. Rapid movement of families due to priorities of job function has made the extended family of in-laws and grandparents more and more distant. Consequently, close friends tend to come in professional relationships more and more. Work and relaxation get mixed in together and intimacy often becomes a problem.

There is the additional complication of learning and education. Education here is meant in the broader sense of total life learning and not just education through a school or institution. As women become more and more liberated, the traditional roles of housewife and stabilizer are disappearing. She often feels that it would be helpful to her growth to return to some educational pursuit, be it a university or a series of art classes. But because society is moving so quickly she learns at a faster rate than she would have ten years ago. Her husband, whom she sees a little less now, and whose interests are now different to hers, learns through his job at another rate of speed. The children, going to grade school, listening to *Sesame Street,* learn at another rate of speed. Alvin Toffler says:

> *"It is possible to demonstrate that, even in a relatively stagnant society, the mathematical odds are heavily stacked against any couple achieving the ideal parallel growth. The odds for success positively plummet, however, when the rate of change in society accelerates as it is now doing. In a fast-moving society, in which many things change, not once, but repeatedly, in which the husband moves up and down a variety of economic and social scales, in which the family is again and again torn loose from home and community, in which individuals move further from their parents, further from the religion of origin, and further from traditional values, it is almost miraculous if two people develop at anything like comparable rates"* (Future Shock, p. 222).

What would permit a family to survive in such an environment? A quick and oversimple answer might look to the above and say: "Surely more sharing by all members of the family would help." And, yes, I really suppose it would. The deeper implication of this is that they would need to understand intimacy well, and be able not only to share knowledge and differences, but their deepest fears, anguishes, hates, loves and aspirations together. Any marriage counselor will tell you this is not the most common thing in the world.

Time: A Conclusion

We have viewed time in three dimensions: past as pioneer man; present and past as man consumed and marketed; and, thirdly, man as he faces the future. Each one of these has a personal, as well as a social, dimension. Each one faces man as an individual in a collective setting, and asks him to make a choice. However, the past and the present are far more active in imposing values on us than the future. Both pioneer man with his rugged independence, and consumer man with his function orientation, are asking us to view the world in a particular way. They are asking us to have a particular set of values. As we shall see later in the book, associated with the past are also inner feelings of guilt and celebration that indicate internal values. We need to sort out the good from the bad, in order that we can deal better with the present and future.

In dealing with the future, man must know who he is, know his place, know his limits, in order that he can adapt. He must be able to deal with the multitude of alternatives and choose creatively. Man's inability to choose is part and parcel of the inner condition of anxiety. Choosing and knowing how to choose is, as we shall see, the first step in valuing. The future differs from the past in that it presents possibilities rather than any set values.

The question of choice and being able to choose, so critical to the identity of any human being, brings us to a point where we need to see how time and space are interrelated. People who feel they can't choose where they are going, what their life direction should be, or even what to say at social gatherings, feel trapped or hemmed in. We talk about claustrophobia. They cannot choose in time, and they feel space is closing in on them.

SPACE

Have you ever played Blind Man's Bluff? Children play it at parties, and some adults play it at sensitivity groups. The idea is that people stand in a circle and someone is in the middle with his or her eyes blindfolded. They are then turned around a few times, so that their sense of direction is lost. When they touch someone else in the group, then that person goes in the circle. There is another exercise called a trust walk. The person is blindfolded as before, and then led on a walk by a friend as an act of trust.

If you have experienced this, you might reflect on some of the feelings you had at the time. I know for myself, and others I have seen do this, that there is a feeling of uneasiness that goes along with the loss of control. After all, I have lost a very important part of my sensory equipment. I cannot control my movement in space so easily. That is to say, by putting on a blindfold, my space becomes limited. James Fitch describes this:

"Life is coexistent and coextensive with the external natural environment in which the body is submerged. The body's dependence upon this external environment is absolute —in the fullest sense of the word, uterine. And yet, unlike the womb, the external environment does not afford optimum conditions for the existence of the individual. The animal body, for its survival, maintains its own special internal environment. In *man, this internal environment is so distinct in its nature and so constant in its properties, that it has been given its own name, 'homeostasis.' Since the natural environment is anything but constant in either time or space, the contradictions between internal requirements and external conditions are normally stressful"* (James Marston Fitch, Environmental Psychology, p. 76).

Man's Environment: How We Fit

The world is man's natural environment, and as James Fitch points out, it is stressful on him. Like the other animals, in order to survive man has to adjust to his environment. Birds have feathers to keep them warm in cold weather, and monkeys have fur. But man, more than the animals, needs to modify his environment, his space, in order to survive. The house and the building are examples of modified environment for survival against the elements—for example, the igloo of the Eskimo, or even the tent of the state park camper. Fitch states:

"Thus man was compelled to invent architecture in order to become man. By means of it he surrounded himself with a new environment, tailored to his specifications; a 'third' environment interposed between him and the world. Architecture is thus an instrument whose central function is to intervene in man's favor. The building—and, by extension, the city—has the function of lightening the stress of life; of taking the raw environmental load off man's shoulders; of permitting homo fabricans to focus his energies upon productive work" (James Fitch, p. 79).

Man modified his environment in order to survive. But a beautiful cathedral or a Michelangelo's David is hardly an instrument of survival. To modify the environment is also a creative act that frees man from that same environment. So it is that *work* is man modifying his environment. Work is not only a necessity of life that one has to accept if one is to make a living in this society of ours, it is, as Erich Fromm points out, man's liberator.

Work as Man's Liberator?

"Unless man exploits others, he has to work in order to live. However primitive and simple his method of work may be, by the very fact of production, he has risen above the animal kingdom; rightly has he been defined as 'the animal that produces.' But work is not only an inescapable necessity for man. Work is also his liberator from nature, his creator as a social and independent being" (The Sane Society, p. 159).

Why is it that work becomes the liberator? Because as man molds his space, modifies the environment outside of himself, he becomes a part of it, and so changes and remolds himself. As a social worker, for example, works with clients and sees them change, she sees herself in them and changes herself to become a different person.

This is seen in particular in the history of art. Kenneth Clark, in his wonderful book called *Civilization*, points out that by viewing man's art one views man himself at any given age, in a way that no history book will ever be able to help us. A piece of art tells about a man's inner creative spirit, his behavior and his

Work as Work

underlying values. For example, we can view the emergence of cathedrals like Chartres in the twelfth century, standing firmly on the ground with a new confidence and hope not reflected in earlier centuries. The Vikings, for example, left little for us to observe other than their ships, which, although fragile in appearance, managed to travel half the globe. Their presence are the reminder of a fearful people who seemed to make change and the unsecure a part of their existence. They had no roots, nothing much that was permanent to leave us; they are a stark contrast to the cathedrals of Europe one sees in the twelfth and thirteenth centuries which in Viking terms are very non-functional.

Another example in art, and interesting in terms of present change, and the role of women in society, is the varied image of woman through the centuries. Up until the eleventh and twelfth centuries, women in European art were often caricatured much like the modern-day ill-tempered mother-in-law, and were usually part and parcel of labor forces, as for example in the building of Chartres Cathedral. Then, suddenly at the end of the twelfth century, there arose a different attitude and women became frail and even adored. The cult of the Blessed Virgin up until that time simply had not been so popular. Then her statues full of feminine beauty appeared all over Europe. Art as a way in which man modifies his space here illustrates a radical change in attitude toward women. Values central to people's lives are involved. It will be interesting to see what happens to the place of women in art in the next few years.

One of the highest ideals of work, Fromm points out, related to the thirteenth- and fourteenth-century view of craftmanship, is when there is no ulterior motive other than the product for its own sake and the process of its creation. The worker controls his own work, and finds meaning therefore in the creative act. Work and play were not split like they are today. But, when consumer man emerged, work, instead of freeing man, began to dominate him.

> "With the collapse of the medieval structure, and the beginning of the modern mode of production, the meaning and function of work changed fundamentally, especially in the Protestant countries. Man, being afraid of his newly won freedom, was obsessed by the need to subdue his doubts and fears by developing a feverish activity. The outcome of this activity, success or failure, decided his salvation, indicating whether he was among the saved or lost souls. Work, instead of being an activity satisfying in itself and pleasurable, became a duty and an obsession" (The Sane Society, p. 160).

Work moves from a creative self-satisfying act to becoming a duty in a consumer man. The final stage is the definition of work as that which a man does when the machine cannot do it. We have come the full circle, from modified environment as lightening man's load, offering him a setting where he can become his most creative self, to the other side of the circle where work becomes a new and burdensome environment.

Man and Creativity
What is a creative or a non-creative setting? The creative setting is where man is free to choose new creative alternatives for his life. A non-creative setting is one where openly or subtly values are being imposed because of the limited choices being offered.

As an example I will take my six-year-old son, Martin, in his first year of grade school. He was attending a small public school outside a large city in the midwest. As his report cards would come in, his teacher told us that his progress was excellent, and all his work tended to be B+ or A. However, even though his report cards were good, Martin did not seem to agree. In addition he often seemed nervous and complained of stomach aches about once a week as the school year went on. To make a long story short, we investigated and found that the teacher, who was a lady in her late sixties, found the class of thirty very difficult to handle. Martin and six or seven others were seen as the fast learners. That is to say, they finished their work before the others. The teacher then, to keep them occupied, gave them extra paper work to do which was always a repeat, with slight variation, of what they had already done. She insisted that they sit silently in their seats to do it. As a consequence he became very bored and would stare out of the window. The teacher would then tell the advanced students that, if they had not finished their work, they would have to finish the next day—but that they must catch up. Martin who was naturally bored, as well as angry, then would get behind and be afraid to go to school. The conflict was resolved by talking to the teacher, who agreed to allow my wife and several other mothers, whom she organized, to take the students who had finished their work to another part of the room and tell them stories with discussions. Unfortunately, most problems of this nature are not solved so easily.

In terms of space and work, children have a natural capacity to enjoy what they are doing, under guidance, when a certain amount of creative freedom is allowed. The teacher was operating under the concept of work as duty. She was production for production's sake orientated. She was very effective in teaching her value system to the children: work is bad and unpleasant. Related to her system of work was her direct use of space: a small desk and chair. The child had restricted space to operate in, and restricted space in the sense of creative tools to use. He really did not have too many alternatives. He could not, as such, form his own values, but only accept or reject hers. The problem was obviated by expanding his space and learning possibilities, which in turn created a new value option: that work as learning may be fun. The point is, then, that space and its use, like time, are very much tied to the way in which we learn the values that we live by.

Inner and Outer Dimensions of Space

As with time, space has its inner and outer dimensions. That is, its effects are not only on the cultural and social realms, but are very much a part of the inner and emotional life of the individual. Edward T. Hall in a book called *The Hidden Dimension* came up with what he calls informal space, which is the space of encounter with others. He sees four such spaces which are put into the category of distances that people need in order to function well.

The first is intimate distance, where the body would touch another body. Sexual intercourse would include this. The use of talking is minimal. The type of talk is deeply personal. It has to do with getting close to another, and of course does not have to be overtly sexual. Counseling is more often than not an exercise, in one way, of intimacy. The point is that there is a space involved

as well as an activity. The second phase is personal distance. Hall places the distance from one and a half to two and a half feet. It would be the kind of distance husband and wife might normally stand in relationship to each other, or best friends. Thirdly, there is social distance. This is party and business acquaintance distance. Finally there is public distance. This is the distance of formality that keeps strangers strangers.

The point of the latter was not to categorize all the types of space there are, but to illustrate once again how value and space are intertwined. The closer the distance, the more I as a person am exposed, and the more will my values, thoughts and feelings be visible. For example, along with distances goes an interesting set of environmental modifiers. With intimate space goes the whole question of the clothes I wear. If I wear a black suit and red tie every day, unless it is a uniform, it probably says something about the way I perceive my environment, the people I meet in business and so on.

Personal space perhaps points to such things as the car I drive, the hobbies I have. In the social and public sphere, we get to the house or apartment I live in, the job I have, all pointing to my use of space and the values that I own. This does not mean that all people who drive a Cadillac have the same values—of course not. It only means that if you asked a Cadillac owner why he bought the car he owns, his answer would say something about his values.

Inner and Cosmic Space

Finally, two aspects of space that need mention—inner and cosmic space. We started this section by talking about how man needed to modify his environment to live. Then in terms of the ideal of work, he became a part of that environment and so grew. The better side of man as such is reflected in the arts, as his inner potential bursts forth exposing all men to new dimensions. This is the inner creative spirit that men like Teilhard de Chardin

speak of. Work then is man modifying his environment not only to survive but to become as fully human as possible. This can only be understood in the larger dimension of history, since environment has been progressively modified over the centuries. But when work becomes duty or a substitute for the machine, then man becomes dehumanized. He becomes poor.

Awareness of cosmic space, or the more extensive dimension of space beyond individual man, to the creation itself, comes as a person actually takes on responsibility for space beyond his or her own territory. Why do people buy Standard Amoco lead-free gasoline? To prevent pollution of our air? Because they care about creation? It would seem to me that some buy it because it is better for their personal space, their car. Others, reading about the new pollution monster, stir deep inside with a secret fear, and see pollution encroaching on intimate space. Others live in the country, but travel a great deal and see it moving in on their social and public spheres. A few have another sensitivity to the creation itself and the progress of man as a whole. This is the awareness of cosmic space.

A Limited Example

This chapter has dealt with the issues of time and space as they impinge upon us and affect our lives and the values that we have. By looking at time and the images it gives us, such as that of pioneer and consumer man, we can see what values the unthinking can be drawn into. That is to say, the majority of people that we will run into operate with values that they are not aware that they have. When those values affect their behavior to the extent of making social and human relations impossible, they will go to a counselor of some sort or perhaps resort to some other comfort like alcohol in excess.

The Problem of Limitations

The basis for so many of our problems is the sense of our own personal limitations. The irony is that the basis for growth is also our acceptance of limitations, because it is the starting point for the daily evaluations we need to make if we are to choose creatively. The problem is when we do not want to face our limitations but deny them, and live as if we do not have any. The most basic of human limitations is the body and the fact that we are all going to die one day. Yet, the reality is that many people deny that they are getting older every day. Miami Beach is full of people over sixty years of age dressed as if they are teenagers, trying to recapture the past, not ever seeing the beauty and dignity of the older person. Value clarification is the beginning of seeing where I am now in my own life journey, so that knowing where I am, I can move ahead more creatively.

Case Example

John and Mary had been married for eighteen years and have six teenage young people ranging from fourteen to nineteen years of age. Two of the young people are girls. They are the two youngest.

The mother and father came to see me for counseling; they said that they argued so much over the children, they thought it must be having a bad influence on them. My response was to say that I would like to see the whole family. Over a period of time the following became evident.

John who was a very successful business man, and who now had his own manufacturing plant, grew up during the depression days, and experienced his own father, whom he was very close to, losing his business several times. "Yes, it was hard on us," he would say, "and I was about to make sure that did not happen in my own family." He reviewed several experiences where his family suffered when he was a child because his father did not know how to handle money properly. Through this history, John became a man who was always fearful of failing, even though he was always successful, and so kept a very tight hold on the money in the house, making the children work hard for anything they got.

Mary, on the other hand, never seemed to know where the money went, and felt the children never listened to her. They listened to her husband but he was always working and never wanted to get involved when he got home. Mary interestingly enough also experienced a rugged depression years history. There was a difference in her situation in that she had several brothers and she did not have to work in the same way her husband did. She also grew up with the thought that neither she nor her children were going to have those experiences that she had—money was not going to be a problem. Consequently, she felt insecure if she was not buying things. She hoarded or collected things much like her husband did money. They both were operating on the same value priority—security. Without going into too many of the details, I want to describe a value clarification technique used on the whole family which can be a part of an experience for your own group or family discussion.

Experience II

First, Ranking Sheets I and II were given to each member of the family (below).

RANKING I	SELF-RANKING II
IMAGINATION —inspirational, creativity more important, search, process of developing and experimenting (or something like that)	*SECURITY*
FUNCTION—gets job done, operates chiefly from the point of view of use or accomplishment, emphasis on task-oriented relations (or thereabouts)	*WORK*
IDEAS—getting idea across is more important, intellectual approach, understanding entire process is basic (or somewhere in that ball park)	*RELIGION*
FEELINGS—feelings are more important than getting job done; where individuals are within a program or project, persons and feelings are seen as important as how a task develops	*RECREATION*

The headings: Imagination, Function, Ideas and Feelings are four parts of the personality. Each part is equally important. They are based on Jung's concept of personality, and are used only to test and stimulate value-directed discussion. What the family was asked to do was simply rank the four parts in the order they felt was true of the way they behaved, and then to test it out with the rest of the family to see if it was true. The idea is that depending on how a person would list them could say a great deal about that person through a discussion. For example, the kind of person that might make a good artist would probably put imagination first, then feelings or ideas second and so on. An accountant would probably have function first and ideas second. Now all these things are equally important and it is just a matter of where your priorities happen to be.

Having done Ranking I, they were asked to do Self-Ranking II. Here as before the idea is to put everything in the order you think is true of your behavior. In this case, the things ranked were: Security, Work, Religion and Recreation.

After they had all done the exercise, they were asked to repeat the first exercise in terms of what they thought others expected of them. Well, the results were quite a revelation to the whole family, but especially to Mary and John. John and Mary came out as follows:

John
Function
Ideas
Imagination
Feelings

Mary
Feelings
Imagination
Ideas
Function

When the six teenagers all did theirs, they all came out different. What was startling to them was that when they were asked to put down what was expected of them, the boys all came out like their father, and the girls all put "feelings" first, with a variation underneath.

When they did the second ranking, John and Mary came out as follows:

John	*Mary*
Work	Religion
Security	Security
Religion	Work
Recreation	Recreation

Almost all of their teenagers had the following:

Recreation
Security
Work
Religion

Drawing Conclusions from Value Clarification

Now what does all this mean, other than that the family disagreed over most of their priorities? Well, I suppose we could come to a lot of conclusions, but the important thing about value clarification is that the conclusions only come from the persons doing the clarifying. If you did the above, you should make your own conclusions. The kind of questions to ask are: Are my rankings the same as I would want them to be, or are they different? Are the rankings very different from what others and I expect they should be? These were the kinds of questions John and Mary's family were asked to consider. Let us now look at some of the conclusions they came to. First they found that all their arguing was not over the difference in ranking so much as the fact of trying to impose them upon one another. The question was asked to the teenagers: Who do you think are the most important persons in your family? They had little trouble making a decision. Dad was the most important because he brought the most money in. He provided for everyone. Mom was second because she looked after everyone and worked hard, even though she did not bring any money in. The teenagers were listed according to age, the oldest being the most important, because he was able to do more around the house. Importance and doing were seen as the same thing. In terms of our earlier discussion, they all appear to be very much in the consumer man's consciousness.

As they all looked closer at the problem they began to see that they were all categorizing themselves according to their parents, and especially according to their father's ranking. Did this cause a problem? With this family, no. Why? Both John and Mary were as surprised at the results as everyone else. With Mary and John, work and security were very close together. The result was that they unintentionally taught their children that security and work should be the most important values.

As we looked at what religion meant for Mary, it turned out to be very closely related to work and security. Her religion was more concerned with what she did (in her mind) than what she was. Consequently, she belonged to so many organizations that she had very little time for her family. Doing these things, she said, gave her a sense of security. Both she and her husband agreed that when they did relax they felt guilty. The implication of Consumer Consciousness is that if you do not work you are of no use. Of course, with everybody running around doing things they had no time for each other. Intimacy was a problem in their family.

The children's value rankings were only a problem when they felt guilty for not having the same ranking as Dad. When this happens, everyone gets angry at one another, making for a very unhappy family.

When the family was able to see how they were imposing their values on each other, things began to change. One of the central reasons they were able to look at their family differently was that they did not realize how much they were imposing on each other. After several value clarifications, they were able to discuss as a family what values they would like to have and what could be done about it, how they could balance recreation with work and how religion could be more meaningful to them.

Conclusion   In conclusion, we might ask: Is it so bad to have a bit of pioneer or consumer man in me? Is it so bad to find myself anxious about the future? After all, I have three teenage daughters. So what if I am work-oriented—it provides my family with security and education.

The answer is that it is by no means bad, it is a statement of who I am. That is never bad. The problem comes when I do not know who I am, and what values I operate under. What is being suggested is that by making clear to myself my value reality, I can better choose my future direction, so as to maximize my potential. We all have a bit of the pioneer man in us, for it has many fine inherent values in it, as does consumer man. The difficulty comes when the negative values in one point of view dominate us to the exclusion of all else. The fact is that the latter is true of a great many people. Value clarification is a method of preventing this and teaching persons to consciously choose their own life direction.

We have spoken all through this chapter about values as the underlying principles that guide the human person in relationship to himself, to others close to him, and to society. In Chapter 2 we are going to look more precisely at the definition of value clarification and the chosen value. Chapter 3 will look more at the values we live by, chosen and otherwise, and the question of value ranking.

2.
Values and
Value Clarification

> *The desire to be elevated above the pressure and "anxiety of the earthbound," as well as the desire to gain a "higher" perspective, a "higher view of things," as Ibsen says, (from which) man may shape, master, or, in a word, appropriate the "known." Such appropriation of the world in the sense of a becoming and realizing the self is termed* **choosing oneself.**
> Ludwig Binswanger, Being in the World

INTRODUCTION

The purpose of this chapter is to point out the distinction between values and value clarification. Also we will look at a definition of a value which is practical in nature, and as such a part of value clarification. The latter part of the chapter will look in detail at what choosing, prizing and acting have to do with the valuing process.

PERSPECTIVES

Historically speaking, there has been no general theory of values. Values were seen to be a study that was more a part of political and economic theory than, say, of philosophy and anthropology. Value in a political and economic sense was seen in terms of utility, monetary exchange and benefit.

The notion of value was not a central issue for the philosopher. Plato conceived of the good, or value, as the culmination of the world of ideas. It was the constructive principle on which the world organizes all its societies and laws.

Aristotle viewed all things technologically. He was also interested, although from a different stance, in the supreme good. He was concerned that we have to choose values. He pointed out that each value relates to a series of higher values. Each value must have its own end in the overall view of things. As such there is a hierarchy of values.

To the Greek philosopher the question was: What is the good? The next question was: How do I obtain it? If the good is happiness, then how do I become happy in my life? Therefore, the major question of values was one of motivation. So it is that when this was translated into the Christian value system, values were, for the most part, given objectively. Value education then became the imparting of rules to be followed. In other words, if I know the objective values and their priority, the only question then will be: How or what do I do to obtain or develop them? This concept of the objectivity of values continues with us even today.

In fact, when the subject of values started to become of great interest to philosophy, it was Immanuel Kant who was the first to challenge this older concept of values.

For Kant the concept of duty became central. The only thing morally valuable, he said, was "the good will." Reason, now, and not God, is the source of the moral law. The point is that for him there is now an ordering of the world and life from within. This is totally different from the objective sensory view of Aristotle.

With the advent of psychoanalysis, educational psychology and the whole existentialist movement, there has been to a large extent a swing to the subjective point of view. Hence, we have a whole series of new questions arising in the past century:

"How objective or subjective is a man's value system?"
"What is the relationship between a man's values and his own self-realization of them?"

"Can value clarifying occur without a discussion of the intrinsic worth of certain values?"

"What is the relationship of personal values and human growth?"

"What is the place of value formation in educational process?"

Existentialism

It is not my purpose here to cover the whole history of philosophy in regard to values. However, it is important that we see that the modern definitions and approaches to values are not new but do in fact come out of a history. In the history of philosophy we see that Kant poses a new point of view. The totality of our world is not so much objective, but the inner ordering of things must be taken into account. That is to say, the question is raised of how I know that what I see is not totally subjective, that it is not ordered from within. Another philosopher who should be mentioned is Schliermacher. According to his philosophy, more than ever before, the whole idea of subjectivity in relationship to a person's feelings was examined. From these philosophers bursts forth the whole existential movement with names like Nietzsche, Kierkegaard, Heidegger, Sartre, Binswanger, and, in the United States, persons like Bugental. To the existentialist, the central question is: "Who am I?"—that is to say: What is the essential relationship of my existence to my consciousness? Hence, the question of choice is central to the existentialist, for what I choose has a great deal to do with the question of identity and what I shall become.

"Choice, be it of a particular action or of a whole life's commitment, presupposes a rising or lifting of oneself above the particular worldly situation and thus above the ambit of the known and the seen. But what does this "above" mean? As Nietzsche so eloquently described in the preface to Human, All Too Human, *it does not mean the adventurers' 'circumnavigation of the world' in the sense of worldly experience; it means, rather, the strenuous and painful scaling of the 'rungs of the ladder' of the problem of evaluation, i.e., of establishing an order of preference"* (Binswanger, Being in the World, p. 345).

So we see in Binswanger and Nietzsche, as in all the existentialists, an emphasis on choice. It is the choosing toward authentic being. An important aspect of the choosing and becoming is the choice of alternatives—what Sartre calls the possibles. That is to say, as we look at the whole aspect of time, the future contains within it possibilities or ranges of alternatives. It is these from which we choose. Sartre in his book *Being and Nothingness* discusses being as value:

"It would be absurd to say that the world as it is known is known as mine. Yet this quality of 'my-ness' in the world is a fugitive structure, always present, a structure which I live. The world is mine because it is haunted by possibles, and the consciousness of each of these is a possible self-consciousness which I am; it is these possibles as such which give the world its unity and its meaning as the world" (p. 158).

As we shall see later, this whole world of future possibilities has a great deal to do with the development of the imagination because it is in the imagination that I fantasize and dream of possibles. Implicit in what Sartre says in the last quotation is the movement toward action. In all the existential writers, especially those who are psychoanalytic in their emphasis, it is the doing that is equally important to choice.

Psychoanalysis
The whole human potential movement that we hear so much about today with emphasis on words like actualization is an emphasis on the need to act out of the variety of options. So, it is a very practical philosophy especially when it is applied psychoanalytically as a method of healing or therapy. It is evident, then, that as we talk about a philosophy of values and as we move into the modern era, we automatically move into the question of a psychology of values. I am speaking here, of course, of those fields of psychology that deal primarily with human development.

PSYCHOLOGY AND EDUCATION

In this portion of the chapter, we will examine some of the insights which varied disciplines bring to these questions, both in the effort to clarify our own specific area of interest and also to aid us in finally defining these illusive and varied words.

With the advent of psychoanalysis came such giants as

Freud, Jung, and Sullivan. This new analytical movement was both clinical and objective in its approach on the one hand and yet very subjective in that it dealt with the inner man on the other hand. So it is, as we look at different psychological points of view, that we can still see the same philosophical battle between the objectivity of things and the ordering of the environment from the outside, over against the view that the environment is really ordered from our own personal perception of things from the inside. It is here that the question of values and valuing is becoming of predominant interest. Modern psychology has had great influence on education at this point.

One particular and very major contribution that the psychoanalysts made which affects very much the study of axiology or values is the notion of development and formation. Up until the early part of this century the idea of the formation of a person's values was for the most part connected to the idea of morality and was seen as an objective reality. That is to say, in order to live the authentic life, especially in the religious thought such as Christianity, one had to possess certain values in a given hierarchy. Since the hierarchy was considered known, it was only a question of how to live them. Therefore, educational theories were orientated around the idea of telling the person what the values were in order that they could live them. There was an explicit acceptance of the theory that the cognitive, the area of reason, was the most important influence on a person. In other words, if the person understood the information, he would then act. Value formation was then seen, for the most part, as something that was taught cognitively to a person. Students were given the information and then it was expected that they would act on that information. Many manuals were produced, especially in the area of religious institutions, that would give instructions on what you had to do in order to become a moral person who had these sets of values. They would talk about the development of virtues, such things as patience, how to deal with anger, and so on. The formation of character (and of values) was seen as coming from authority outside the young child. The teacher or the parent would instruct the child on how he should behave. The child was seen as a primitive, ignorant, and immature person, and therefore needing the instruction and guidance. With the introduction of psychology and the thought of such people as Sigmund Freud, an entirely different point of view emerged.

In the new point of view, it was pointed out that formation of the human personality was natural and developmental. It was further posited that all persons went through similar and consecutive physical and mental developmental periods in their life. Freud saw this developmental process in terms of the oral, anal, and phallic stages of development. Further, it became evident that how a child or person would develop did depend to a great degree on what he learned from his environment. Primarily this meant his mother and his father and the other influences on his life such as the educational and social realm. However, the learning that took place was not seen as being basically cognitive, especially in the early years, but rather learning that was assimilated by the child imitating his parents. That is to say, he would learn something from the way in which the parents behaved toward him. It was thought that if the child did not have certain elements in his life such as, for example, enough security or love, he would develop a personality that was deficient in helping him to cope with society. Exponents of this point of view held that the formation of personality was simply an instinctive development, and in this sense man is very much the same as an animal.

Super-Ego, Id, Ego

In the Freudian outlook on reality, there was the development of what was called the super-ego. The super-ego was seen as a balancing factor between the outside environment which would impose norms and insist on limits on the person's behavior, and the inner ragings of the primitive aspect of the person's personality called the id. Freud considered the id to be an unconscious force, an inner part of man, whereas the super-ego was very much a conscious force and really an appeaser of the external and internal environments. So it was that he conceived a third element that stood between the super-ego and the id, called the ego, whose development has very much to do with the whole question of the identity and development of the more human aspects of the person. It needs to be pointed out that Freud is probably the greatest thinker in this realm and as such has influenced all other thinkers. The neo-Freudians such as Erik Erikson have developed Freud's view into a stance toward man and his environment which emphasizes man's authenticity. It was Freud who first developed in detail the whole idea of psychosocial development which is further explored culturally in the writings of Erikson. A more subjective and we might say inner-world orientation is that of Carl Jung who also saw the ego as standing between the conscious and unconscious as did Freud. But Jung understood the idea of ego as being a complex which constituted the center of consciousness. This ego that stood between the conscious and unconscious world was something that was primitive in the sense that it was developing and that as it developed it brought about the union of the two psychic systems, consciousness and unconsciousness, so that the ego developed into something which is called the self. The self was seen as the last point in the road of what Jung called individuation, which is another word for self-realization.

Psychosynthesis

Assagioli has developed a theory of psychology called psychosynthesis, which has a similar concept developed from Jung. He talks about the little self and the big self rather than the ego and the self. He has the following to say about this:

"Very often patients ask for specific clarification on the quality of the self and of the so-called higher experiences. In such cases we explain some of the main characteristics. The chief quality is the experience of synthesis or the realization of individuality and universality. The real distinguishing factor between the little self and the higher self is that the little self is

acutely aware of itself as a distinct, separate individual, and a sense of solitude or separation sometimes comes in the existential experience. In contrast, the experience of the spiritual self is a sense of freedom, of expansion, of communication with other selves and with reality, and there is a sense of universality" (Assagioli, Psychosynthesis, p. 87).

Potential and Self-Discovery

As we move through this psychological movement, we see a movement that is more and more concerned with the maximum development of the human being called authentic existence. This realm of identity and future aspiration and goals led to the area of values as a particular interest to many people. The development of values, then, has to do with the formation of one's identity and development which is intricately related to one's life experience. The following question, again from Assagioli, might help us to see that connection a little more clearly.

"The persisting resistance to and a denial of values among many psychologists can be explained, we think, historically. In the eighteenth century there were fixed sets of so-called objective values, ethical and religious, imposed from without by authority, often rigid and sometimes even inhuman. Inevitably, there is often an uprising, a revolt against such authoritarian values and dogmatic theories, and so the pendulum has swung to the other extreme. Now it is time to try to find the middle path, to empirically endeavor to establish the relative values based on vital criteria" (p. 89).

What is being stated here is that man has abilities and potentialities. It is to this point that this book is directed. Rather than discussing the relative merits of this or that value or its objective rationale, we would like to explore how things become values and how people are aided, educationally, by the opportunity to clarify their own personal values and their relative importance to them. The examination of the intrinsic nature and worth of specific values might be the realm of the moralist or the religionist; the task of knowing who I am and what I value, so that I can choose rationally and intelligently the direction of my life, is legitimately the realm of the educator. The more I, as an educator, know of the valuing process, the less likely I am to impose values on my students and the less likely I am to leave them with no opportunities to find direction for their lives. Either extreme is reprehensible for the educator; but there is, in fact, a middle road which we are considering. According to the developmental process being discussed here, it would be regressive to revert to the older notion that values are objectively taught. Each person must discover what his values are as he experiences life. Each person must search out the alternatives in his life from which he can choose.

This then would be the difference between clarification as a science over against an interest in the intrinsic nature of values as a science, which was the predominant interest of philosophy. It was William James who pointed out that psychology was a science, whereas education is an art. It is at this point that we need to look at some of the educational psychologists. This book is primarily interested more in the area of value clarification, which is an art, and not so much in the investigations of philosophy or the science of psychology. The discussion of psychology and philosophy presented here is to put value clarification in historical perspective.

EDUCATIONAL PSYCHOLOGY

As psychologists spoke to the emotional development of the child, naturally there was an influence in the whole realm of education. Historically it was assumed that the behavior of a child, "the perfect gentleman" or "ideal lady," would become the ideal through the virtues and habits that they were told to assume. However, when the idea of development through relationship became obvious, then suddenly the idea of education became expanded to be something beyond a cognitive practice to the question of "How do I teach a child to behave virtuously?"—to the question of "How do I facilitate a child's value system?"

John Dewey and Jean Piaget

The two central philosophical and psychological influences in this century are John Dewey and Jean Piaget. Dewey was interested in the developmental stages of growth and felt that the child's educational experience was not something that was given to him from the outside but something that he had to discover. It would be from this discovery, this relationship, that his own value system and his total personality would develop. So the problem of teaching was a problem of inducing personal experiences for the child. Questions were raised as to how the subject would become a part of the experience for the child. Dewey, like William James, wanted to point out that the problem of the teacher is different from that of the scientist. So for Dewey it was not so much the subject matter that was important in the sense of relaying knowledge and content to the child, as it was a matter of the subject matter as it was related to the growing experience of the child.

For Dewey, the experiencing child discovers values in nature. You might say then that experience has within it the values which are to be discovered. This relates to the idea of a person with a whole series of alternatives from which he will choose. For Dewey, values were not something to be philosophized on but rather they were a practical matter that was discovered by the child in his living experience. He was concerned not so much with the theory of values, but with a methodology, a way of choosing, a way of deciding what option among other options would be the most creative and satisfying. It was assumed that this would be achieved by a teacher who would facilitate this action as a guide rather than one who would in an authoritarian manner tell the child what it is that he should choose. What is interesting with Dewey is that, although there is this implicit trust in the positive

potential of the child to discover values through his own experience, which therefore implies the acceptance of the concept of
the inner ordering of things, there is also, on the other hand, a real
acceptance of the Aristotelian idea of objectivity, which is that the
child discovers out of his experience and so orders from what he
sees around him what his own inner values will be. It is because
of this emphasis on the experiencing of the child that many have
accused Dewey of not really being balanced enough in the area of
the cognitive. The irony is that there is a sense in which he places
a great deal of emphasis on man's reason in that he puts trust in
persons to discover their own cognitive input.

Probably the most influential developmental psychologist
in the area of education is Piaget, who links the cognitive as well
as the affective development of the child very much to the normal
psychosocial development as outlined in Freud. The affective domain or the domain of values and feelings takes equal importance
with the cognitive domain in Piaget. The following quotation will
give some indication of this:

"The first moral feelings ensue from the unilateral respect of the young child for his parents or other adults and how this respect leads to the formation of a morality of obedience or heteronomy. A new feeling, which arises as a function of corporation among children and which social life engenders, consists essentially of mutual respect. There is mutual respect when two individuals attribute to each other equivalent personal value and do not confine themselves to evaluating each other's specific actions. Genetically, mutual respect stems from unilateral respect. Frequently an individual feels that another person is superior in some respect while there is reciprocity in other respects. If this is the case, we have a mutual global respect in all friendships based on esteem, in all collaborations which exclude authority, etc.

"Profound transformations occur in affectivity during middle childhood. Cooperation among individuals coordinates their points of view into a reciprocity which assures both the autonomy of the individual and the cohesion of the group. Similarly, the grouping of intellectual operations place diverse intuitive points of view in a reversible set that is free of contradiction. Thus, affectivity from 7-12 years is characterized by the appearance of new moral feelings and, above all, by an organization of will, which culminates in a better integration of self and a more effective regulation of affective life" (Piaget, Six Psychological Studies, pp. 54-55).

In Piaget, the whole developmental process of the child is related to the whole development of the self which in turn is a valuing self. Therefore, the development of self and the development of values are parallel. This, of course, is the same kind of thing we see in Jung, Sullivan, and, for that matter, Freud. At the same time, there is a very strong implication that values develop not as a purely inner matter, but only in relationship to other people. Thus, Dewey and Piaget hold that the child learns from his or her experiencing in relationship to other people. In Erikson's terms, this would be the whole transformation of the personality related to the development of the concept of authority as initially being on the outside to move to the development of the self as one becomes one's own authority in relationship to self, others, and total environment—or, briefly, the movement from external to internal authority.

The important contribution of people like Dewey and Piaget is that the child is the most important factor in his own education and development. This development occurs through the interaction of the child with self, his relationships with others and the total environment. For example, the educational environment, both in relationship to the teacher and the teaching materials, is very important. The child grows, his fantasy life develops, and he slowly modifies his view of the world through the experiences of that world which he receives. Therefore, the more constructive and non-threatening those experiences are, the more secure and free the child is to develop creatively.

As the child grows physically, he has more apparatus in which to understand the experiences that he receives. He may be exploring things with his mouth, and later with his eyes and hands, and later with voice and touch and interaction. Through the experiences that he has had, the child will be able to hear certain things and see certain things. He will learn more permanently from them depending on what his experiences have been like previously. Piaget points out the importance of this physical development in order to understand the whole learning procedure.

As the child develops his intelligence and his cognitive abilities and his reason, he is then better able to integrate the facts of experience into his total developmental process. That is to say, the child must continually be able to learn to be able to deal with the increasing amount of possibilities that are open to him. It is only recently with books like Toffler's *Future Shock* that we realize that the ability to deal with an increasing amount of alternatives is not merely a matter of the cognitive and reasonable side of us, but has much more to do with how we have been trained in our whole affective domain. It was the latter that was pointed out by Piaget many years ago and is now beginning to be realized as essential. Therefore, perhaps the major contribution of Piaget is that he insisted on the unity of the cognitive and affective domains.

Learning and the Ethic of Balance

Essential here is what John Hendrix calls the ethic of balance. This means that as we talk about these things, we should never assume any one view to be correct, but always try to get balance into everything. It should not be just the affective domain or the cognitive domain, but the right balance of all these things.

This ethic of balance must be stressed at every level and aspect of education. There has been, on the one hand, great emphasis on the cognitive, on learning facts and figures, on learning content. However, on the other hand, there has been a swing by many of the so-called progressives to emphasize affective domain. We need to remember that we should not overstress one or the other, but rather to experiment and discover what the most practical balance for the health of the child should be.

"Affectivity is nothing without intelligence. Intelligence furnishes affectivity with its means and clarifies its ends. It is erroneous and mythical to attribute the cause of development of great ancestral tendencies as though activities and biological growth were by nature foreign to reason. In reality, the most profound tendency of all human activity is progression toward equilibrium. Reason, which expresses the highest form of equilibrium, reunites intelligence and affectivity" (Jean Piaget, Six Psychological Studies, pp. 69-70).

So the question is how is this kind of psychology applied to the educational situation? Silberman in his book *Crisis in the Classroom* has the following to say in regard to the kinds of teaching that agree with Piaget's psychology:

"A big part of the teacher's artistry, clearly, must be defined and provide an appropriate relationship between what is to be learned, the way it is to be learned, and the stage the child is in—what the American psychologist J. McV. Hunt calls 'The problem of the match.'"

Silberman goes on to say that the teacher must be very flexible. This means creating situations where structures can be discovered and which encourage the child to experiment, to manipulate things and symbols, and discover the validity and truth of things for himself. One of the important discoveries of modern education is that the child learns at his own rate and not at some previously programmed rate of the teacher or the administration or the school. Silberman quotes Piaget as saying that the principal goal of education is as follows:

> *"To create men who are capable of doing new things, not simply of repeating what other generations have done— men who are creative, inventive, and discoverers"* (p. 219).

As Silberman points out, in referring to David Hawkins of the University of Colorado, it is as if the child is being taught to learn the genuine understanding of matching Buber's "I," "thou" and "it" relationships. The emphasis here is that the teacher should be equally concerned with the emotional and affective growth of the child as he should be with the cognitive growth of the child, since, in reality, both are part of the same unity.

A VALUE DEFINITION I

Definition of a Value

A value is something that is chosen from alternatives, and is acted upon, and enhances creative integration and development of human personality. This definition is just a beginning for us to reflect on and is not one that I think is necessarily comprehensive or total. First of all, what we are saying in the definition is that we are concerned with that area of evaluation that is subjective to human personality. That is to say, we are not concerned about values in terms of comparing the American dollar, for example, with the British pound as an economic theory. In referring to the whole existential movement, we are pointing out that a value is something that is chosen from alternatives and is acted upon.

In Sartre's terms, this is choice from the "possibles." In terms of creative behavior, the action or the commitment to the choice is as important as the choice itself, and is, therefore, integral to the definition of a value. The whole area of formation of personality and the idea of value as being something of worth point to a definition of value in terms of that which enhances human development. What "enhances human development" may be theoretically arguable and unclear.

This functional definition mainly means that something would not be a value if the choice was intentionally destructive. So, I would suggest that something would be a value if the person thought that it would be creative. In experiencing that his behavior was destructive, I would assume that for the normal personality there would be a revaluing process that would go on and that the value could change. This definition of a value is defined in terms of the valuing process more than it is in terms of what a value is intrinsically, from a philosophical point of view. The reason is that the concern of this book is of values and the relationship to value clarification.

Definition of Value Clarification

By value clarification is understood a methodology or process by which we help persons to discover through their behavior, through their feelings, through their ideas, what important choices they have made that they are continually, in fact, acting upon in and through their lives. If a person is living on sets of values assimilated from his upbringing rather than chosen, then he is moving in directions and has goals that are hidden from him and that he is not aware of. It is only as I clarify what choices there are which have a major influence on my personality that I can really understand who I am and where it is that I am going. I can hardly understand where I am going and what goals I want to form if I am not aware of choices I have already made. Most people that I come in contact with through counseling and through teaching are quite unaware of what their underlying motivations and values are. This is quite evident when we see people who say, "I really want to do well in the world, but I don't seem to know how to get along with certain people." Or, "I love teaching, but the students seem to turn me off." "I just can't understand my kids; I guess it must be the generation gap." These kinds of statements really are indicators that persons are baffled at the discrepancy between what they want to be and what they appear to be to other people. In most cases, it is because they don't understand what their underlying values are or even that their values are different from their children's. Value clarification is a method that helps people to clarify what these underlying choices are.

Example

I was teaching group dynamics and values in a college course. One way in which the students in the class were to be tested in terms of what they had gained from the class and whether or not they would get a passing or failing mark was to be dependent on their participation in the classroom. This was to be judged partly by themselves. In the middle of this process, I interviewed each student independently so they could feel more free to speak than they would in front of the class about how well they had done over the year. One student by the name of George was decidedly withdrawn for the whole year and it was thought by myself and my assistant that it would be better to try to encourage him to talk but not push him. We felt that his basic need was in the area of development of personality, and that if we pushed him too far, he might withdraw. Throughout the year, he was encouraged to share as much as he could, and did so, but with a great deal of anxiety. In a personal interview with him afterward he related how in his life experience it had become a value for him not to speak up in classroom situations or in any place where there were any authorities, since when he had done so in the past, he had been hurt. He related one instance in the Army when he had spoken up honestly about some of the activities going on in his company in the area of stealing and was told by the rest of his friends that they didn't want anything more to do with him. He said that they told him that he had "ratted on them."

He went on to say, "What is more, the sergeant that I told this to also disrespected me for telling him the information, even though he had asked for it in the first place." He went on to say, "If you do trust people and speak honestly, you'll get hurt. So I have decided that from now on, even though I want to say the things I think are right, I refuse to say anything, otherwise I will get hurt. So I've decided to keep as quiet as I can and get through this class with as little participation as possible."

As we looked at the matter a little more closely, we decided that the value which he originally had was honesty. He had been told that if he was honest, this would be good for him. He discovered in his own experience that honesty, rather than enhance his human development, proved to make him a more lonely person. However, he did not conclude that dishonesty was a value that he should choose, but rather decided to choose that honesty was not a value and to remain silent when people asked him for it. We talked and I asked him what it was that disturbed him about all these experiences. He was able to relate that below the honesty there was a need for companionship and friendship that he felt he had. He felt that by being honest he would have this companionship, but found it not to be so. He also reported that since that time and since he had decided not to be honest, he, in fact, had become even more lonely in his life. We talked several times together and George decided that he would like to tell the class about his concern and see what other people felt.

George's revelation to the class turned out to be a very productive experience. The results were along the following lines.

George discovered that the value that he really had was intimacy. Intimacy may be described as sharing with another significant person repeatedly my deepest feelings, aspirations, hopes, values, and goals, and where the other person will share his deepest feelings with me. Honesty had been an expression of this with other people. However, George had discovered that not only did they not reciprocate, but they actually separated themselves from him and rejected him. As he clarified the matter, he saw there was a difference between intimacy with one person and intimacy with all people. The question was raised, "Is it possible to be honest with all people?" The problem was solved for George personally by relating it to the question of value. The question was then put in terms of: "Your need for honesty appears to be your need for intimacy. If this is to be a value, George, then it is to be something chosen from alternatives, something that you act on, and something that enhances your personal development. How could this be a value for you in such a way that it would develop your personality?" Several alternatives were given to George, one of which was to be honest to this degree with a significant other person who can equally share his or her needs with him. Other possibilities suggested were getting into an encounter group situation with a professional person present, or even into counseling. As it happens, through George's sharing in the group that we had, he made new friends where he was able to find this outlet. The question is, "What was the problem that George originally had and why was it that his trust in the first place as a value was destructive to him, whereas it was not destructive in the second place?" The answer is that George, somewhere in his upbringing and probably through his parents or through his learning experiences, had learned that honesty meant to be totally honest with all people at all times and that he had not clarified the reality that some people are unable to receive honesty. Some people would be unable to be as honest as he was, and so on.

The final conclusion was that George was able to define the value of honesty as being as open with one's feelings, aspirations, and anxieties, etc., to the extent the other is able to receive, whoever the other may be—and, secondly, to find someone with whom he can be that honest within some kind of repeated situation. In other words, honesty only became a value for him when he was able to choose it and act on it in a way in which it was, in fact, a creative integrative force in his development. Therefore, in that it did not work the first time, he was finally forced to clarify and be more specific in terms of what the value of honesty really was for him. What caused him to go wrong was the fact that he hadn't clarified some underlying assumptions which he had about the concept of honesty. Coming from a strong, fundamental religious background, he was brought up with the idea that we should all love everybody all the time and trust all people. The problem was, of course, that he had never been taught of a difference between trusting a person's potential and a person's behavior on the other hand. All this is a way of saying, I suppose, that he was immature and a little naive in this area of his life. However, it was also true that most of the other students in the class were able to relate similar situations.

As described by the example above, it is by defining a value in terms of the valuing process that we are dealing with the area of value clarification. To say I have a value is one thing; it may not mean very much unless I define exactly and specifically what it is we mean by that value operationally. For example, if I say that for me a wife would be a value, that simply is not good enough unless I define exactly what I mean by wife and what the relationship would mean to me and my human development. Likewise, in defining honesty, George was able to see that what he had considered previously to be honesty was not a value, since it alienated him from people rather than bringing him closer and helping his development.

A VALUE DEFINITION II

The second definition is offered as an additional piece of information on which we might reflect in order to try to come to grips with what we understand by value. Please look at the following diagram.

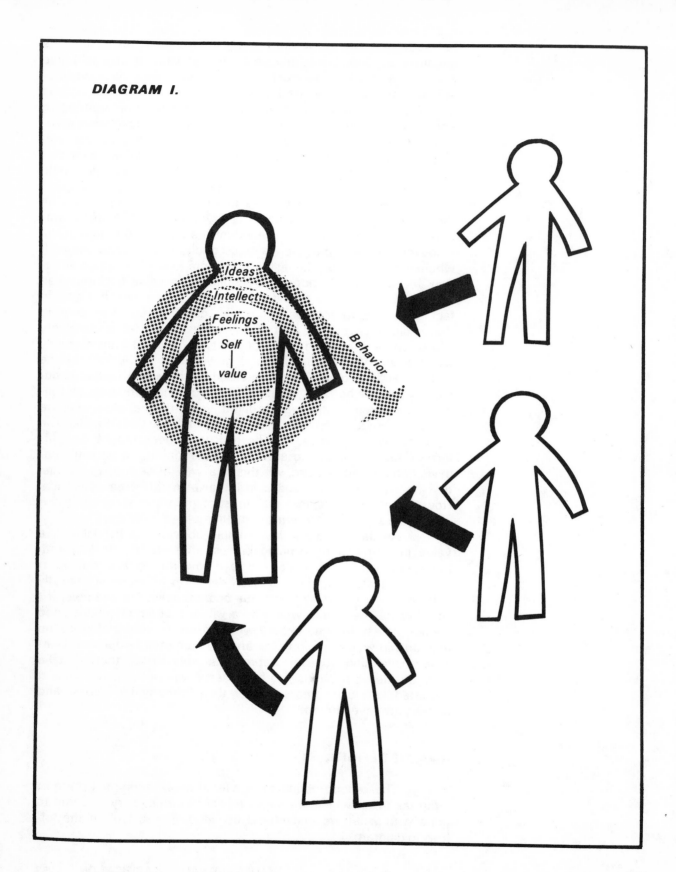

DIAGRAM I.

Ideas
Intellect
Feelings
Self
|
value

Behavior

Definition II: *A value is the stance that the self takes to the total environment as expressed through its behavior, ideas, body, and feelings, and imagination.* The above definition, of course, relates very much to the Jungian and Piagerian view of man, where the self is the central dynamic force in the human being that expresses itself through the totality of the personality. We mentioned earlier in speaking of ego that this was the element that stood between conscious and unconscious, and that self was more of the developed person as the outer environment and inner environment were integrated in some meaningful way in the identity process.

The above definition then relates very much to the idea of the valuing process where the stance of the self to the outside world changes as the person grows. The self continually develops so that values can never be static but are being rechosen as the self re-evaluates the outside world. As the self makes its stance to the outside world, in terms of the mother, and later in terms of the father, brother, sister, and the total environment through school, society, and so on, it evaluates, makes fresh choices, and develops a value system which is an inherent part of the development of self.

It follows that the intellect which here is seen as the outer ring is one of those rational forces in man that evaluates the outer environment and so modifies the self's view of the world as it evaluates and makes value choices. At the same time, ideas, feelings, body (in the way we were talking about it in Chapter 1) and the outer behavior of the person are all value indicators. Value indicators are things that point to the real inner values of the person. This means that values are never necessarily formed permanently, but are always in constant change with some values being dropped and others being incorporated. Value indicators may also become values if they are chosen in a specific way. As we shall see later, some values need to be permanent.

A VALUE DEFINITION III

This next definition of a value was made in a book called *Values and Teaching* by Louise Raths, Merrill Harmin and Sidney R. Simon. This value definition also emphasizes the process of valuing and, as such, is very helpful in the area of value clarification.

The authors define the process of valuing as having seven aspects and make it clear that unless all seven aspects are present, then what the person has chosen is not a value. They also state that a value has seven criteria which can be divided into three categories: (1) choosing; (2) prizing; (3) acting.

In the area of choice, it is stated that the value must be chosen freely. There must be no coercion but the person makes a free choice and is totally accountable for the choice he makes. Secondly, the choice must be from alternatives. If there were not any alternatives, then really there would be no free choice in the

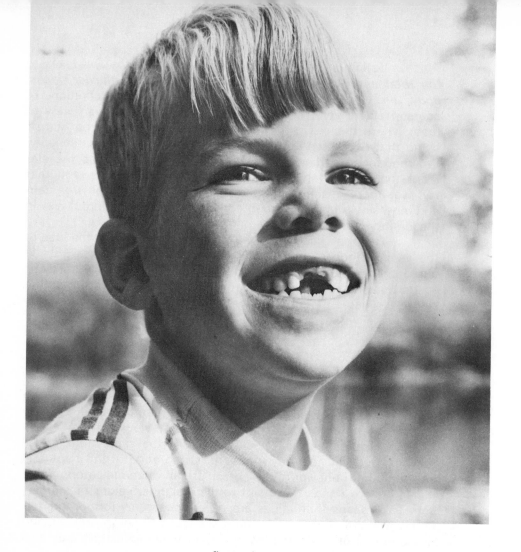

first place; one would only be able to accept what they were faced with. They give an example of the fact that we may be able to choose various types of foods, but we cannot choose whether we eat or not, so eating is not a value. The way we eat might be a value. The third aspect of choice is the thoughtful consideration of the consequences of each of the alternatives. Therefore, choices which were made without thought or impulsively would not constitute a valuing process. Therefore, for these authors, a value can only emerge with the consideration of a range of alternatives and consequences.

The second range of the aspects of value process was prizing and the prizing has two areas. One, that what is chosen should be prized and cherished. By this is meant that a person who chooses a value must be happy about what he is choosing and hold it as something dear to him. The second aspect of prizing is the area of affirmation—namely, that after we have chosen something from the alternatives and are proud with it, we are now glad to be associated with it and would be willing to admit so publicly. In other words, we will champion the cause of our choice and would not be ashamed that we have made that decision.

The third aspect of the value process also consists of two points. The first is that we would act upon our choice. One way in which we would see that what we had valued was a value would be simply to ask whether we had acted on it or whether it was something we are still thinking about, in which case it wouldn't be a value. There must be commitment and action which would change your behavior and which would be evident to other people before there is a value present.

The last aspect, the seventh, and the other side of acting, is that it should be repeated action. If something really is a value, we will not only act on it, we will act on it repeatedly, and as such it will show up in several situations.

A summary of Raths', Harmin's and Simon's definition is as follows:

CHOOSING:
1. To choose freely.
2. To choose from alternatives.
3. To choose from alternatives after considering the consequences of each alternative.

PRIZING:
4. Cherishing and being happy with the choice.
5. Willing to affirm the choice publicly.

ACTING:
6. Actually doing something with a choice.
7. Acting repeatedly in some pattern of life.

The beauty of this definition is that it emphasizes the process of valuing throughout the seven aspects. It clearly expresses all the views of what a value is and what the valuing process is as developed in recent psychology and philosophy. It takes in the aspects of choice, action, and prizing, and moreover it spells out what each of those means in a much more specific manner. This makes the definition of a value very practical in the area of helping a person understand whether or not what he has chosen is a value. A person may say, for example, "Oh, yes, I value very much that we do something about changing the problem of institutional racism in our country. And that is very much a value for me." The question that will check whether this is a value according to the definition is: "How recently did you act on it and how often do you act on it?" The person might reply, "Oh, well, I don't act on it because of other things I am doing. I don't have time, but it is very important to me." The response might be, "Well, that is a potential value, but not a value. A value is something that you are actually acting on."

THE VALUE INDICATOR

A value indicator is simply something which does not meet all seven criteria of choices. For example, if we have something operating in us that comes up to only six of these criteria, then this would be a value indicator. In this sense, a value indicator is anything which, by its nature, is moving toward a partially formed value. Anything which does not meet all seven criteria approaches a value, but is not a value. Other value indicators would be aspirations that I like but do not have at this time and, as such, I may have chosen but I have not yet acted on. Other value indicators are *interests, feelings, beliefs, attitudes,* and *convictions* that I may have. We will be looking very closely at some of these value indicators later on when we look at the problems of guilt, anxiety, and poverty.

The definition of a value indicator by Raths, Harmin, and Simon is a good one. However, it would seem to me that often a value indicator does not indicate a partially formed value, as much as it indicates a whole mixture of things, some of which may be actual values—so that when we get into the area of value indicators, especially as they relate to such things as attitudes, the picture often gets very complicated indeed.

VALUING AND CHOOSING

A value is something that is chosen. This presumes that to have values indicates a certain amount of awareness of the possible alternatives on the part of the person doing the valuing. Valuing, therefore, is integral to the idea of discovery, formation and identity of the human being at whatever level that person may be. The whole matter of choice becomes crucial. The idea of having chosen something immediately implies the idea that there must have been alternatives from which the person made the choice. Moreover, to make the choice basically implies that the person considered the various alternatives within that choice. To choose is a creative act. To be not allowed to choose or to be told in an authoritarian way what to do is in a sense dehumanizing, because it does not permit a person to become himself.

Example   I was struck a year or so ago when I was counseling a family who had a seven-year-old son. John was giving them a great deal of trouble in the area of discipline in the home and at school. His mother complained that he was a bad boy basically. She was at the end of the road with him, for no matter what she did, he would disagree with her. In this manner he vitiated any of her attempts to discipline him. She also reported that the teacher had complained of his behavior. It was my responsibility to consult the school psychologist and inquire about the difficulty. When I phoned, the psychologist said he was not sure at all if the child did have a problem. In fact, testing showed that the boy was very bright indeed. The psychologist was questioning whether or not the problem was with the teacher in the school.

In the meantime, I asked to see the husband as well as the wife to discuss the matter of the boy's discipline. The father supported the mother by saying the boy was a problem. I asked if they could explain exactly what the problem was. The mother related how each night for the last several months she had put John to bed at the hour of seven o'clock and told him to go straight to sleep—but he would not go to sleep. Instead, he played with his toys and continually shouted downstairs for his mother. If she did not come, he would scream. She told how he would keep this up until 11 or 12 at night and keep her awake. The husband did shiftwork and often wouldn't be home until the evening. When he did come home, he argued with the mother about why the boy was not asleep, at which time the boy usually would go to bed and fall asleep. The mother thought he did this to get back at her.

At the first interview the boy would get off his chair and crawl underneath my chair and desk and all over the room looking at various objects in the room. The mother would shout at him, "Sit in the chair, be quiet, and don't you dare move." The father would sit silently. The boy would sit for a few minutes, get fidgety and then start crawling on the floor again. I made a point of not saying anything, but just observing. After a time the mother started to get angry with me and started telling me to discipline the boy. I asked her why the crawling worried her so. I pointed out that many of the things are colored and interesting, and that I thought it was good that he would be interested. She replied, "I was nervous because I thought you would be upset at his behavior." I asked her if she thought anyone else was upset at her son's behavior. She replied, "Well, the school was." She thought for a while and then said, "And my mother comes over quite a few times and she also thinks he should be disciplined more."

As we talked, her son became very interested in a dictating machine that I had. I excused myself from the parents and spent a little time showing him how it worked. He was very pleased indeed. After that I said to him, "John, I would like to speak to your mother and father for a little while now. Would you like to join the conversation or would you like to sit and be quiet?" He said that he thought he would like to be quiet. A little later he began to talk and butt into the conversation. Finally, at the end of the interview I suggested to John that he could have several alternatives that he might like to explore the next time he came with his mother and father. One could be that he could spend some time with me beforehand looking at the machine, and then sit quietly afterward. Or another could be that he could join in the conversation with his mother and father and myself and afterward I would spend some time with the machine with him. A third possibility I suggested was that he could crawl about on the floor just as he did when he first came in, and then sit quietly or join in the conversation, but not be allowed to play with the machine. All the alternatives were presented to him in such a way that he felt no imposition and that he could choose which one of the alternatives he would like to do. John was very pleased at being able to choose.

The next time they came, John agreed to sit silently and then he would have his opportunity to explore the machine with me afterward. A little time after we had started the conversation, John interrupted and started to get off his chair. "Oh," I said, "you have decided to choose the other option where you'll move about on the floor for a little while and then sit silently for the rest of the time?" "Oh, no" said John, "I want to play with the machine." I then repeated the choices that I had given John and had him choose again and said maybe that he had forgotten. He smiled and said that he hadn't forgotten and that he would sit and be quiet for the rest of the interview.

The parents, Mr. and Mrs. Jackson, were amazed that he did sit quietly. Interestingly enough, they were also amazed that I did spend some time with him at the end. Both Mr. Jackson and Mrs. Jackson related how their own upbringing had not given them any choices and that they felt that children should respect their elders. Then the question was posed as to how the child could respect them if they hadn't given him the opportunity to respect them since they had given him no choice. How would he learn what respect means? The Jackson family was satisfying to work with in that they wanted to change. When they saw the alternatives to the previous way in which they had been doing their discipline, they were very ready to choose and try a different path.

What happened finally with this family was that they tried a different range of choices from which John could choose. Some of the different choices were as follows:

1. He could go to bed at eight o'clock and go to sleep immediately.

2. He could go to bed at seven o'clock and play for an hour and then go to sleep.

3. He could watch television until 7:30, play for half an hour in bed, and then go to sleep.

The point is that the boy was given a range of alternatives from which he could choose. He actually delighted in the choices, and they did not have too many more difficulties with him in regard to his discipline at home. This whole experience probably helped the parents more than it did the child. In not being able to see alternatives which they could give him, they were reflecting a background where they were not able to choose because they had never been taught the practice of choice. The discipline system which they were imposing on the child was not a value chosen by them, but rather something assimilated from their own background. When they were able to look at it and see the possibility of other alternatives, they automatically produced a more freeing environment.

Following this I was able to get together with the psychologist at the school who discovered that the teacher in the classroom was imposing the same form of disciplinary measures on the boy as the mother had been. The boy, being very intelligent, was able to think up all sorts of alternatives which would make the teacher angry and upset. He was moved to another class where he was able to use his intelligence more appropriately and where the teacher was more flexible. He was able to use his creative ability to a positive end which would be more integrative of his personality and his development. The tragedy so often is that the children do not have enough affirmation at their age to stand up to the teacher in such a way and thus usually acquiesce. Often crushed by parents and teachers, the child becomes apathetic to the whole learning process. It is interesting that the boy's bad behavior was not a negative thing in this sense, but rather a strong value indicator of his need to be himself.

Not all problems are solved as easily as the one of John. But many problems are solved when persons are given a creative choice. It is also possible, of course, that a person could choose badly. The art in posing choices, especially in the discipline of children, is that the range of choices are protective in such a way that the child can choose only creatively and not in a way that would hurt him. Unfortunately, the same possibilities are not always available for the adult. We are confronted with the fact that much of our behavior is not chosen. We are influenced greatly by habits and rules that were imposed, but not necessarily chosen. In the above example, this lady really felt with great conviction—and acted on her conviction—that her method of discipline was the right way. For all intents and purposes, her behavior appeared to be a value and, as such, would act as powerfully as any value. However, she was discovering that her discipline was not helping the integration and creative development of the personality of her child or herself. In fact, there had really been no choice because she had never been given a series of alternatives from which to choose in the first place in her own upbringing. Hence, in the classroom, whether it be in a religious education class or in the public school, value formation is impossible if, in the process, a child is not given alternatives from which he may choose.

Limitations

There are problems in the whole question of choice. The main one can only be raised, but certainly not solved. If valuing is choosing from alternatives after considering the consequences of all those alternatives, then how many alternatives are there and how many consequences to the alternatives should I have questioned? In reality, many choices that we make are simply not based on all the alternatives. Choice confronts man with his own limitations of who he is. For this reason, valuing is always a process, since once having made a value choice, it is possible that later on I will see other alternatives and other consequences and change my choice. I am therefore confronted with the reality that the valuing process for man must mean that I make the best choices I can within my human limitation. That limitation, of course, would also be an expression of where I am in my life process.

An example of man's limitations is the whole problem of Future Shock—namely, that we are living in a world where we are confronted not only with alternatives, but with an ever-increasing number of alternatives. The problem is in considering

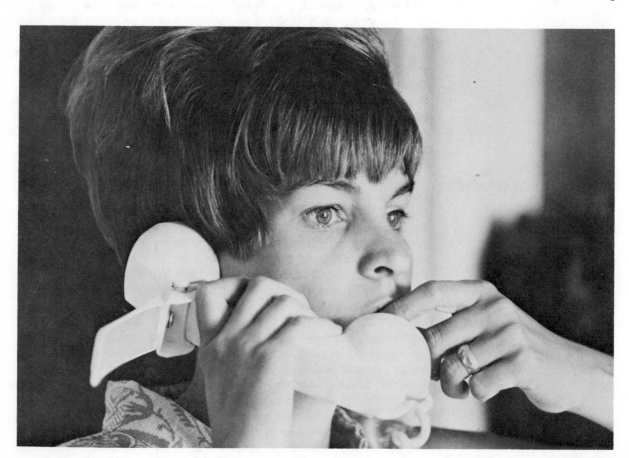

the choices I have to make and in considering the consequences. The range of choices is so great that I am confronted with my limitations as a human being. The responsibility and consequences implied cause man anxiety today. For each choice I do make, there is the possibility of failing and making a bad choice. Therefore, the greater number of choices there are, the greater chance of failure and the greater amount of anxiety. Anxiety is one of those things that restricts my ability to choose. Thus another aspect of the whole area of value clarification as we face the future is teaching people how to choose from a large range of alternatives on the one hand, and teaching people how to see alternatives on the other hand, when their ability to perceive the variables in a situation is restricted. With the seven-year-old boy, John, he was unable to have a range of alternatives from which he could choose because of his parents' restrictions. His parents were unable to see the alternatives because of their life-style. In this case, it was a matter of expanding their alternatives. The other side of that picture might be when John gets to the age of eighteen and he is confronted with a whole series of courses and electives he wants to take at college. Unless he has been trained in dealing with alternatives and in his ability to choose, he is confronted with a situation that is even more overwhelming to him than the one where he had no choice at all.

The question of choosing as a part of valuing is a whole area in which people need to be trained and helped. On the one hand, we need to develop the creative imagination of people in order that they can see alternatives from which to choose so that their life may be value-directed and they may increase in their sense of identity. On the other hand, we need to train people in how to deal with increasing numbers of alternatives in order that the choices they do make will be ones that were made sensibly and from an educated mind in the best sense of the word. When I choose, I am involved in the valuing process, and as such I am involved in a responsible act. The point is here only to suggest that the problem of choice is a complicated one. A part of the educational process, whether it be parent-child relationships or a therapeutic relationship, is that it should expand people's imagination in order that they can see alternatives, and train people to deal with situations that present more alternatives than the person may be able to tolerate.

VALUING AND BEHAVIOR

An intrinsic part of the valuing process, as we said, is choice, but choice is sterile without action. To have chosen is one thing, but to have acted on that choice often is another thing. As an example of this, I was giving a conference in value clarification to a group of fifteen persons who were involved in joint man-woman administrations. The goal of the conference was to help them see how as men and women they could work together more closely and at the same time treat each other as equals. In one administrative unit of three people, there was a man and two women. The man's name was Ray and before the conference he had contracted some kind of virus. His work involved directing a number of conferences of an educational nature and, as such, he felt that a lot of people were relying on him. He had been sick for three weeks and yet was present at this conference. Not only this, he was stating continually that he had to be at three other conferences during the next week and a half before he could go into the hospital. Through a process of value clarification that was used in the conferences, it became evident to him and to the two women he was working with that he did have difficulty in handing over the responsibility of his job. I remember clearly sitting in a small office with the three of them while Ray stated clearly his realization, in terms of what his values were, that he would definitely choose to hand over the responsibility to the other two women and that he was not omnipotent, and, as such, should be in the hospital. There was a period of silence. The statement was then made, "If you feel that is true, why don't you make arrangements to go in the hospital?" He replied, "I cannot go now; I have these other conferences." It was then pointed out to him that he said he had chosen to delegate his authority, that he should be in the hospital, and that if that were true, why would there be any reason why he could not go "now"? I have seen this kind of confrontation many times. One often sees a turning point where this person has chosen, but hesitates to act. To actually take action upon a choice is more threatening than making the choice.

After considering for a long time and arguing, he decided that he would follow through with what he had said. One might say that it was difficult for him, but that it was also a growth period, because the value was completed when, in fact, he acted upon it. In terms of the third definition, we would say that it would not be a value until it became a part of him to the extent that he acted upon it in all similar types of situations. Also, in terms of the other definitions, it would have to be a choice that would aid his integrative and creative development. This was a case where it was very evident indeed that not to go to the hospital would be very uncreative, since the man was sick.

It seems to me that the idea of action, to have acted recently and to act consistently and repeatedly, is really the "nitty gritty." There are many instances where a person states that he has this or that value where the question can be raised, "Are you acting on it?" One clear example of this has been in working with clergy, who often state to me that the value they have is to love and reach out to other people, to care for other people. It would seem that this has been a very strong theological value in their seminary upbringing, but when the question was raised: "Have you made a concrete effort to reach out to others around you recently and do you make concrete efforts to do it repeatedly?" all too often they would say, "I really don't. I guess it isn't really a value." I'm not suggesting this is true of all clergy. I am simply saying this is an example of where a group of people were trained to think that the belief and acceptance of a value meant that they had the value itself. In fact, unless they act upon it consistently and consciously, in a chosen way, it is not in reality a value.

VALUING AND CELEBRATING

The other part of valuing, which Simon, Raths, and Harmin refer to as the cherishing and prizing of the original choice, I have placed here as third in the order of things. The reason it is placed at the third point is that I feel that the prizing comes at the same time as the acting out or the behavioral extension of choice. As we noted before, choice confronts man very much with his limitations. From the existential point of view, man is faced with his contingency. Man is continually confronted with the fact that he is in reality frail as compared with the rest of the creation. I could be here today and gone tomorrow. Ultimately, I will die. I am limited in what I can do. As a person, I am limited by my nature. If I am a person who has lost the use of one hand, for example, I am limited by that fact in what I can do in terms of work priorities and so on. So am I limited as a human being in what I can choose. I am limited in any series of choices that I make in that I don't know what all the consequences are. Therefore, the fact of choice, as we noted before, brings me face to face with the reality of my limitations, which for some can be very anxiety-provoking. The whole area of valuing, the valuing process, and value clarification of its very nature confronts a person with the reality of who he is. That is to say, it confronts him with what his limits are and what he has chosen for his values and, as a result, what he has chosen for his behavior, goals, and style of life. To be happy with, to cherish, or to prize, therefore, the choice that has been made seriously in terms of a value decision means ultimately to have confronted what my limitations are. Since this is a rare opportunity and a rare event, the valuing process ultimately is difficult, but it is also extremely productive in the development of an integral and creative person. Central, therefore, to the idea of being happy with my choice is the idea of being happy with where I am at this particular point in my life's growth.

The person who is happy with his present state is a person who, having come to grips with his limitations, sees them as not a negative influence, but rather as a neuter point of where he is and a point from which he wants to proceed and grow. Central to the valuing process, as we said in the first definition, is that the choice we make be productive in terms of the integration and development of my human personality.

The integral person makes a choice that permits his normal emotional, psychological, and spiritual development to proceed.

Primary Values

One value necessary for man is to reach out and affirm other people as being of value. There are choices a person can

make from alternatives, and this is a primary value. The reason we call these primary values is that apparently if one knew what the alternatives were, one would perhaps choose to always affirm other people. The problem is, however, that in counseling a lot of people do in fact choose the alternative of not reaching out and are not concerned whether they become developed human beings, but are more often more concerned with their immediate comfort. So, in reality, a person can be happy with a value choice even though another choice would be much more helpful in his over-all development. The reason I am bringing this in at this time is that a painful situation that may make a person feel unhappy in the short run may also be more productive in the long run. Therefore, I think it needs to be said that in addition to being happy about my value choice, it has to be a choice that involves the creative development rather than the destructive development of the personality. We might reply by saying, "Does this mean a person cannot destroy himself or cannot choose to destroy himself?" The answer, of course, is: "Yes, a person can choose to destroy himself." He may, in fact, do so because he believes that it is for the betterment of the creative integration of his or other persons' personalities.

REDEFINITION

In retrospect, then, we define a value as being the stance that the self takes to the world through the feelings, ideas, imagination, and behavior of the individual. The valuing process comes about through the free choice of the individual within a particular stage of his formation with its given limitations. This choice must consider the consequences or the alternatives that are evident and must be, of course, a choice from alternatives. Essential to the valuing process also is that the choice must have been acted upon and become a permanent part of the life plan of the person if it is to be called a value. Finally, the person must be happy with the choice, and the choice must be one that enhances the development, emotional and spiritual, of that individual.

In order to clarify whether or not a given thing is a value or not, I should ask myself the following questions about it:

1. *Was the value chosen from a range of alternatives that I was aware of?*

2. *Did I consider the consequences of those alternatives that I was aware of?*

3. *Is this value evident in my behavior? That is to say, have I acted on it recently?*

4. *Do I act on this value repeatedly in some fashion through a variety of similar experiences?*

5. *Am I happy and pleased with the choice?*

6. *Am I willing to state it publicly?*

7. *Does the value enhance, and not impede, the development of my emotional and spiritual well-being?*

66

This is, of course, a slight modification of the Simon, Raths, and Harmin definition, but the criteria still stand. If I cannot answer yes to all of the above questions, then what I am speaking of is not the fully developed value. The next question that has to be asked is: How many chosen values, since the above is a chosen value, do we, in fact, live by? Is it possible that the majority of values we have are part and parcel of our personality and assimilated from our upbringing? Would we choose the values which we become aware of? This whole question brings up the problem of the various types of values that there are. This we are going to deal with in the next chapter.

3.
Values Here, Values There, Values Everywhere

> *Wherever men forget their mere man's nature,*
> *Thinking a thought too high, they have no use*
> *Of their huge bulk and boldness, but they fall*
> *On most untoward disasters sent by Heaven.*
>   Sophocles, Ajax

In this chapter, we are going to deal with the question: How does a person achieve the ability to choose his own values? What happens to a child, to a young person growing up, to enable them to choose creatively from alternatives and to have the inner strength and ability to act on those alternatives? Another way of placing the question is: What kinds of things have to happen to a person to enable that person to become his own authority, making his own decisions rather than depending on the decisions of others most of the time?

Values and the Child

THE CHILD. (See Diagrams A, B, and C) In speaking about the child, Carl Rogers feels that the child immediately begins to have a clear approach to values. That is, he prefers some things and rejects others. Now, clearly this preference and judgment is influenced largely by the mother and father in the early stages of development. He copies them sometimes. He mimics them or does opposite things to annoy them.

> *"Hunger is negatively valued. His expression of this often comes through loud and clear.*
> *"Food is positively valued. But when he is satisfied, food is negatively valued, and the same milk he responded to so eagerly is now spit out, or the breast which seemed so satisfying is now rejected as he turns his head away from the nipple with an amusing facial expression of disgust and revulsion.*
> *"He values security and the holding and caressing which seem to communicate security.*
> *"He values new experience for its own sake, and we observe this in his obvious pleasure in discovering his toes, in his searching movements, and in his endless curiosity.*
> *"He shows a clear negative valuing of pain, bitter tastes, and sudden loud sounds"* (Freedom to Learn, p. 242).

Rogers wants to point out that the source of the evaluating process always starts within oneself even when the child is very young. He even goes on to say that when the infant is very young, he is not concerned about the values of his parents. He only reacts to them in the ways expressed above. This points very much to the valuing criteria that would say to a parent: "Your child learns from your behavior, from your reaction to him more than from whatever you say."

Original Value Formers

The environment in which the child finds himself, to which the child reacts, as he discovers what he likes and what he does not like, is very important. *Those aspects of that environment that affect the child's ability to choose from alternatives and to act at this stage are called original value formers.* They are all those aspects of his environment which will affect his later ability to make clear value choices. That is to say, if credibility is given to a child's fantasy world or to his value as a person or to his ability to make his own choices, these things will very much affect his later ability to choose his own values. (See Diagrams A and C)

Although it is evident that there are many original value

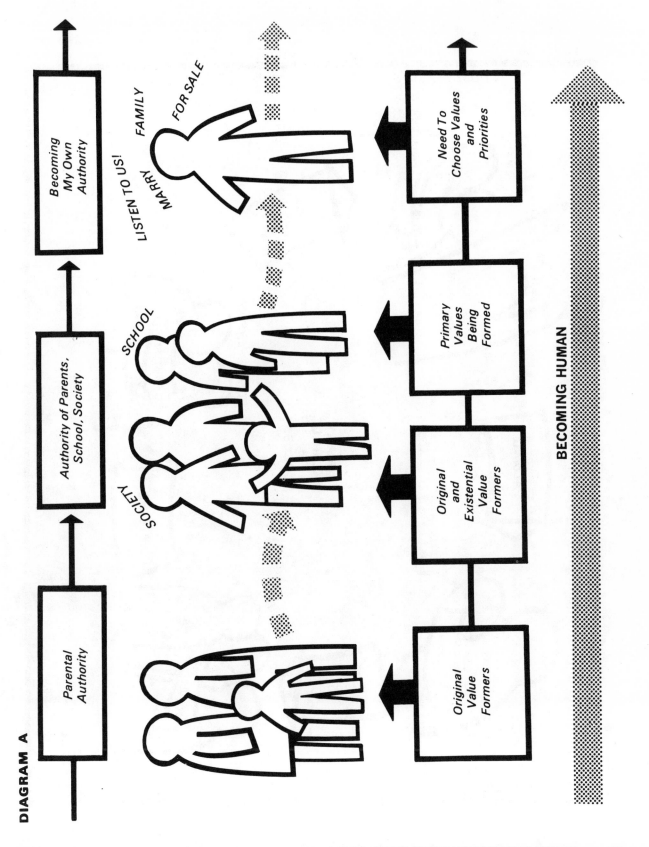

DIAGRAM A

Parental Authority

Authority of Parents, School, Society

Becoming My Own Authority

Original Value Formers

Original and Existential Value Formers

Primary Values Being Formed

Need To Choose Values and Priorities

SOCIETY

SCHOOL

LISTEN TO US!

MARRY

FAMILY

FOR SALE

BECOMING HUMAN

DIAGRAM B

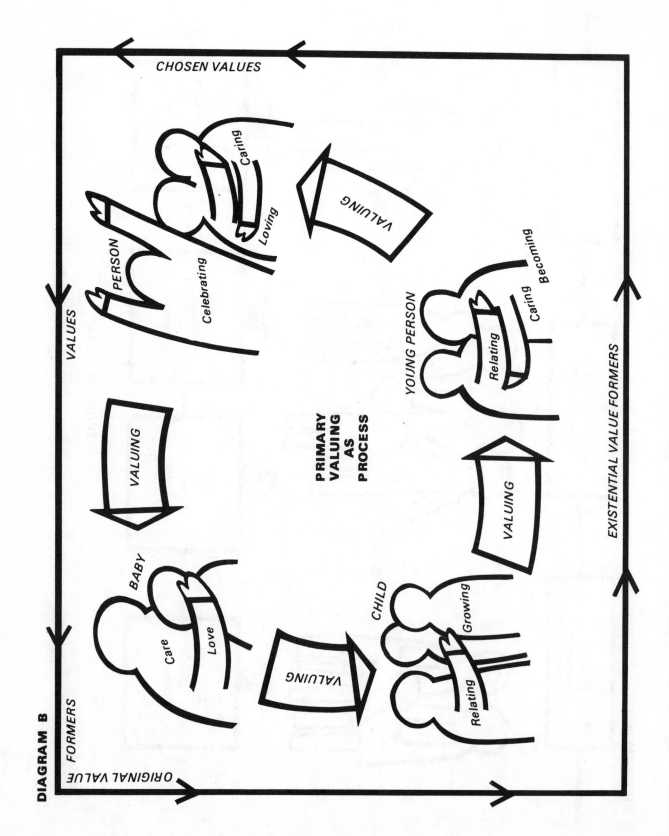

CHOSEN VALUES

VALUES

PERSON

Caring

Loving

Celebrating

VALUING

YOUNG PERSON

Relating

Caring

Becoming

EXISTENTIAL VALUE FORMERS

PRIMARY VALUING AS PROCESS

VALUING

VALUING

CHILD

Relating

Growing

VALUING

BABY

Care

Love

FORMERS

ORIGINAL VALUE

DIAGRAM C

EXAMPLES OF VALUE FORMATION

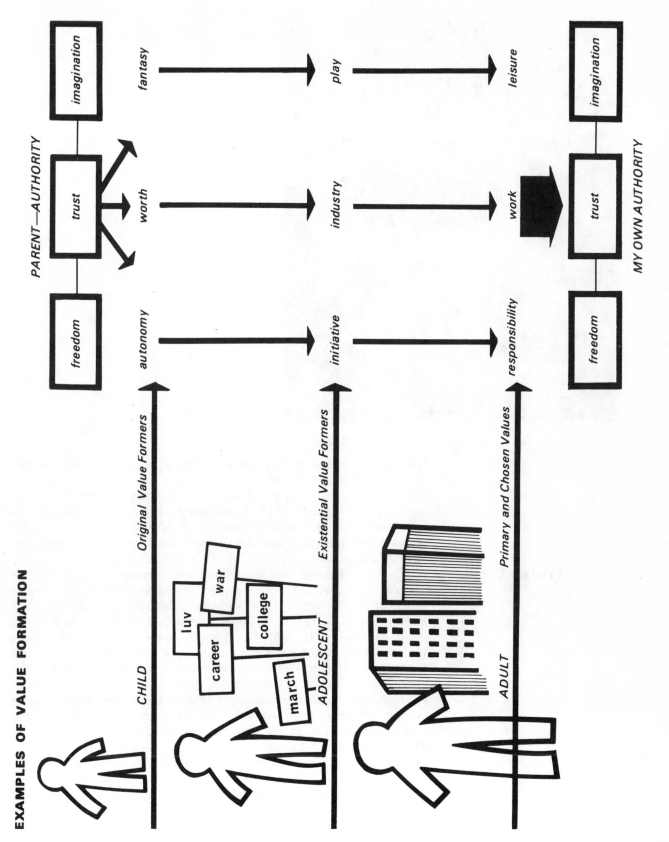

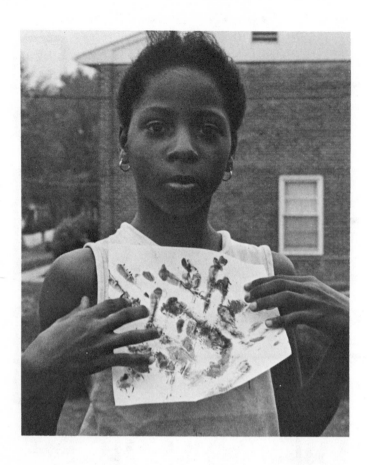

formers, there are some that are more essential than others. We can see, for example, that in order for a child to grow he must have a certain amount of freedom. He must be allowed to use his imagination. The use of his intelligence must be encouraged if he is to survive in our school systems. Now all these original value formers will later on grow into chosen values such as intelligence, leisure, and so on.

Primary Values

But, having said this, there are certain values which we call primary that are necessary for a person to be able to live creatively in the world. That is to say, although a person may have many values, there are at least a couple that he must have in order to survive. In terms of original value formers, this means that the child must have certain primary value formers that will finally result in those other values that we spoke of. Basically, the infant needs love and will tend to behave in ways as a result of which he will receive experiences of love and of being told that he is good or worthwhile. As such, he responds to discipline or the loss of affection from his parents or from his brothers or sisters. The ways in which he receives love and is taught to get love from people are what we call aspects of the environment.

The point is that there must be some elements in this environment which will permit the child to grow in such a way that he will have the ability to choose those values in later life

74

that are necessary for his creative development. There are many values that could be considered as basic and necessary. Examples of such values would be responsibility, work, leisure, or freedom. However, there are, in this author's opinion, two values which are considered to be primary. The first would be the value of *self-value* or the intrinsic knowledge that I am of worth to others. The second would be the *value of others*. Other people argue that there are more than two primary values. Aldous Huxley, for example, adds intelligence to that list. In referring to primary values in this text, we are talking of those two just mentioned.

If these two primary values are important, then, in the development of a child, a loving and caring environment which affirms the worth and value of the child is necessary. Hence, among the original value formers there needs to be the presence of love and trust.

Values and the Adolescent

ADOLESCENT. (See Diagrams A, B, and C) As the child grows and he begins to discover how to choose behavior that will get him the love and affection that he wants, as well as the kind of behavior which gets him those pleasures which he seeks, he will actually be experimenting with choice and the consequences of choice. In the earlier stages, his choices are restricted by parental authority. Then his choices are restricted by the authority of school and teacher. Slowly but surely he begins to make his own choices and to take responsibility for his acts. This process is that of a person, any person, becoming his own authority. Sadly, in our own society many people never become their own authority but remain always dependent on others or on the whims and directions of advertising and media.

Identity and Healthy Development

In good healthy development, a person becomes more able to choose and act, or, as we say, they become more aware of their identity. This identity crisis is usually placed in the adolescent period. (I would like to mention at this point that the teenage period or the adolescent period may extend over a whole person's lifetime and is not necessarily psychologically restricted to the years between twelve and twenty.)

This movement toward identity is evident in several ways:

1. People tend to move away from the pretense of playing a role and to place more emphasis on honest communication to the best of their ability.

2. There is a movement away from over-dependence on the expectations of other people and toward the idea of feeling joy and happiness in making my own choices and deciding my own life patterns. This is marked by the lack of fear in choice; there is more of a sense of adventure and determination.

3. Those aspects of one's behavior that point to the underlying values emerge as being positive and not things to be feared. That is to say, a person values his ability to express his feelings and is not overly threatened by reflection on inconsistent behavior. He delights in fantasy and imagination and does not always fear that someone will find out what he is really thinking.

4. There is a marked appearance of the value of self as a person comes to feel that he can make a contribution to any setting. He is not afraid that what he says will be laughed at because he knows that what he has is of value. There is, then, at the same time an automatic valuing of others which always goes along with the valuing of self. This is true because the person will begin to communicate more honestly, trusting the response of others and knowing that if that response is negative he will be able to handle it because he has an automatic awareness of his own positive side.

5. The person begins to develop an increased ability to see alternatives as a development of the creative side of his imagination. He is not overwhelmed by his alternatives as in a state of anxiety, but rather delights in them and begins to see them as possibilities for creative growth.

6. The person moves toward deeper feelings of intimacy of others as a positive value. He does not fear closeness and in-depth communication as a threat to himself. Self is valued highly.

The above process is the development of authority and therefore the development of a person's ability to choose his own values through his life-cycle experience. The question of identity or coming to grips with my authority centers in many writers, such as Erikson, for example, in the adolescent period. The reason that this period is often seen as one where the identity issue is most crucial comes from the fact that during this period in a person's life he is confronted with leaving home, starting college, joining the army, getting a new job, meeting members of the opposite sex and getting married. This is the period of time when the person approaches increased needs to be intimate in the area of long-term relationships with other people. All these things confront a person with a multiplicity of choices which will affect his life-style to a very great degree.

**Significant Persons
as Value Formers**

It is becoming apparent, then, that when we speak of original value formers, we are speaking primarily of the influence of significant persons and their attitudes and the environment they create. Such significant persons could be parents, brothers or sisters, teachers, and possibly employers. Such original value formers are primarily relational—dealing with the early experience of an individual's relationship to others. When educators or psychologists concern themselves with those elements of a person's development which ultimately affect their ability to deal well with other persons, they are usually reflecting upon the positive and negative experiences in a person's life which are the original value formers.

**Existential
Value Formers**

However, there are other value formers which center on other experiences. For the sake of clarity, we have referred to them as *existential value formers*. Existential value formers confront a person with his total human reality in the face of the world. They prompt a man to question the meaning of his nature as a human being among other human beings in the world. The issues of death and limitation and creativity and the totality of life are involved in the area of existential value formers.

The issues raised in terms of existential value formers are broader, therefore, than the self-significant other issues raised by original value formers. Because of this fact, normally, existential value formers begin to influence people at a later stage of their development, particularly during the adolescent period when most people confront a broader span of life decisions.

The existential value formers will normally prompt a person to become more aware of the need to choose creatively, of the question of his personal responsibility to act, of the fact that he is, at root, a lonely person, and of the facts of death and sickness and limitation to his life. I say that "normally" his awareness of these issues will occur during adolescence; however, environment can finally shelter him from any such consideration and will, in fact, delay or prolong the process of value formation which we usually identify with adolescents.

Values and the Adult

THE ADULT. The word adult here is simply used to describe that part of a person that has gone past the childhood and adolescent periods of development. Some people never get past those stages. It is simply a word that helps us describe the valuing process in any well-developed human being. Obviously, all adults are not mature. The point is that by the time a person has got to this point, hopefully he would have had enough original and existential value formation experiences so that he would now begin to develop his own personality by being able to choose his own values. It is here that we encounter the necessity of the choice and development of primary values.

As characteristics of the mature person, Rogers feels that values are not held rigidly but are continually changing. This, of course, is related to the fact that my choices change continually because, as I grow older and more mature, I continually see more alternatives. Another way in which a person grows in maturity is that not only are the values chosen by the person, but the person also begins to recognize the imposition and expectations of another so that the person is able to differentiate between his values and the values of other people.

Thirdly, like the infant, the person not only finds a locus of evaluation within himself, but recognizes it as such and is able to choose values more openly. He would then be more cognizant of what that choice meant in terms of behavior and action. Thus it becomes evident that the valuing process and the choosing of values to which we referred in the previous chapter is not a simple matter, but one that can develop only after a long period of value formation through the processes that we have enunciated above. The less of a human being that I am, the less identity I have, the more difficult it is for me to make my own choices, and the more I am at the whim or the fate of others.

Diagram A

THE DIAGRAMS. In the diagrams A, B, and C, I have tried to illustrate some of the process outlined above. In Diagram A we see the development of a person, starting with the major influence of parental authority and moving to the idea of becoming his own authority as an adult. The adult here chooses for himself and reflects and evaluates the expectations of others rather than always blindly trying to live up to them. Original value formers are seen as starting at childbirth and moving through the totality of life. Existential value formers come later as the child develops, and primary values perhaps begin to be involved as a person becomes a teenager.

Diagram B

In Diagram B the same process is evaluated but refers only to primary values. The primary values of self-worth and valuing of others come about through the environment of love and care that a child first receives as a baby. This is the original value former which carries on through childhood as he begins to relate to other people and begins to utilize this care and test it out. As he becomes a teenager, a person finds caring relationships with members of the opposite sex and is confronted with not only choice but responsibility as here he encounters the existential value former.

All the while this process has been taking place through the various relationships that a person has received. Finally, the adult begins valuing others by celebrating his own choices and his ability to choose to love and care for others as a person.

Diagram C

In Diagram C we see some examples of value formation. We see the environment of parental authority as examples of freedom, trust, and imagination. This means that the environment positively regards these three examples. The results on such experiences in a child will be the original value formers, i.e., the appreciation of autonomy, worth, and fantasy. These three formers in the adolescent, as he begins to choose and face the world, will result in the existential values of initiative, industry, and play. These, in turn, could result in the chosen values of responsibility, work, and leisure in the adult. From these final values he would then begin to create his own environment of freedom, trust, and imagination.

Autonomy as a Value

Other examples of value formers are autonomy and the use of the imagination. With autonomy as an example, we might first ask what kind of environment would permit autonomy to be an original value former. The kind of environment which would allow autonomy to be an original value former would be, in particular, the one of freedom. (See Diagram C) That is to say, the child would have to experience a sufficient amount of freedom as well as control to experience autonomy at a very early stage in his life.

What is understood by autonomy is the experience of a child to be able to make choices which are his own and to experience positive consequences as a result. A great deal in psychoanalytical literature has been written about toilet training, asserting that if you push a child to use his sphincter muscles too rapidly, he loses control and does not learn choice as a positive experience. As such, this affects his whole attitude of choice in the area of giving and taking in later life. In terms of valuing, this would mean that he was not given sufficient autonomy to be able to learn how to choose.

As the child becomes older and moves toward the teenage years, this early experience of alternatives becomes for him the ability to utilize inner creative initiative. He becomes interested in things, but does not drop interest rapidly because he knows that there are choices available to him. He can, by his own direction, create things and fantasies in his own imagination. If he has had bad experiences where choice led to unhappy experiences, then he is going to lack initiative at a later stage. In a sense, initiative will be more a threat of failure than a promise of success.

When the person becomes a young man or woman, autonomy and initiative have now prepared this person for responsibility. That is to say, responsibility is not only whether I choose and act, but also whether I am willing to accept the consequences of the choice. This, of course, can become a value.

Once the person reaches this stage there are several values that could have come out of the original value former which was autonomy. Another example would be freedom. As such, it would be a chosen value to such a degree that he consistently selects environments of freedom for himself and those he relates to as lover, parent, teacher, etc. It will, then, be a consequence of the original freedom that his parents originally allowed him. In this example, we might say that autonomy, initiative, and freedom were value formers. Freedom originally given and responsibility finally obtained are examples of chosen values that can result from this original value formation.

Imagination as a Value Former

Our other example that we mentioned above was *imagination*. Imagination, of course, is a natural part of any human being; however, the positive regard for this element in the child can affect the original and existential value formers experienced by the child and, therefore, his chosen values. If the parents value imagination, a child's fantasy world will be seen as essential and important. His playing, his getting on the floor with different things, will be seen as important. The parents wouldn't laugh at his dreams and his world, but rather would participate in them. Parents who, unfortunately, regard the fantasies of a child as unreal or just childish of course restrict the possibility for the development of a person's imagination later on in life.

As this child develops, fantasy becomes play. Play, it seems to me, carries on all through life, but so often it is relegated only to the pre-school years. Often, when the child goes to school in the primary years, he is told that he will have play periods, but that is only because of the adjustment needed. Play is seen as often that which is childish and regressive. However, it is essential as an extension of the original value former of fantasy, and its absence leads to the repression of a most valuable side of the human person. Repression of the imagination, repression of fantasy, can lead to serious mental illness later on or minimally to states of boredom and uncreativeness affecting a person's whole life-style, work, and human relationships.

In the adult the value formers of fantasy, imagination, and play now act on a person in terms of values chosen in the present as an adult. What values? The major value is that of leisure. To

see recreation, recuperation, festivity, and celebration as a necessary part of my existence is to give balance to my life. All these values are essential and come to being in a person only as they have had the possibility of formation through original value formers earlier in life.

TIME AND DEVELOPMENT

As was noted in the introduction of this chapter, a child learns through his social development. Several writers have pointed out that this development moves through several given stages. The point is that a healthy development through these stages prepares the child intellectually and emotionally to be able to choose the kinds of values and direction in life which he wants.

To avoid adverse trends of behavior, the child needs to have received certain things in his emotional development. For this reason it is important for us to briefly look at the developmental trend and to be aware of the time factor involved. Following this we will explore a number of influences which seem to clarify the notion of original value formers.

Piaget's Stages of Child Development

In Piaget, the development of the child is seen in a balance of the intellectual and the affective elements. In addition to this, development is organized along intrapersonal and social lines. Within this context, six stages of development are noted:

1. The reflex or hereditary stage at which the first instinctual nutritional drives and the first emotions appear.

2. The stage of the first motor habits and of the first organized precepts, as well as of the first differentiated emotions.

3. The stage of sensorimotor or practical intelligence (prior to language), of elementary affective organization, and of the first external affective fixations.

These first three stages constitute the infancy period— from birth till the age of 1 ½ to 2 years—i.e., the period prior to the development of language and thought as such.

4. The stage of intuitive intelligence, of spontaneous interpersonal feelings, and of social relationships in which the child is subordinate to the adult (ages 2 to 7 years, or "early childhood").

5. The stage of concrete intellectual operations (the beginning of logic) and of moral and social feelings of cooperation (ages 7 to 11 or 12, or "middle childhood").

6. The stage of abstract intellectual operations, of the formation of the personality, and of affective and intellectual entry into the society of adults (adolescence) (Piaget, Six Psychological Studies, pp. 5-6).

In reflecting on values, it is important to realize that values are beginning to be chosen at the fifth stage according to Piaget. However, it is clear that the way in which they are chosen is dependent upon the positive growth that has occurred in the preceding four stages. In other words, it is important that the child's emotions have developed so that he can differentiate them and manipulate them creatively. Hence, what we are referring to is the nature of a healthy personality which has been formed in such a way that values can be chosen at a later date.

Erikson and Human Development

Another developmental cycle that we should just look at briefly in order to get a wider perspective is that of Erik H. Erikson. Erikson posits eight stages in the psychological and social development of a human being. The first six are stages which take a person up to the end of adolescence and in this way make a good comparison with Piaget.

1. *Basic Trust versus Basic Mistrust.* This is important to the totality of life and is not restricted to childhood only. The point is that in the first year or so of the development of the child, a sense of being cared for, looked after, and protected by the mother is essential. This is needed if the child is to develop a trust in people which will carry on through the rest of his life. Babies are vulnerable, and as such there is a question of what must not be done with a child at this stage, so that he will not develop a feeling of mistrust in people rather than trust.

2. *Autonomy versus Shame and Doubt.* For the psychoanalyst, the years between two and five are close to the anal stage and are concerned with the whole business of muscle control as the child learns to hold onto and let go of things. In terms of the total development, he is involved in learning through his parents how to gain a sense of self-control without losing self-esteem. He learns to use all of his muscles and begins to feel a sense of accomplishment. With sufficient support from his parents and other adults around him, he confronts his limitations without feeling a sense of failure.

3. *Initiative versus Guilt.* In this stage the social sphere begins to expand, and so the child is confronted with an ever-wider range of alternatives and possibilities. He begins to be able to command the language which increases his whole communication. As his language and locomotion expand, he is confronted with an even larger series of possibilities in the area of his imagination which may be frightening to him. As a person becomes aware of more alternatives, he becomes aware of the possibility of greater failure as well as his guilt as he fails himself and others. In the Freudian viewpoint, it is during this stage that the child has greater interaction with his parents. As he develops his communication skills and the greater possibility of social mobility, he has to confront all sorts of feelings of which he was not previously aware.

4. *Industry versus Inferiority.* This is the stage that goes from seven to twelve years of age and is very much like Stage 5 in Piaget. In this stage the child becomes very enthusiastic about learning. He wants to be shown how to get busy with something and with other people. This is the stage where, in all cultures, children go to school and are taught. The danger is that a sense of inadequacy or inferiority may be developed by not dealing with

the creative will of the child. The child needs to have recognition of things that he does and thus he learns a sense of accomplishment. The child becomes very function-orientated and needs to learn to differentiate between work and play. All too often school systems have emphasized the work aspect and regarded play as something only for small children, and so they have eliminated for many people a real appreciation of the later development of leisure.

5. *Identity versus Identity Diffusion.* This stage is the beginning of puberty and adolescence. The child experiences physical changes and is encountering rapid changes in the world around him. He is preparing for college or the possibility of marriage in the future. He is experiencing a rapid increase in alternatives. There is an increase of responsibility—more than he has had to deal with before. Erikson points out that the identity reached in this stage is more than the sum of the childhood identifications. It is the new man who now builds on all development of past experiences in a new way. These past experiences, which in terms of values we are calling value formers, are essential if a person is to be able to deal with his life at this stage. The problem is that if the child has not been given sufficient foundation at previous stages, he is likely at this point to take on other people's identity, that is to say, take on the values of his peers or continue with the values of his parents—which may be inadequate in his new life. At this stage, identity means choosing his own life direction, his own values and priorities, and not depending so much on the priorities of other people.

6. *Intimacy and Solidarity versus Isolation.* This is really the first stage of adulthood, but it is mentioned here since it does complete the adolescent period. The whole question of intimacy and the ability to share deeply with another person rests squarely on the shoulders of all the other stages. I can't share unless I can trust, for example. I can't form a solid married life and an intimate direction if I am not sure where I am in terms of my identity. The problem of this stage is that as my ability to be intimate breaks down, I become isolated and alienated from the world.

The main point in going over the idea of personality formation above is simply to point out that the personality and the values within the personality are developed over a period of time. They are developed as a person grows in relationships.

Piaget and Erikson, and Original Value Formers

Now to relate this overview of Piaget and Erikson to original value formers, let us brainstorm for a moment on the two systems of social development listed in the last section. They will indicate elements needed for a healthy value system. Here is a list of some of the important elements we might come up with. Some of these words are taken directly from the vocabulary used in the systems delineated by Erikson and Piaget. Some of the following words are just inferred.

trust	*play*
initiative	*intuition*
ideas	*control*
joy	*feelings*
industry	*autonomy*
imagination	

At this point evaluate these two lists according to your position of what has been important in your early life in forming values. What elements in these two lists would you change? What elements would you add? Make your own list. Include in your list elements important to yourself and important to your ability to relate.

For the moment, let us take three or four of the words listed and see how they might operate as value formers in the area of self, others (society), and world. In doing so, we will be exploring the influence of original value formers on the individual's value system.

Trust: Essential to Primary Values Development

Trust versus mistrust is, of course, the first stage in Erikson's development. And as such, he calls it basic trust. That is to say, it is basic to the whole system of trust that the human being will need for his growth during the total development of his life. Therefore, each of the positive words in Erikson's life stages is important to the formation of our values. However, trust is the most basic. In fact, if the proper environment is not present, the child will not develop the right attitude of trust in regard to himself, or others, or creation itself. Let us briefly analyze this.

Trust is first formed as the person relates primarily to the mother in the first year of development. To put it another way, if a small child was treated very badly by the first person that he or she ever related to, then obviously the child will develop toward mistrust. So often, in counseling, one will be confronted with a married couple where one will refuse to change on the grounds that he does not trust the other.

In relationship of the self to the self, trust is essential in the development of what we refer to as primary values. The primary value that I would allude to here is the value of self-worth. Self-worth is defined as the conviction that other people, if they really knew me, would see me as a person of value. Without exploring this any further, I simply wish to point out that if I do not have the basic elements of trust within my system, I will not believe people when they say I am worth a great deal. As such, the value of self-worth is impossible for me.

Related to this trust element are other words we could have put in our brainstorm list, such as listening or honesty. If I have no trust in people, honesty becomes impossible. If I have no trust in people, listening becomes distorted.

When Trust Breaks Down

A breakdown of trust often occurs when the parents have expectations of a child which the child feels he cannot live up to. This is borne out not only in the home, but also in school systems. In fact, numerous recent educational studies have indicated that the expectations that a teacher has for a class of students does, in fact, affect their learning ability. If the teacher has low expectations (low trust in the students), the students perform below their ability and consequently validate the lack of trust by their behavior. It is interesting to note how much recent educational theory has been attempting to face this issue of trust and expectation in classrooms, whether in suburbia or inner city areas. A school system predicated upon distrust and the consequent highly authoritarian structure and demeaning attitude toward the students produces, it seems, reduced performance and an irresponsible student body.

An example of this was a young man I knew who was very intelligent and very clever in terms of abstract sciences, but he had a father who was an athlete and who put a great deal of emphasis on sports. His son, who had less physical capabilities than his father, grew up feeling that his skills were not to be trusted because he was not a sportsman!

Not only can a man be distrustful of himself and his own worth; he can also develop attitudes and methods of behavior which are based on his mistrust of others. Generally speaking, that mistrust will show itself in various attempts at manipulation and control of those around him. To control and be manipulative is a choice which we are taught in our early years and through the various experiences of our life. If the pain of life is too great, this desire to control might eventually lead to the extreme of choosing not to communicate at all—the ultimate in control and manipulation. A person's life experience (original and existential value formers) could lead him to a deliberate choice of pragmatic non-values in order to "survive."

When we manipulate people, we are attempting to control rather than trust the response of others. Hence, trust as an original value former is very operative. Whenever we encounter such controlling behavior, we almost always get angry. The mistake is in feeling that we have to control people in order to gain them. If I have the value of friendship but lose all my friends by controlling or manipulating them, it is because the original value former of trust is not active.

If I have been taught to choose to mistrust myself and to

mistrust others, I am likely to extend that pragmatic non-value to yet another area, to the creation and environment around me. Once a person has moved into the kind of relationship with people that is controlling in nature, then that person ultimately needs to control his environment to his own end. The created order, therefore, of non-human objects is usually seen as valuable only insofar as it meets that person's ends.

In order for man to respect the created order—the rivers, the fields, and so on—he must see it as that which contributes toward the humanizing of man. Therefore, when trust is broken down as an original value former, and man's relationship with man, with society, is in a state of alienation, then he is unable to relate to creation as being of value. The creation cannot be a humanizing factor for him unless he sees humanity as positive and trustful.

One of the clearest examples I have seen of this was watching a television interview of the manager of one of the large steel plants in a large urban area. The purpose of the interview was to discuss the reality of the miserable effect upon the area of pollution in the form of chemicals in the air.

The point was being made that smoke pours down streets daily, gets into people's lungs, and makes the city a very unpleasant place to live in. The interviewer asked the manager of the works, "Are you not concerned about this?" The reply came back, "Why should I be concerned, since the major motivation of most of the people in our factories is to earn money?" He went on to say that he and his superiors provided income and money for these people and that the employees were not concerned about pollution any more than he was.

Now this is not to say that he represented all management in all steel factories. It does, however, point out the connection between the need of man to be considerate of his fellow worker as a part of the continuum which permits him to be concerned about the creation itself. In this case, the man was concerned about neither.

Many of the advertisements for lead-free gasoline talk about their concern for "you" while they are talking about their concern for pollution. The underlying original value former of trust, then, is absolutely essential in the development later on of the choice of values, not only self-value, but a value of others and even of the world itself. As man fails to trust himself, he tries to control other people around him. The control moves out from friends to people, often en masse.

We see thousands trapped in the ghettos of our city who are, in fact, under all sorts of discrimination and control. The person from the low economic area, for example, may not get a job when he tells the interviewer where he lives. He may not get credit when he tells the store owner what his income is. This, however, is often not so easy to see as a man being controlled by another individual. As we move across to the national dimension and the international dimension and look at war, we see countries trying to manipulate other countries.

Autonomy and Initiative

Other examples of original value formers that were noted were, for example, in the area of *autonomy* and *initiative*. The whole relationship of the teacher and of the parent to the child in teaching him and permitting him to be autonomous in given areas in the early stages of life is essential to the development of responsibility later on in life. If a child is not allowed to choose early in his life and discover the fruits of his choice as being positive, then, of course, he will be deficient in his whole pattern of choice throughout the rest of his life. Choice, as we have noted in the last chapter, is essential to the development of values. This is, therefore, another example of a very important original value former.

In the area of self, if I cannot choose, I begin to doubt my own self-worth. Why? Because if I can't choose, I become dependent on other people and dependent on their affirmation of my value. My value, therefore, is dependent on others rather than on my own potential and choice.

In the area of my relationship to other people and society, I become a dependent person who can only receive what others give and am unable to create the society that I would wish for. Further, as has been pointed out previously, without self-directed creative relationships the creation tends to be something that is abused rather than something which enhances my humanization.

Values become impossible if I am not aware of the need for value formers. Original value formers, then, are essential in the education and parental upbringing of children. The teacher and parent need to develop such things as trust and choice if value formation is to become possible in our children.

THE EXISTENTIAL VALUE FORMER AND COMPUTER MAN

The question to ask in regard to value formers is: Is the reality in which I find myself, both by my existential nature and by the needs which have to be supplied from my environment as in the original value formers, the totality of who I am?

As we look at original value formers, one might ask the question: How much love and caring does anyone need in order to have the trust to be able to choose completely freely? Values are something that are chosen freely and acted upon. How can I choose freely if I am dependent on so many needs and factors which affect my life? Frankl writes on this point:

> "*Man, as the finite being he basically is, will never be able to free himself completely from the ties which bind him to the various realms wherein he is confronted by unalterable conditions. Nevertheless, there is always a certain residue of freedom left to his decisions. For within the limits—however restricted they may be—he can move freely; and only by this very stand which he takes toward whatever conditions he may face*

does he prove to be a truly human being. This holds true with regard to biological and psychological as well as sociological facts and factors. Social environment, hereditary endowment and instinctual drives can limit the scope of man's freedom, but in themselves they can never totally blur the human capacity to take a stand toward all these conditions" (Psychotherapy and Existentialism, pp. 59-60).

Frankl's statement is just one of many expressions of the realization of man's capacity for freedom and choice. If we are to discover our identity and if we are to clarify values, we can never get away from the underlying needs that we all personally have. Freedom to choose, then, is freedom to choose from alternatives. It can never mean all the alternatives; it can only mean some of them, depending on my own particular limitations in this situation. The existence of that capacity cannot be forgotten while we are discussing values and value formers. To say, as we have in the past section, that certain psychic-socio experiences affect the values which man chooses is to say that man is affected by experiences but can still take a stand toward them; it is *not* to say that man is totally controlled by these experiences.

Balancing Man's Potential and His Limits

To enter into the mystery of the balance between the potential of man and his limits is really to enter into the mystery of man himself. Yet, we cannot really understand the significance of values which are authentically chosen without reflecting upon the process of choice and the influences on that process. When we spoke of original value formers, we were examining one source of these influences. In this section, we would like to examine another source.

One of the basic conditions of man flows from the very fact that he is limited—limited in his existence, his choices, his actions, his relationships. Every time we sense that limitation, we are put into the position described by Frankl; we are called upon to take a stand toward that limitation. As man comes to grips with his limitation, we are in the area of what we are calling existential value formers. They, like the original value formers, will influence our choice of values.

The series of diagrams in this chapter are really a combination of many of the themes and concerns which occupy the attention of many existential thinkers for the past century. It is included here merely to chart a suggestion, a hint, with which each of you can play. The themes are not exclusive, the lists not complete, the concerns not iron-clad, but they should touch some of your concerns. They should remind you of moments and thoughts and feelings which have struck you. As we progress through the discussion of the diagram(s), we will be following the varied paths modern man can take, in the fact of his existence, toward the choice of his values.

Man's Limitations

We need, within this context, to look at some of the limitations which man faces in order that we can begin to evaluate the formation of values which result from an awareness of these limits. For the sake of this issue, we have selected four basic limits which face every man and will analyze how he can cope with them. The limits are simply:

Limited being: Physically he will die; emotionally he can cope with just so much.

Limited choice: From the maze of alternatives open to any man, he can choose just one, know just so many, imagine the full implications of only a few.

Limited action: When I make a choice a reality by action, I bear the brunt of responsibility for the consequences.

Separateness: I stand faced with these limits by myself, apart from others.

The awareness of each of these conditions of limits on my existence affects the individual in different ways. As such, they are value formers. Let us examine their effect on people.

We need, within this context, to look at some of the limitations that man is faced with in order to begin to evaluate the formation of values and what it is we need to be aware of in some degree.

LIMITED BEING. Every human being is, of course, ultimately limited in what is physically and emotionally possible of him. That is to say, we are all going to die one day, and as such we are limited in our life span, for example. This is what the existentialists call contingency. This simply means: "I am here today, but I could be gone tomorrow." Put in terms of earlier chapters, "I cannot control the future, I do not in fact know what is going to happen, and as such my very existence is in some ways always tenuous."

Some of the elements that result from this situation in which we find ourselves are: body, feelings, faith, trust. Now, what do I mean by this? First of all, my limited condition really faces me with the reality that I am growing up, that I will get older, that I will die. This confronts me with the whole reality of my body. The spatial concept here would be very much the idea of self. As one is confronted with one's limitations in the area of body, feelings are automatically present through the body (refer to Diagram III).

Several months ago I was working as a consultant to a team of single women teachers who were living together in the same house. Three of the teachers were having difficulty in working and living together. One young lady, twenty-four years of age, continually complained that the other two with whom she was having the conflict were insensitive to her feelings. The other two, on the other hand, complained that she was not interested in what they were doing in their work situation. The one young lady, June, was an artist, while the other two were principals in a school. In order to help them come to grips with the conflict, I asked the three of them to do a diagram of some tension or conflict that came to mind in their past history. You might at this point try a similar diagram for yourself. Diagram IV is an example.

In the picture we see a series of circles. Now the idea is to simply pick a particular conflict in the past and to diagram it by

DIAGRAM III

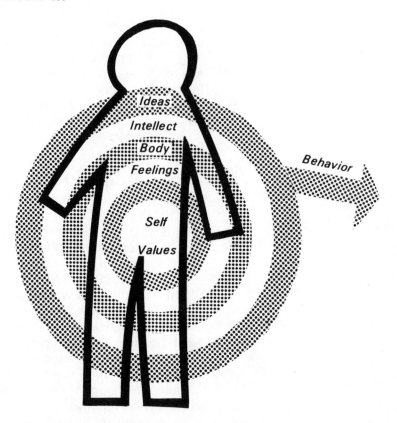

drawing the circles. The size of the circle represents how important that particular person whom the circle represents was in relationship to the other person's diagram. The distance between the circles represents emotional distances. What *importance* and *emotional* mean is up to the person who is drawing the picture.

The reason for doing the diagrams was not to get into a counseling session with the three people, but rather to help them see how they relate differently in conflict situations. In this particular instance, the girl June related how close she was to her father after the death of her mother when she was a small child, a fact unknown to the other two teachers she was living with. The two teachers, on the other hand, related the difficulties they had in administrative situations in dealing with conflicts between other teachers. Their priority was more functional—getting the job done. And the priority of June was more in the area of feelings.

As we talked more and more about this, the three girls became aware that June was far more sensitive in the area of feelings and far more apt to get depressed occasionally and to be overwhelmed by situations. All of this was within her normal functioning and was not at all to be seen in the area of what we might normally call mental ill-health. It was simply where her personality was.

DIAGRAM IV

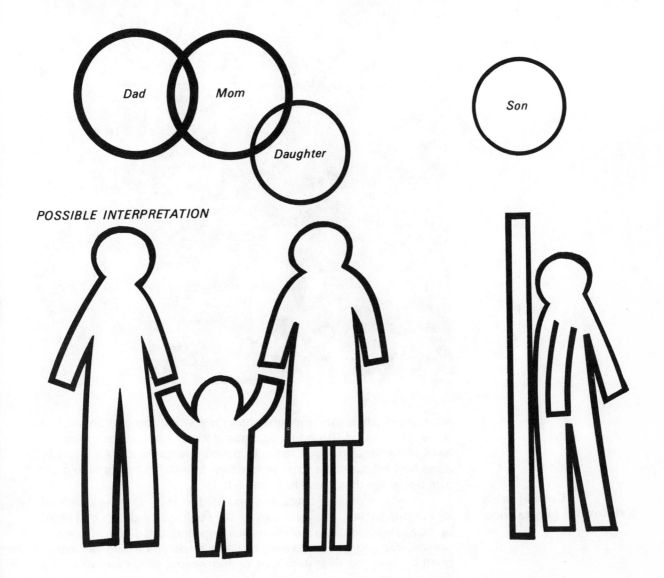

POSSIBLE INTERPRETATION

It was pointed out to the three of them that when a person is confronted with the reality of death, as was June, the person frequently is much more aware of her contingency as a human being. She is more aware of death and that sort of limitation in her life. She tended, therefore, to get much more emotional about things, since she was much more aware of the fearful possibilities. However, it was also clear that she had a deeper ability to feel and could, therefore, be more sensitive to other people and, as a consequence, was the type of artist whose feelings were very evident in her paintings.

The other two teachers then became aware of their need to be more sensitive to her, but also to tell her what her limita-

tions were when they thought she was getting too emotional. The three of them had to come to grips with the difference in feeling level because of the difference in their life experience. As a result, June had to put more trust in her two friends that they would affirm her when they knew how she felt.

Coping with Existential Limitations

As a person takes a stand in the face of his existential limitation, certain tensions can arise. Feelings of death or failure or powerlessness can be overwhelming and can flood in upon a person, causing a whole series of value decisions which can either contribute to the destruction or strengthening of his authority. All that we are attempting here is to point out that such tensions do influence our choices and an awareness of them can increase our capacity to choose intelligently.

Feelings are existential, that is to say, an integral part of the human being. They can be repressed. One way of dealing with my fear is to push it down and not acknowledge it. The two teachers in the above example decided to make feelings part of their value systems. They chose to express their feelings as a positive attribute in the creative development of their relationship with June. It was a value because it was chosen and acted upon, and they were happy with it. They did, in fact, have a choice not to express their feelings in this way. Hence, it could be argued that it was a value in the way in which they utilized the feelings.

LIMITED CHOICE. Another reality that confronts us is that we as human beings are able to choose. If we never chose we would, of course, become less than fully human. We would be contingent upon all the whims of other people. The reason I have said limited choice is simply, as we have noted in the previous chapter, that choice means alternatives.

I cannot choose unless there are alternatives. But since I cannot know what all the alternatives are, my choice is always limited.

Other Examples. In the latter few pages we have dealt with trust as an original value former. That is to say, trust is necessary as a part of the human experience in order for values in the area of human relationships, such as self-value and value of others, to form. This was one example, although admittedly a very basic example. There are other examples that could be taken, such as play.

Play is very important to the child, especially as his ability to walk about and manipulate his arms and legs as well as his imagination becomes developed. The young child, before he or she learns to speak, is involved in all sorts of playful activities. Now, certainly, these activities are egocentric and center, for the most part, around his view of the world.

As he grows older, play continues to be a very important activity and takes on new dimensions as he makes relationships with other young children. Play prepares children for the world and the society that they are going to live in. They learn in a fantasy world about good and evil, about life and death, through the simple games of cowboys and Indians, for example. Perhaps they can deal with the violence that is in the world and on TV by playing these games.

Play is very important for the understanding of leisure. As we shall see later, it is leisure that makes prayer and contemplation and some of the higher things of civilization a possibility. Play, then, like trust, is a value former. If it has not been developed well, the values that could ensue from it may also not form.

The way that a child develops his play and is allowed to see it as something of value will relate to how he develops his use of the imagination. It will also develop the possibility of work and leisure as values in his later life.

It is sad that so often a child is made to believe after he goes to school, especially after he has been in two or three grades, that play really is a childish thing. Play is often seen as useless because it is non-functional. A child who learns these kinds of things in a school system may also learn the negative side, namely that function—to do—is the only value that a person should have. Many people I meet have confused their work as their total worth.

If this observation about play and its importance is valid, then it is incumbent upon the educator to rethink the number and extent of creative, pleasurable experiences that are provided for students. If the school experience simply validates work, production, and performance without incorporating other occasions for fantasy, "playing around" with ideas and materials, non-graded creative and imaginative moments, it will simply be hampering the formation of the playful and creative side of man. In a world which requires a broader ability of fantasy and creativity just to survive, in a world where leisure becomes both a greater opportunity and a greater burden every year, the school can ill afford to serve in this hampering process.

Alternatives increase as I grow up from being a child with fantasy and imagination into the world of increased information and cognitive ability. Hence, we might say that some of the value formers are imagination, ideas, creativity, and meanings.

Creative Alternatives to Limited Choice

The extent to which I develop my imagination, the extent to which I develop my ideas, will be the extent to which creative alternatives are available to me. The way in which I have been taught to deal with the choices that are available to me will be to the extent that creativity is a positive value former.

Here again, there are negative possibilities. To the extent that I am not able to choose in my life, life becomes meaningless to me. If I feel inferior in the area of ideas and have been continually made to feel that I am a failure in my schoolwork, I am likely to become an anti-intellectual. The anti-intellectual element is destructive in that it does not allow me the availability of certain alternatives. Of course, this depends on the degree to which a person is anti-intellectual. If this was an extreme, it would be destructive.

The availability of alternatives is very much a part of my imaginative process. A typical example here that is so obvious is the area of sexuality. The puritan attitude in this country toward sex has had a rather sad effect on many marriages in terms of creative sexuality.

This is manifested by the excessive amount of sexual movies and literature that is available throughout the society. As an advertising friend of mine once said to me, "If you want to sell anything from soap to furniture, make sure that you get sex or children into the ad copy." This would very much indicate that the past has been marked by repression of sexual fantasy by many. Look at the incredible salability of such books as *The Sensuous Woman*, which after all should not be shocking to a normal married couple.

Also, as was pointed out in the first chapter, priority has been given to function as a primary existential value former rather than imagination in our society. The problem here is that if this has meant repression of the imagination, then it has meant to a large degree perhaps repression of creativity.

One might say that smoke pouring down the streets of Los Angeles or Gary, Indiana is a symbol of the lack of imagination of modern man as he discovers his own creation. The problems of pollution, or the problems of the ghetto as an unattractive, uncreative environment, relate then directly to the problem of the education of man in the area of choice and creativity.

Creativity, ideas, and imagination as value formers, then, should be considered as a balancing factor in much of our educational process as temporary values for some people. For example, if we should turn to the test in the first chapter and do it again, we might be able to reflect on it in a different way.

Obviously, if this analysis of man coming to grips with limited choices in his life is accurate, then the educational implications are immense. We live in a world where the alternatives open to men are becoming more and more varied; and if we are to prepare students who can come to grips with their own limitedness in the midst of all these choices, we must gear our educational efforts to a greater and greater emphasis on the use of imagination and creativity. They are the "tools" of choice.

In the past, an emphasis on docility, memory, instant feedback of prepackaged data, getting prepared for an already defined job in our society, performance according to already prescribed norms—all of these served to reduce the areas of creative and imaginative thought in students. The "rewards" of the educational system were not given to the "dreamer" but to the worker; not to the one who played with an idea, but to the one who remembered it; not to the one who relished the new, but to the one who cherished the old. That must change, and it is one of the most basic challenges of educational reformers.

For the moment, let us "play" with this idea for ourselves by working the following diagramic game.

DIAGRAMIC GAME
EXISTENTIAL VALUE FORMERS AND TENSIONS 1.

LIMITED BEING

Confronts Me With

CONTINGENCY

VALUE FORMERS	POSSIBLE TENSIONS

Physical Body:
    Health
    Exercise
    Eating
    Care
    Security
 	
Feelings:
    Joy
    Enthusiasm
    Accomplishment
    Security
	Physical Body:
	    Powerlessness
	    Death
	    Illness
	    Hospitals
	    Age
	
	Feelings:
	    Repression of:
	    Anger
	    Fear

DIAGRAMIC GAME
EXISTENTIAL VALUE FORMERS AND TENSIONS 2.

LIMITED BEING

Confronts Me With

[Contingency? What is your word?]

- -

Your Own List of Value Formers	Your Own List of Tensions

DIAGRAMIC GAME
EXISTENTIAL VALUE FORMERS AND TENSIONS 3.

LIMITED CHOICE

Confronts Me With

ALTERNATIVES

VALUE FORMERS	POSSIBLE TENSIONS
Meanings	Meaninglessness
Imagination	Anti-Intellect
Ideas	Repressed Imagination
Creativity	Destructiveness
Intuition	

DIAGRAMIC GAME
EXISTENTIAL VALUE FORMERS AND TENSIONS 4.

LIMITED CHOICE

Confronts Me With

[Alternatives! What is your word?]

Your Own List of Value Formers	Your Own List of Tensions

LIMITED ACTION. Action and choice are very close to-gether. However, the difference is that choice does emphasize the imagination, and, as such, places itself in the future in terms of a time span. That is to say, imagination, as we noted in Chapter 1, is in the future. Action is in the present. Therefore, it does differ from choice.

Once I have acted, I have already chosen from the various alternatives that I see are open to me. One of the problems that I am faced with is my limited ability to choose and to act. I am not perfect. Therefore, I can fail; I can make a mistake. Therefore, with every action that I take, there is a possibility that I can take the wrong action. If I am not grounded in the understanding of my limitations as a human being which I see as good or at least neuter, then I could be overwhelmed with the anxiety of possible failure.

I am confronted with the whole question of my responsibility. When my wife and I were going to buy a house for the first time, we were delighted at the adventure of looking over several houses, exploring different possibilities, and so on. We were delighted when we found the house that we wanted to buy. However, it was not until I had to sign the papers and take responsibility that I became suddenly less adventurous and a good deal more fearful.

Action-Responsibility, and All That It Entails

Act, then, means responsibility. It also means possible failure. However, the more I have expanded ability to choose and see alternatives, each failure offers another possibility of success. To live by values, a person must learn to act on his values. A great deal of attention will be given to this in the next section on primary values.

Action means involvement. The more I act, the more I get involved not only in people but also in the created order itself. In addition, I come to a greater awareness of who I am, my identity. This is true because as I act, I see in perspective through my experience more of my failures and my successes. (One definition of mental ill health is when a person does not learn from experience.)

The tensions that can arise from a person who has not had enough value formers developed in his life can lead him to refuse to act, resulting in such things as rebellion, boredom, blame, apathy, and so on.

The fact that my choices are limited, in that I never know what all the alternatives are, means, of course, that my actions are also limited. The difference, however, is that the more I am aware of my limitations, the greater will be my anxiety at the point at which I need to do something.

The following dialogue will illustrate the point. It took place between a counselor and an employee of a furniture factory who had decided to leave the factory and go back to college and get a degree.

Counselor: Are you sure that you want to leave the factory where you are working, or are you just saying that?

Client: Yes, I've decided to leave. Those people I work with are an ignorant group of people anyway. I'm going to college, get a degree, earn more money, and make something of myself. My girl friend is enthusiastic about it, and I can see no reason why I shouldn't go ahead.

Counselor: What about the financial side of it?

Client: I have the G.I. Bill and a couple of thousand dollars I've saved up. I really shouldn't have any problems at all.

Counselor: Well, fine. When are you going to quit your job and start school?

DIAGRAMIC GAME
EXISTENTIAL VALUE FORMERS AND TENSIONS 5.

LIMITED ACT

Confronts Me With

RESPONSIBILITY

VALUE FORMERS	POSSIBLE TENSIONS
Involvement	Rebellion
Identity	Guilt
Function	Blame
Autonomy	Apathy

DIAGRAMIC GAME
EXISTENTIAL VALUE FORMERS AND TENSIONS 6.

LIMITED ACT

Confronts Me With

[Responsibility! What is your word?]

Your Own List of Value Formers	Your Own List of Tensions

Client:	I don't know. I haven't decided that yet. *(Hesitation in his voice)*
Counselor:	You haven't decided when yet?
Client:	No, I haven't. I guess I should do something about it.
Counselor:	You don't seem too certain. Did you inquire at any of the colleges that I gave you the names and telephone numbers of last week?
Client:	No, I didn't, but I'll do it sometime in the future. I think college is what I need.
Counselor:	Why don't you call the colleges now? I have a telephone here, and you could at least get some information directly.
Client:	*(Becoming nervous)* Well, I don't know. I could do it tomorrow or perhaps the next day.
Counselor:	You really are nervous about this, aren't you?
Client:	Yes, I guess I'm not sure that I have the ability and I may not be able to make it. Academically, I mean.

The latter dialogue is probably very common to many school counselors who get involved in their students or, for that matter, to many guidance counselors in a number of situations. At the beginning of the conversation, the client was very adamant, even angry, about going to school, even to the point of running his fellow workers down. He was protesting too much, it seemed. As the conversation went on, he was able to dream about what he would like to do and would appear to have made the choice to act. At the point at which he was given the opportunity to act, he became very nervous and was confronted with his own limits. That is to say, he did not trust his own potential. He was able to make creative choices but feared the limits of his action. Such an example is very common and points out the clear distinction of the reality of our limits for all of us.

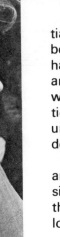

LIMITS OF SEPARATENESS. The last of our four existential realities is separateness. This relates very much to limited being in that as I am a human person in the world, with a body, I have to face the fact that I am separate from others. Psychoanalytically, I was separated from my mother's womb where there was unity, and I seek that same unity in marriage and in relationships with others, and, if I am a mystic, with creation and the universe itself. Finally, I am faced also with my separateness in death. I am confronted with the fact of being apart from others.

In terms of what we have been saying, this means that I am faced with my need to choose from alternatives, to be responsible, and to act. The main existential value former here, then, is the experience of trusting, relatedness and what we ultimately call love.

Love is a basic human need which is as necessary as food or warmth. People who have not had sufficient love as a value

DIAGRAMIC GAME
EXISTENTIAL VALUE FORMERS AND TENSIONS 7.

LIMITS OF SEPARATENESS

Confronts Me With

APARTNESS

VALUE FORMERS	POSSIBLE TENSIONS
Love	Withdrawal
Unity	Dependent Manipulation
Affection	Domination
Adoration	Suicide
Closeness	Loneliness

DIAGRAMIC GAME
EXISTENTIAL VALUE FORMERS AND TENSIONS 8.

LIMITS OF SEPARATENESS

Confronts Me With

[Apartness! What is your word?]

- -

Your Own List of Value Formers	Your Own List of Tensions

former because of unfortunate life experiences may withdraw from people or move into the kind of manipulations that we spoke of under original value formers.

The limits, then, of my separateness or my apartness from man are the limits to which intimacy and relationship are possible. That is to say, to be separate from people ultimately can confront me with the reality of death itself. I am born into the world as a separate entity and I die alone. Therefore, the whole business of separation confronts a man with the whole wider complex subject, for example, of separation anxiety. To be separate from people is for some people a very anxiety-provoking phenomenon.

It has often been pointed out to me in talking to people who were dying that a major part of the process of dying and the remorse that a person has is not so much over the point of physical death as it is over the loss of friends, wife, husband, and so on. The confrontation with death, for most people in my experience, has been the loneliness and the separation from those with whom we worked so hard all our lives to build relationships. The limits of separateness, then, are the limits that we are confronted with ultimately in death itself, as we realize that all relationships end up in our apartness from people.

The question of the limits of separateness and how people feel this so often was brought home to me with particular emphasis when I worked abroad for several years. One of the jobs that I had was a counselor for persons who had been living in other cultures. It is here that we talk about the whole problem of culture shock.

That is what happens to a person when he moves often from one country to another or even from one town to another town. The person often becomes nervous and depressed and seems to go through all the feelings of grief that a dying person or people at a person's funeral are often confronted with. The common element is the separateness, the fact of having left people behind, having broken relationships, having been confronted with the limitations of intimacy in the kind of world in which I live.

Future Shock and Separateness

It is here, in particular, that the whole question of Toffler and Future Shock are so relevant, in that separateness, lack of intimacy, and rapid problems of change confronting us with separation are so much a part of our new and rapidly-moving world. The problem of separation anxiety is one that has always been a part of the process of training the counselor as he separates from a client who has been with him for a number of months, for example. It is a part of the training of the grief counselor, the minister, as he sits by a death bed. It has been a part of the training in management relations as people are confronted with changes of staff and organization. It has, for many years, been a part of the training of the overseas missionaries and for people such as those in the Peace Corps as they change from one culture to another. The fact of separation, the limitations it imposes on us and confronts us with, then, is a very important part of the existential value formation of an individual in change.

PRIMARY VALUES AND AUTHENTIC MAN

After our discussion of original and existential value formers, we can begin to explore true values which fulfill the definitions given in Chapter 2. These are the values which are actually chosen, acted upon, and make the person happy and contribute to his authentic development. I would like to delineate the two types of such values—primary and chosen.

Primary Values

It is my view that primary values are so essential to the growth of man that they merit specific explanation in themselves. By primary values are understood values that are chosen, acted upon, that a person is happy with, that are necessary for the authentic development of man. A psychologist might argue that his goal is to help people to become functional in society, as contributors rather than as destructors of that society. For this, the person would need these primary values.

Moreover, it is my thought that the primary value is defined as the value which helps a human being to develop to the best of his capacity and, as such, has a goal, beyond the normal functioning in society, to exceptional functioning. This is, then, a spiritual development. It is a development toward human self-realization. Cornelius J. Van der Poel has the following to say about this:

> "Human self-realization may be described briefly as the development of the human potentials. In normal circumstances, this development goes on all the time. This applies not only to the individual but also to humanity as a whole. Consequently, the values which are to be realized and the norms which describe how these values are best expressed in human life and society are never static, but are subject to constant change" (The Search for Human Values, p. 80).

Primary values are those values which are basic and as such are necessary for development to take place. They are the values that Van der Poel says are normal to natural development. The problem is, of course, that we don't always know what normal development is. It would appear to depend on the natural assimilation of a basic amount of love, trust, and stability in our upbringing—that is to say, the development of the original value formers. My experience leads me to postulate two basic primary values: *self-value* and the *value of significant others*.

William Glasser has come to this same postulation in his clinical observations:

Being Loved and Loving, and a Feeling of Worth

> "Now that we have seen that an involvement with someone you care for and who you are convinced cares for you is the key to fulfilling the basic needs, we can proceed to a discussion of the needs themselves. For in therapy we recognize two basic needs—needs which cause suffering unless they are fulfilled.
>
> "It is generally accepted that all humans have the same physiological and psychological needs. Competent people may

EXISTENTIAL FORMERS AND PRIMARY VALUES

EXISTENTIAL REALITY	LIMITED BEING	LIMITED CHOICE	LIMITED ACTION	LIMITED SEPARATENESS
CONFRONTS US WITH	Contingency	Alternatives	Responsibility	Apartness
SOME POSSIBLE EXISTENTIAL VALUE FORMERS	Trust Faith Feeling Body	Meaning Imagination Ideas Creativity	Involvement Identity Function Unity	Relatedness Unity Love
PRIMARY VALUES POSSIBLE	Self-Value Value Others	Value of Creation (God) Self-Value	Value the Other	Value Self as Total Worth Value Others as Total Worth
SOME CHOSEN VALUES	Society Mankind	Leisure Creation (World)	Value Others Dedication in Work as Purpose	Intimacy Mystic Unity Contemplation (Prayer)
EMPHASIZED SPACE	Self Neighbor	Self World	Self Limited World	Self Cosmic Space (Universe)

EXISTENTIAL VALUE FORMERS AND TENSIONS

EXISTENTIAL REALITY	LIMITED BEING	LIMITED CHOICE	LIMITED ACTION	LIMITS OF SEPARATENESS
CONFRONTS US WITH	Contingency	Alternatives	Responsibility	Apartness
SOME POSSIBLE EXISTENTIAL VALUE FORMERS	Trust Faith Feeling Body	Meanings Imagination Ideas Creativity	Involvement Identity Function Unity-Power	Relatedness Unity-Affection Love
SOME POSSIBLE RESULTANT TENSIONS	Death Powerlessness Denial of Feelings	Meaninglessness Anti-Intellect Repress Imagination Destructiveness	Withdrawal Guilt Blame Boredom Rebellion Apathy	Withdrawal Top Dog/Under Dog Controls Alienation
TIME SPACE ELEMENTS EMPHASIZED	Future Self	Present-Future Self World	Past-Present Self-Others	Present Self-Others

describe or label these needs differently, but no one seriously disputes that in all cultures and in all degrees of civilization men have the same essential needs. It is also generally accepted that needs do not vary with age, sex, or race. A Chinese infant girl has the same needs as a Swedish king. The fulfillment of the physiological needs for food, warmth, and the rest are really the concern of psychiatry. Psychiatry must be concerned with two basic psychological needs: **the need to love and be loved and the need to feel that we are worthwhile to ourselves and to others**" (Reality Therapy: A New Approach to Psychiatry, p. 9).

As a psychiatrist, Glasser is primarily concerned with the area of basic needs, rather than with the broader complex of all the needs which contribute to full human growth and life. When we talk about primary values, we are examining the broader concerns. It is possible that Ivan Illich, as an educator, will serve to keep this distinction in mind for the remainder of this chapter and the next.

"All of us are crippled—some physically, some mentally, some emotionally. We must therefore strive cooperatively to create the new world. There is no time left for destruction, for

hatred, for anger. We must build, in hope and joy and celebration. Let us meet the new era of abundance with self-chosen work and freedom to follow the drum of one's own heart. Let us recognize that a striving for self-realization, for poetry and play, is basic to man once his needs for food, clothing, and shelter have been met—that we will choose those areas of activity which will contribute to our own development and will be meaningful to our society" (Celebration of Awareness: A Call for Institutional Revolution, p. 16).

Self-Value and Primary Value

The first two primary values will be defined, then, as follows:

1. *Self-Value.* To accept that I am of (infinite) total worth to significant others.

2. *The second primary value.* That others are of (infinite) total worth also.

The perspective here is that Illich is speaking of self-realization as a possibility when very basic things like need for food and so on have been fulfilled. In an emotional context, it would mean that self-realization only becomes possible when we have sufficient original and existential value formers that have been dealt with by us in our emotional development. In addition, there are certain basic values which are the foundation of any healthy value system; these we call primary.

I value self when I recognize my imagination and my ideas and my feelings and my body and what I do as being of value. Repression of my imagination or a playing down of my intellectual capabilities whatever they may be or avoidance of my feelings would be expressions of non-self-value. The expression of Glasser of being worthwhile to myself and others is very close to what we have termed here as self-value.

Self-value is: the acceptance of myself in that significant others who would know me would see me as being of value.

As I Am, So Are Others

The second primary value, which is as important as the first, is that I would see others as of being of great value. Since I am of value, others must also be of value. But what does it mean to be of value? Does it mean that I do a good job? Does it mean I am a good garage mechanic or a good artist? Or does it mean more than that? In terms of the chart and the way it is being defined here, self-value relates to trust, my feelings, my imagination, my creativity, and to my ability to function, to get involved with people, and to love.

These two primary values are not possible except in relationship to each other. That is to say, I will not be able to affirm others as being of total worth unless I have been affirmed myself. In order for these to be a value, they must be chosen by me as being of particular importance and they must be acted upon by me repeatedly in some form or other.

As I am valued, or affirmed, I am able to value and affirm others. However, this is not an unconditional acceptance of all a person *does,* but of all a person *is.* What love is about is separating behavior from the intrinsic value of the person. I can see you as being of total worth—your ideas, your imagination, your whole person. At the same time, as an act of love, of valuing you, I can reject your bad behavior. Valuing, then, has to do with facing and confronting a person's bad behavior and not letting it slide under the table. By the same token, to know I am of value does not mean that I think that I am "the greatest person in the world." It is to know that I am of value to significant other persons. It is to know what my limitations are. My value is not omnipotence or grandiosity, but simply who I am, with my limits and my potential.

For most people, then, these two values operate as original value formers, or, in Glasser's terms, at the level of need. In order to contribute to extra developmental growth, they must become chosen forms and, as such, values.

Refusing To Value Others

It really is important to distinguish between self-value and the value of others as original value formers and as chosen primary values. Very few people would consciously deny that they value themselves and value others; however, their behavior, their choices, their conscious and unconscious defense mechanisms might simply serve to show that such a denial is true. People who are overwhelmed with their own limitations or who have been so deeply betrayed by others might, in fact, be operating on the non-value of distrust of self and others. That distrust is a non-value because it can contribute to nothing but the regression of their own personhood and the personhood of those around them.

To work through a sense of our own limits and the limits of others is the human growth process, which brings us to a point where we will be able to deliberately *choose* to value ourselves as we are, and others as they are. That is the process of making the value formers true values and is one of the chief goals of this book and any educational or helping process.

We all need to be valued, and people who refuse to value others lose their friends. Why? Because those who take and never give, who never value or affirm people outside of themselves, soon tire and drain their friends. The tragedy for many is that they do not realize that they are not valuers and are not aware of how devaluing they are.

Many people who control and manipulate others really are not aware of how damaging this is to their relationships and themselves. The idea of "the man for others" is the idea of the valuing person. Once a man has recognized that trust is integral to valuing, he will try to avoid manipulation and withdrawal, because it would be a sign of not trusting, and therefore not valuing. To control another's actions is to prevent that person from trusting another; it limits an infinite potential in a massive human network. Self-realization is vocational. It reaches out beyond the individual but at the same time concerns itself very much with the innate goodness of every single individual.

The value of God or the quality of adoration would be considered by many to be another primary value. In my opinion, it is not so much a primary value as it is a development of a value from the expanded awareness of the human being and flows naturally from the two primary values listed. For this reason, value formation, for example, in public schools does not need to concern itself with the problems of the religious interpreter. It is in this respect that I do not see the latter as a primary value, but rather a value that is of central importance to the religious person.

It seems necessary to add this because it is so easy to feel that a value must necessarily have something to do with a specific moral code or set of religious truths. That is not necessarily true, particularly when we are speaking of primary values. They are simply the basic foundation of human growth needed to develop *any* value system. In their regard, the task of the educator is not to prescribe certain behavior or judge certain ethical views, but rather to provide an atmosphere that promotes and proclaims the value of each student in such a manner that he is able to both come to know and accept himself and others. Without this self-acceptance and the acceptance of others, he is incapable of authentic growth and human interaction. The approach, therefore, is basically non-judgmental, accepting, and trusting, in contrast to ethical polemics and institutional manipulation and imposition. As we shall see throughout this book, this is a central point.

Primary Values Development and Man and Art

It is interesting to me how the development of these primary values are seen throughout civilization itself, especially through man and art. In Kenneth Clark's book, *Civilization,* he notes how in the fifth and sixth centuries woman is seen as a rather heavy and undelightful creature. Then, as we move into the medieval period, she suddenly becomes dainty, rather beautiful, often in the form of the Virgin. That is to say, she is beautiful and frail, but more beautiful when she is a virgin. And so it is only recently in our own social history that we see woman in a sense being emancipated, as being basically of great worth in her own particularity (which is a pre-condition for a positive self-image).

Similar, also, is the development of the crucifix in Christian art. To quote Kenneth Clark:

> "We have grown so used to the idea that the crucifixion is the supreme symbol of Christianity that it is a shock to realize how late in the history of Christian art its power was recognized. In the first art of Christianity it hardly appears; and the earliest example, on the doors of Santa Sabina in Rome, is stuck away in a corner, almost out of sight. The simple fact is that the early Church needed converts, and from this point of view the crucifixion was not an encouraging subject.
> "The men of the tenth century not only recognized the meaning of Christ's sacrifice in physical terms, they were able fully to sublimate it into ritual" (Civilization, p. 29).

What does this prove? No matter how sophisticated some theologians and thinkers in our early periods of history were, man more generally reacted to art forms with a concern about his self-value.

As we move into the tenth century with the emergence of the crucifixion as a common art form, so man's attitude toward his limitations also changes as he confronts this through art. In addition, this form impresses symbolically upon man the need for sacrifice as a valuing of the worth of others. Seeing himself of great worth, Christ had infinite trust in God and died for the value of man. It is interesting that the emergence of the valuing of woman appears in art around about the same period of history.

THE CHOSEN VALUE

In this chapter we have examined the whole area of original value formers, existential value formers, and primary values. We have noted again and again that the difference between a need or attitude, a value former, and the chosen value is in the fact of choice.

The chosen value is something that is chosen from alternatives, that the person is happy with, and that the person acts on. Therefore, many of those things that we call value indicators

or value formers could be values if they were chosen in the way indicated. As we look at value formers, we can see how these would lead into the development of value choices.

For example, if we were to take elements such as trust, faith, body, and feelings, which result in the need to value self and others, we then move into specific types of values. How many values could a person have in regard to society? Or how many values could a man have in regard to mankind? The answer is many. But, as we shall see later, in reality he will only have time for very few.

Significance of Time

Time is a large and significant element. It tells us not only where our values are, but how many we can have. For example, in the area of mankind and society, a man could have many values connected with work. Maybe he has a value for biochemical engineering as a means to curbing pollution, or a value which says he must do anything in order to change society. His value then may consist in being a unifying change agent. The most important point is that *each person must describe specifically and exactly for himself what his or her values are.* The exceptions to this are the primary values listed above.

From the elements of choice, imagination, and creativity come such values as leisure. How do I specifically use my leisure? If it is a value, I will act on it and will have chosen it and will be happy with it. But its identity is specific to me. Leisure could be study or contemplation or many other things.

From the idea of choice and creativity might come my whole attitude toward the world and creation which could give me many other values. Perhaps I am a "community organization man" as a consequence of my values and interests in pollution or welfare rights or whatever.

In the area of action comes the whole possibility of the value of work and the specific work that I do. What is work and what does it have to be in order to be a value to me?

Finally, there is the whole area of apartness and love. This brings about other kinds of values, such as the value of intimacy or the value of prayer, of mystic unity. Thus, from our existential situation, from our life background, emerges the possibility of the many values that we can, as individuals, choose.

Having defined values in so many ways, we now come to the point where we must examine the reality that time and space does press upon us, telling us that we cannot, in fact, have many values. Why? Because man is limited, and he is limited within the framework of time. This comes to the issue, then, of not simply what do I value, but what is the *priority* of my values?

I have heard many a person tell me that study was a value for them. When I asked them how many hours they had studied, they would say that they hadn't studied for the last seven or eight months. In my view, study was not a value for them since they did not act on it. It may have been a value indicator, something that was an ideal or a goal for them, but it was not a value. Is that a negative response? No! It is simply a statement of limitation.

I may have many things that I would like to value, but I have no time. The question of value ranking and priorities and what they mean in my life and in my behavior are, therefore, essential to me and dictate probably more than any other aspect of value clarification who I am and what my life direction will be.

The values that I have in relationship to myself are one thing; the values that I have in relationship to others and creation are another. The amount of time I put on self-values or the amount of time I put on world values or society will direct my behavior and life-style in relationship to the world and society. Is it possible, for example, that the ghetto exists not because people are devaluing others, but simply because they have no time in their priorities? And if that is the case, does it make any difference or the pain any less for the people who live there? In the next chapter we will start to look at ways of clarifying some of these things through the method of value ranking.

4.
Priorities and World View

"Set all things in their own peculiar place
And know that order is the greatest grace."

John Dryden

INTRODUCTION

In the last chapter we discussed the primary and chosen values which an individual might have. Here we wish to explore the interrelationship of values within any individual, realizing that a person can take a number of value stances on an almost unlimited number of issues in his life.

For example, depending upon the depth and extent of priority which a person places upon his own self-worth and the worth of others (the primary values mentioned previously), an individual will have differing stances on such interpersonal issues as *intimacy, authority, freedom, control, sexuality,* and *love*—to name just a few. As a person investigates how he reacts to any of these issues, he will, in turn, be coming to grips with a variety of other values and priorities which he has within his life.

Any of these issues can serve as the "window" or entrance way through which to begin the value clarifying process. And yet, that list is not exhaustive either. Other issues which closely affect a man's behavior and attitudes could include such varied items as the *meaning of work, the use of leisure, the place of money in his life, the roles determined by society for him, his place in business or community or family, his use of time, the images of self, others, or the world which were presented to him through his educational experiences,* etc. Even this listing is not exhaustive, and with some reflection the reader will be able to conceive of other areas and issues which are value-laden in the life of individuals.

What this indicates, of course, is the simple fact that rarely will anyone be able to come to grips with one isolated value without considering at the same time the interrelationship of that value with many others. This chapter will investigate that interrelationship under the topic of "value ranking." Here, as in previous chapters, the examples used are not the only possible avenues of clarification. Any of the issues mentioned previously, together with any other issues which the reader might have thought of, could serve as well. What is important, then, is to reflect on the *process* being used, realizing that that process has varied applications beyond those described here.

Feelings Evoked by Value Ranking Process

It might also be helpful at the outset to attach some typical feelings to this value ranking process. If a person's values are ranked in a manner which is comfortable to him and to the expectation of those around him and the institutions which are meaningful to him, he will experience feelings of *joy, hope, creativity, support, and freedom.* On the other hand, if there is an unresolved conflict of values, either within himself, or in relationship to others and their expectations for him, he will experience feelings of *anguish, trappedness, boredom, insecurity, and control.*

Throughout the chapter, many of these themes will be explored or at least alluded to, as we investigate the valuing process and value ranking process which man must accomplish to be authentically himself.

RANKING AS WHERE THE ACTION IS

In our original definition of values we saw the value as the stance that the self takes to the external environment. This view is narrow in that we rarely view the world by placing emphasis on one value. Life is simply more complicated.

Illustration of Priorities

Usually we view the world through sets of priorities that we have. It may be that friends are very important to me. But if I am the type of person that places high priority on studying, I may have little time for friends. In this example, the ranking would have been as follows:

1. Studying
2. Friends

In such an example, the value of studying is important. The value of friends can also be very important. However, consider an individual with the opposite ranking, namely:

1. Friends
2. Studying

In each case, both values are very important, but the reverse order would in fact change the behavior of the person. The latter individual would spend more time with friends. This person might, for example, be more of an extrovert and more social in his thinking, whereas the former individual would probably be more inward-thinking and more happy living in a world of ideas rather than people.

Neither ranking is correct. When the rankings are reversed, one is confronted with a different behavior, a different world view, in fact a different person. Values as individually chosen elements in a person's life are very important; however, the variety and ranking of these individually chosen elements are at least equally as important.

Case Study: Mr. and Mrs. Marshall

The Marshalls had been coming to me for marriage counseling for several weeks. It became rapidly evident to me that their priorities and their use of time was saying a great deal about their conflict. The Marshalls had been married for a couple of years, had no children, and owned a small but very pleasant house.

Mrs. Marshall worked a full eight-hour day and spent 1 ½ hours each day commuting to a local city. She admitted that financially she did not need to work, but that it gave her a sense of security. She spoke quite freely, and it became obvious that although work was a preoccupation, it was not her sole or predominant interest. She spoke a great deal about her house. She spent a lot of time in cleaning and redecorating. She complained that her husband took insufficient interest in her and that they spent very little time together.

I asked Mrs. Marshall to list what she thought might be five important things to her in her life and then to rank them in order. Her listing came out as follows:

1. Work
2. House
3. Money
4. Husband
5. Recreation

Mr. Marshall was on the swing-shift. He worked three shifts circulating over the seven-day week period. As a consequence, he would often be working during his wife's two days off, which were always on the weekend. He received a good salary, but his job was repetitive and uninteresting. He worked on an assembly line in a large factory. He did not wish to change his work; rather he placed emphasis on recreation. When Mr. Marshall talked prior to the counseling sessions, his major preoccupation would be with sports and fishing. He liked to go fishing with one of his friends on his days off. He was concerned about money, but it would appear that it was his wife's preoccupation with it that was more of the problem than his own interest. Therefore, when I asked him to come up with five important items, he listed them as follows:

1. Recreation alone
2. Money
3. Baseball
4. Wife
5. Work

The simple listing of these two lists and placing them side by side was quite a surprise to the Marshalls.

Mrs. Marshall	Mr. Marshall
Work	Recreation alone
House	Money
Money	Baseball
Husband	Wife
Recreation	Work

(A note on the process to this point: First of all, what is important is that this was their own listing, their own priorities, accomplished without any judgments by others. Secondly, the simple doing of it was a mutual confrontation without too much threat. Thirdly, the comparison of the two listings was an even greater surprise to them.)

As the Marshall family continued to investigate their differences, they decided that they would like to choose a new life-style. After several interviews and a lot of hard work, they both chose the following new lists:

Mrs. Marshall	Mr. Marshall
Self	Self
Husband	Wife
Recreation	Recreation together
Work	Baseball
House	Work

To begin with, each list now contains a new expression not found previously, namely the priority of "self." This normally happens when individuals begin clarifying their values and their ranking of values. In the case of Mrs. Marshall, as she began to think out what money meant to her, the term "security" kept occurring. As she attempted to explore this need and its effect on her, she began to realize that she had a basic need for personal affirmation which money had served to provide for her. Yet the underlying need was self, not money, and the same sort of process was operative in Mr. Marshall's self-examination.

She also decided that she wanted her husband to come first, and thus work would come lower down the list. This meant that she would have to make an effort to spend more time with her husband in the form of recreation. Quite obviously, this meant a major behavioral change. She had to change her job so that she could be with her husband during his days off. (He could have changed his job, but in their case it was simpler for her to make the change.)

Mr. Marshall also dropped the word "money" and placed "self" at the top of the list for the same reason as his wife. With their new work arrangement they were able to go fishing together. Baseball for him was really recreation alone through the television. Mrs. Marshall had no interest in this area.

In order for this to become a value ranking, the Marshalls had to work very hard at the behavioral changes necessary to bring about this new priority. It meant job changes, dealing with personal anxiety, and a whole change in life-style.

(Another note on the whole process: *value ranking like the valuing process has to be chosen, prized, and acted upon. It has to be something that contributes to the creative development of the personality. It is an active celebration of a person's limitations as he comes to grips with his priorities, in time, through new behavioral patterns.*)

BEEF STEW RANKING

What we have been describing to this point is conscious, deliberate process which a mature person can use to arrive at a fairly well-articulated, thoughtful and deliberate ranking of chosen values. However, just as we have mentioned concerning values themselves, ranking is a maturing process and takes years of living and emotional growth. In younger children and even in adults who have never really reflected on any of this, ranking will be done, but rather than a ranking of chosen values, it will be a ranking of various *priorities* which occur to the individual as a result of the influence of original value formers, various value indicators, and possibly a value or two. The result of this ranking of priorities will be the development of certain *attitudes* in which many of the priorities are either unconscious or unclear, and therefore unchosen. In fact, if the clarifying process is accomplished, they might even want to reject certain priorities. *Growth and personal identity are accomplished when an individual has the opportunity to clarify his attitudes, weigh the priorities operative in the formation of those attitudes and come to chosen value rankings which please him.* In fact, it is to this aim that this whole exploration of values and their ranking is directed.

In the educational process, whether it be a child in a family, in a Sunday school, or in the public school, exercises in ranking of priorities are essential and most helpful as a part of developmental valuing process.

The following exercises will help us to start thinking practically in this direction. Ultimately, all such exercises should be developed by you for your particular situation. This exercise is very simple, does not have to take very much time, and can be used anywhere with practically any grade at school—that is to say, with grades 1 or 2 upward. As the child gets older, the kind of listings can become more sophisticated.

First Exercise   First, we choose a value-laden area. Then we choose one word to depict the area. Sample words might be money, love or school, or any of the other areas mentioned in the introduction to this chapter. The idea is to mention a word and then ask the person to list four more words that come to mind when the word is mentioned. For myself, the listing would appear as follows. Take the time right now to compose your own list for each of the three areas of "money," "love" and "school."

Money	Love	School
car	work	teacher
house	play	homework
furniture	family	friends
security	children	art

The next part of the exercise is then to say, "Now, having made the lists, rank the lists in the priority of importance to you." Another variation is to rank them also in terms of how you think they should be.

Several things can be done to make this more interesting and quite helpful. First, discuss these rankings with someone or with different people. (A note on this process: The benefit of sharing with others is that other people have different opinions and different choices. You will probably also find that what you have is acceptable to others.) This simple little process can be a very helpful valuing method. It takes very little time, yet is very important.

As was noted before, the priorities have to be your own unique priorities. For example, a small child would come up with quite different words for school. The kinds of words that a second-grade child might feel are: home, play, friends, and holiday. No matter how the list is articulated, a degree of self-revelation and a deeper insight into another will be accomplished, whether you are a teacher, a parent, a spouse, or a co-worker. Come up with your own list for members of your family or for friends. The following is the list that we came up with as an example:

PLAY
BOATING
ART
FRIENDS
FAMILY COUNCIL
WEEKENDS
MOMMY AND DADDY
BOYSCOUTS
WORK

RANKING AND PRIORITY

An important educational issue that has to be raised as we examine the process whereby children are able to list their priorities and work toward a ranking of values which is done consciously is the issue of indoctrination. Briefly, the issue is simply whether there are certain values which ought to be listed as primary on anyone's ranking list and who has the right to determine them? This is an issue which must be a concern to all educators who work within an educational system founded upon the appreciation of a pluralistic society. Another way of positing this same problem would be simply to ask, "Is there a difference between aiding an individual in personal value clarifying and ranking and subtly or consciously imposing a set of values on another?"

We have noted the importance of teaching a child to list priorities. We have also noted that value ranking is a particular list of priorities chosen by a person. The question needs to be raised: Are there certain values that should be at the head of our list? A well-known educator and writer, Paul Nash, has the following to say:

> *"If we want our children to grow up to be committed men and women, we are faced with two formidable problems: to what should they be committed, and how should we go about helping them to reach commitment? This takes us again into the problem of indoctrination. Aldous Huxley has suggested that an education for freedom must include the 'enunciation of a set of generally acceptable values based upon a solid foundation of facts.' The values he suggests are individual freedom, based on the facts of human diversity and genetic uniqueness; charity and compassion, based on the psychiatrically ascertained fact that love is as necessary as food for human growth; and intelligence, 'without which love is impotent and freedom unattainable.' These facts and values are unexceptionable, but unfortunately Huxley does not meet the problem of how this education is to be achieved"* (Authority and Freedom in Education, p. 311).

Nash goes on to say that these values have been enunciated from pulpits for years. He then raises the question: Should values then be imposed? He then adds that no thoughtful person would leave a child to the ravages of Madison Avenue. He goes on to point out that imposition and indoctrination not only do not work, but are alien to good institutional educational methodology.

What is clearly pointed out in the above quotation is the need for what we have elsewhere called primary values. Huxley has suggested that they are: individual freedom, charity and compassion, and intelligence. Individual freedom is also a part of the valuing process. Obviously, it can be seen as a value especially in the area of human relationships and social reform.

Charity and compassion are related to the two primary values that we have mentioned: self-value and the value of others. Intelligence is the third primary value that Huxley has added.

Nash himself moves toward this as he talks of values in relationship to creativity.

> *"Just as we need to examine more carefully the link between the aesthetic and the ethical, so we need to study the link between creativity and values.*
>
> *"On the practical level, we need to show children that their created gifts should be used not for selfish or destructive ends, but for the service of their fellow man.*
>
> *"How, then, are we to help people distinguish between productive and destructive creativity, between positive and negative creativity? As an initial guide, we might suggest that the kind of creativeness we want to encourage will be characterized by the two criteria of love and joy. If the creative worker works in a spirit of love—love for life, love and respect for himself, his*

work, and his fellow men—we can be happy if we have helped to nurture this creativity" (Paul Nash, Authority and Freedom in Education, p. 267).

The joy aspect which is so important is again a part of the valuing process which we have variously termed celebration or prizing in Simons, Harmin, and Raths' terms. The love element here is the valuing of others and the valuing of self. This is another way of expressing the term love.

Wellspring of Primary Values

We have posited the value of self and the value of others as primary values. There are a number of reasons for this, including, of course, our own Judaeo-Christian ethical background. However, I do not think that the only reason justifying their importance comes from ethical concern. If it did, we might seriously consider whether they are justifiably a concern for an educator in a public school context. To posit these two values as primary for ethical reasons would simply open educators up to renewed concern about the constitutional questions relative to the separation of Church and state.

It is our opinion that these two values can be considered primary simply from psychic-social consideration. Unless an individual values himself, he will not possess a positive self-concept, he will not be able to appreciate his own creativity and potential for growth, and he will be forced to assume a defensive and destructive stance in his interaction with his environment. The amount of research in the areas of education, psychology, and sociology to justify this view is abundant.

By the same token, unless an individual has a degree of value toward others and a corresponding trust of them, his approach to all relationships will be manipulatory, dictatorial, controlling of others, rigid, and totally defensive. His interpersonal relationships will allow for few if any opportunities for love and mutual exchange. His stance toward preferred social order will be non-democratic and non-participatory—a stance which, when pushed to the extreme, is inimical with the American social and political style. It is apparent, therefore, that valuing others and education in arriving at this value is part of the preparation required for a student to serve as a citizen in our society.

It is for this reason that we have used as *examples* of primary values the two so frequently mentioned. Obviously, other individuals might include other values, such as God, religion, spiritual growth, the commandments, the capitalistic system, intelligence, etc., as primary values. Indeed, everyone has the right to include these or others in their personal list of primary values. We have simply centered upon two universal values because of their universality and because they allow us to separate ourselves from the ethical questions which must be cautiously and seriously considered by all educators.

The point of this whole section has been to clarify that although value imposition or indoctrination is alien to the educational process, a human being does need certain primary values if he is to be able to live a creative life. The common primary values that have been enunciated have been the ones of self-value and the valuing of others. Aldous Huxley would also have us include intelligence. As has been previously noted, most theologians would probably also have us include God.

My own opinion is that whatever primary values you think should be included, minimally important are the two values of self and others. We dealt with this in more detail in the last chapter under the heading of primary values.

Normally, self then would come at the top of a person's list. Others would then come further down the list, usually in particular forms, such as: wife, husband, friends, or children. This is not to say that self would never come second to wife or friends, but rather that it is an exception. Many religious writings, including the Bible, state that God should come first. I am not objecting to this point of view, but simply stating that, in my opinion, it is a higher state of development and not something that naturally ensues for most people.

For the development of healthy human beings, the first two primary values are of utmost importance as a part of the educational process. Other things would probably come under religious or spiritual development. This is a sensitive point to many, and the lines need to be drawn and thought out clearly.

Second Exercise

Let us now look at some exercises to try and make this clear.

Self	Others	World
recreation alone	recreation together	nature appreciation
security	friendship	care of rivers
love	wife	air pollution control
love	husband	scrap metal plants
creativity	children	paper recycling plants
affirmation	friends	environmental modification
self-worth	work	

The above lists are simply lists of words that come under the various uses of self, others, and world. The first two, self and others, of course, relate to primary values, and I added the list of world just to expand the idea a little. At this point, take the time to make up your own list and add as many personal things as you can to the lists of self and others. Finally, as an exercise take six words from your own list and rank them in priority, making sure that there are some from self as well as the list of others. You might like to reflect on this with your family. Just placing the list up so others can see without criticism or discussion is very helpful. The point is to see other people's alternatives and relationships. It is a simple way of being yourself.

PRIORITIES AND TIME

It would seem that time is a scarce commodity in our society. Obviously, our work, our leisure, all exist within the dimension of time. Time cannot be accumulated. We cannot build it up or stock it as we do money. However, it is something that people can use, and there is a supply of time.

"But there is also a certain 'demand for time.' Time can be used by individuals in work, with a view to acquiring various goods. Time can also be used in consumption, i.e., the process in which goods are combined with time, in attempts to achieve the ultimate utility in the economic process—material and spiritual well-being. It is important to realize that the consumption requires time just as does production. Such pleasures as a cup of coffee or a good stage play are not in fact pleasurable unless we can devote time to enjoying them" (Staffan B. Linder, The Harried Leisure Class, pp. 2-3).

A point that is often missed is that when we do things, often there are other factors timewise that are involved. As Linder points out, there is the consumption as well as the production of a product. If I am to enjoy clothes that I am wearing, I must take the time to look for them and buy them. If I am to enjoy food that I eat, I must allow time for eating, time for preparation of the food, and time for buying the food. We need to become more aware of the reality of time in our activity.

Why do I need to become more aware of time? Because time relates directly to behavior as a value indicator. How I use my time indicates a great deal about what values I have in the utilizing of time. As such, time can be a very helpful indicator of our life-style. The clarifying of time is often the clarifying of values.

The "Real" and the "Ideal"

The interesting facet of using time in clarifying values and their ranking is that it gives us a chance to distinguish between the "ideal" and the "real." Often, if asked about what is important to us, we will respond by stating what should be important without even averting to what is, in fact, important to us. Assessing our time commitments, then, is a simple way to really test judgments. It is for this reason that we will consider the issue of time in an extended fashion.

Third Exercise

Let us look at this closer by doing two short clarifications of time rankings. Let us first look at work.

Work
1. Regular hours per work day (7 or 8 hours)
2. Other work
3. Worry about my work
4. Recuperation from work
5. Travel from work
6. Study or preparation for work

First, please look over the above list. Decide which of the categories apply to you. If not all the categories apply to you, then rub out those which are not true of your situation. If there are others, then write them in Diagram A. The first category of hours of work means that in your main job you probably work 40 hours a week; just put down the number of hours that is true of your job. If you have a second job, then you put the number of hours for that under "other work." Now make a time ranking list of all the hours per day that you spend for your job in each category.

DIAGRAM A

WORK ORIENTATED TIME SHEET	Amount	Ranking
1. On the job hours		
2. Travel to and from		
3. Extra jobs		
4. Worry about work		
5. Recuperation		
6. Study/preparation for work		

TOTAL WEEK TIME SHEET	Amount	Ranking
1. Total of work orientation time sheet		
2. Time alone		
3. Time with family		
4. Time with friends		
5. Recreation time (can include part of 2, 3, and 4)		
6. Study time (can include part of 1)		
7. Maintenance of house		
8. Shopping, buying clothes		

Consider that the total number of hours that you put in the above listing is what we will call "work." Let us now look at this new ranking.

After Work
1. Work (number of hours above the 40 hour week from the above ranking)
2. Time alone
3. Time with friends
4. Time with family
5. Recreation time
6. Study time
7. Maintenance of house time
8. Time for shopping, buying clothes, etc.

As before, rank how much time you think you use on the average work week for the above. As before, fill in your "time" in Diagram A. As before, eliminate or add words that apply.

The first list, "Work," highlights the number of hours that you spend beyond your official work day time. For example, if you work 7½ hours a day but spend 5 hours a day worrying about that work or studying for that work, then that 5 hours would go down as the number of hours for point 3 on the list. Reflect where you have most of your hour time beyond the normal work week and ask yourself: What does this say about my values?

Often I find in doing this ranking with families that work is a predominant issue. It often points to an underlying value for the need of security. In families who are claiming they have difficulty in communicating with their teenagers, for example, often the majority of the family have more time alone than they realized, meaning that they have a value for self as leisure and in fact do not value a great deal of activity with others. This is not bad, necessarily, but simply a statement of where they are. In this way, time points very much to the behavior setting of the individual.

Not only do jobs and our own personal preferences determine how we use time, but so also does the type of society we live in. At this moment there are particular pressures upon most modern Americans. Each of these pressures implies a specific use of time and a specific expression of values. The next few pages will be spent trying to clarify the values implicit in these pressures which really present themselves as a series of paradoxes.

1. The work week becomes more limited—at the same time that

2. Life seems more hectic—at the same time that

3. More men have more financial resources to explore life—at the same time that—

4. No one has time to think out revised values and choices.

Why is this and what does it imply in terms of values and the ranking of values of twentieth-century man?

The question of time is very essential. It relates to the whole question of our productivity, that is to say, to the way we function with leisure and work. At this point it may be helpful to raise several clarifying questions which will be worth investigation.

One way of raising such questions is to have value continuums. A value continuum is when you have raised a question which has two opposite answers with a line in between. The idea is to ask people to put a mark on the line as to where they think their own position is. Here are some examples:

1. Should I use my time usefully?

All of the time   *Some of the time*

2. Is relaxation necessary?

Some of the time (consistently, planned)   *Rarely (unplanned)*

3. Non-productivity

Is idleness   *Is relaxation*

It may be interesting to create your own continuums which will help you clarify time for yourself or people that you are working with or teaching. These clarifying tests and questions can always be created personally to fit your unique needs.

TIME AND SOCIETY AND PRODUCTION

As we pointed out in Chapter 1, time is very much related to function, to the idea of people producing things. In this society in particular the question has to be asked: Where will increasing consumption and economic growth take us? Will the need for more and more things ever be satisfied? Will we ever have enough time? It is becoming clearer and clearer in our society that more and more time given to people with the shortening of the work week does not necessarily mean that people will have more time for relaxation or for the change of their value system.

A Time for Consuming

The facts are that as people have more time they often seem to spend more time in consumption. They have more time for pleasures, but often use the time in preparing or buying their pleasures. People spend more and more time traveling to shopping centers or in improving their houses. That is to say, maintenance and consumption can become major consumers of time.

The rising production and consumption of goods itself causes a series of inner contradictions which relate very interestingly to our use of time. The following list written by Staffan Linder might be interesting to reflect on. Linder points out that as the efforts of people to achieve growth accelerate in a country where there is an increase of material production and consumption the following are noticeable:

"A. There will be an increasingly hectic tempo of life marked by careful attempts to economize on increasingly scarce items.

"B. There will be an expanding mass of goods, which will make great demands on time in the form of such mainte-

nance and service tasks that cannot very well be mechanized. This will happen in spite of decline in maintenance per item.

"C. Since affluence is only partial, there will be increasing hardships for those whose welfare does not primarily require abundant goods, but the scarce time of their fellow creatures. While the aged, in the beginning of the initial growth period, lacked bed and bread, they will toward the end of the period of growth lack a nurse.

"D. There will be a curious combination of an increasing attachment to goods in general and, owing to a low degree of utilization and a rapid turnover, an increasing indifference to each of them in particular.

"E. There will be a declining competitive position for time devoted to the cultivation of mind and spirit and time spent on certain bodily pleasures.

"F. There will be a declining utility of income but not an exhaustion of wants; in order to achieve some addition to material well-being, increasing attention will, therefore, be given to further economic advances.

"G. In the name of economic progress, there will be increasing emphasis on rational economic policies and behavior, but for this very reason also—as stated by the rationale of increasing irrationality—there will be a growing number of ill-considered decisions.

"H. There will be a new form of economic 'unfreedom' marked not by a fight for economic survival, but by an obsession with growth that sometimes forces us, in the name of registered increases in economic growth, to allocate our economic resources, including time itself, in destructive ways—to destroy God-given bases for life, i.e., air, water, earth natural beauty, and our own heredity" (The Harried Leisure Class, pp. 133-134).

What Linder is pointing to is that with the rapid increase of goods or the pace of life in society, there is a rapid imposition of values on the individual.

Each of Linder's points implies a certain imposed ranking of values. This is very close to what Toffler was speaking of in Chapter 1. As we buy more and more things, earn more and more money, there is increased time needed for maintenance of the money and the things that we buy. For each individual it does not matter whether the items he buys need less and less maintenance. The point is the more things, the more property, the more anything that a person has, the more time he has to take caring for them.

People who have less things are also affected by this same pressure. As time becomes more scarce with maintenance, those people who are under welfare or regarded as the poorer people of society have less people who have time for them. For example, the aged will have less people concerned for them and that is already a growing problem. Even in the ministry, where visiting the aged is a part of their work, very few ministers have actually organized in that direction, and the excuse often given has been the lack of *time*.

As we have an increased attachment to goods, we have an increased indifference to them. The more we are inundated with things, the more we are unlikely to become deeply involved in any one particular thing. For example, our children are continually being taught to do several things at once. What child today can't be playing with a toy or talking to a friend while watching a television program? The consequence often is a lack of intimacy with any of those elements. Friendship can become superficial.

The point well made by Linder is that, with the rapid increase of scarcity of time, there comes the problem of not spending enough time on bodily health or those things which we normally call spiritual development, that is to say, the development of the mind through study, art, and so on. What is implicit here is the idea that people are operating on the idea of function or production as a priority. If time becomes scarce and is pressing upon us, then the priorities that we choose become a major issue.

Time as a value indicator then is a very important factor. As it increases in its scarcity, we are forced more and more to look at our priorities. Priorities or value rankings are then where the action is. As I have less time, the value of intimacy is in danger of being decreased. As I am inundated with more things, more media, more people, and things to do, I have less time for such. As the pressure increases, my human relationships are radically affected. We then see how time and the pressure of time relates to values of self and others.

THE "HARRIED LEISURE CLASS" AND CREATION

As we move beyond self and others, we move into another realm which is equally important, that of creation. If I am inundated by material objects and grow in indifference and apathy toward them, I am in fact becoming indifferent to the non-human order. That is, I am being taught values that are making me apathetic to the created order. Objects are always to be used to my ends. As such, then, we find that water, air, and the created order are there to be utilized to my end. As Linder points out, if I get obsessed by economic survival, then I start using the creation in destructive ways. We see then how value ranking, as it relates to time, relates to self, others, and creation.

Linder goes on to ask the question of how can such a society function and what should its direction be.

> "Its chief characteristic must be, however, that it requires a change of heart of the individual, rather than a change in the political system of the society. The regimen of consumption cannot be abolished collectively through political pressure. A society escaping from the decadence of growth can be formed only by a sum of individuals individually transformed" (Linder, p. 145).

This individual transformation can only occur as people thoughtfully come to grips with their own choice of the use of time, as opposed to the unthinking demands of a consumer age.

Conflict and polarity occur when somebody imposes his value ranking on someone else. The highest possibility then of polarity in a group is when two groups of people or two people have opposite value rankings.

In this sense, imposition is a problem of value ranking. Imposition is when someone imposes his value ranking on you. In other words, he is imposing his priorities on you. When there is conflict, you will find usually that a person is forcing another person to accept his ranking and is not listening or being flexible about the possibility of accepting the other person's ranking.

An example of problems of imposition, polarity, and conflict often comes between young people and their parents over the ranking of the place of people, institutions, and religion. In the popular television series *All in the Family,* the difference between Archie Bunker and his son-in-law is often over these priorities. Often the father will list his priorities as follows:

1. God and the Bible
2. Institutions (Church, law, and government)
3. People

The son-in-law, on the other hand, is continually insisting on the opposite ranking:

The Harried Leisure Class: A Solution

WHO? CARES!

Campus Life

1. People
2. Institutions
3. God and the Bible

As we see, the two rankings are opposite. The point is that both people have the same values, but have them in opposite priority. The conflict takes place when one person tries to impose his ranking on the other person. *Polarity* takes place when both people try to impose their rankings on each other.

Conflict, then, is the imposition by one person or a group of persons on another person or group of persons of a particular list of priorities or values. Polarity is when two groups of people or two people are trying to impose their views upon each other. These views are seen as priority lists. I would include in this the imposition of attitudes on other people. Often, for example, the imposition of negative attitudes upon minority groups is a value ranking situation. That is to say, the attitude is a list of hidden priorities. For example, a person who does not want a Mexican-American to live next door to his house in a particular neighborhood might have the following priorities:

1. Value of my house
2. Status of the neighborhood
3. Self-esteem
4. Worth of other people

An attitude that has that kind of priority listing would, of course, discriminate against any person who in the opinion of the person would reduce the value of his property.

In the classroom, the teacher is often very much aware of this problem as he or she is confronted with students whose parents are continuously pressuring their children to obtain higher grades than those of which they are capable. At the same time, the teacher is often pressed by the administration to produce higher grades in a student. The student often has opinions about what the teacher should be like.

We might take this as an example. What kind of rankings do you think a parent might have of a student/son that could cause conflict? Here is one possibility:

Student/Son	Parents
1. Girl friend	1. Schoolwork
2. Sports	2. Parents
3. Schoolwork	3. Sports
4. Parents	4. Girl friend

A high school student with parents who tried to force him to accept their view would, of course, be in a great deal of conflict with his parents. What kind of ranking would you come up with for the student and his parents, student and teacher, and finally teacher and administrator? Try to come up with some rankings that would indicate conflict or polarity.

Obviously, what we are driving at here is simply to point out that the only way to reduce conflict and the imposition of values is through the creation of freeing environments where each

Role Expectations: Control vs. Freedom

Me and My Role

person is able to choose his own personal values in their given priority. However, there are a number of obstacles which make such a sense of freedom difficult to attain.

Almost all of these obstacles center around the influence which role expectations have in a person's life-style. One person might have a specific role expectation for another; a company might have an expectation of an employee; we might have an expectation for ourselves. In any case, if these expectations vary dramatically from what we really prefer to do, there simply cannot be a sense of freedom to set up our own priorities.

There is a simple technique for discovering whether someone is living under a controlling rather than freeing role expectation. Using any of the value ranking techniques mentioned in this chapter, prompt a person to reflect on the priorities as he would like them to be and then ask him to reflect on how they really are. If there is a large discrepancy between the lists, there is most probably a controlling role expectation operative.

The question might be raised: "Are the lists of priorities that you are living according to your behavior different from what you say you want to be?"

For example, a student might be living the expectation of putting his school first as an A student, his friendship second, and finally sports activities. Consider that the student's average without excessive anxiety was C rather than A and that his predominant interest was sports and friends. Unless the student came to grips with this and dealt with it by challenging his parents or whomever, the anxiety could be very destructive. This is not to say that a student shouldn't strive for an A in his schoolwork; I am simply saying by way of this example that if a student is being forced to do certain work because of someone else's needs rather than his own, then you have a problem of expectations. The expectation here is an imposition of values by another person.

Another example of the problem of expectations is the problem of the ideal image. Many people will become very unhappy not only because they are not living up to the expectations of others, but because they are not living up to some kind of false expectation that they have of themselves. I have counselled many sisters in religious orders who see themselves more as a "sister" than they do as a human being with limitations. One sister who belonged to a teaching order went to college and got a degree that enabled her to teach mathematics. In the counselling process we discovered that her major interest was in art, but for years she had been teaching mathematics. Why? There was a shortage of mathematics teachers, so when she went to college, she felt that she should volunteer to be a mathematics teacher as a sign of her ability to give to God. The problem is that she never really looked at what her limitations and God-given gifts really were. It seems they were not really in the area of mathematics! This discrepancy between her ideal image and her real self caused her a great deal of anxiety and pain.

We see, then, people imposing priorities on themselves as

well as on other people. We might say that people unfortunately manipulate themselves and other people. The problem of manipulation and the problem of imposition of values always cause conflict either within the self or in relationships with other people.

Imposition of values, conflict, and polarity operate at all levels.

1. It operates at the level of a person imposing false sets of priorities on himself.

2. It operates certainly as people impose false priorities on others. For example, the imposition of a parent on a high school student.

3. Thirdly, and just as importantly, people impose all sorts of priorities on others.

Strangely enough, people also impose values on creation, which of course cannot retaliate like people, but can only retaliate in its own destruction. An example is the misuse of water, which is becoming polluted through the imposition of people who place their own priorities on this natural element. It becomes non-usable, and so it retaliates in its silence. What can we say positively about the creative use of freedom?

THE FREEING ENVIRONMENT

In Chapter 2 we pointed out that a chosen value which is so important to life-style and identity consists of at least seven processes. It is something that is chosen freely. It is chosen from alternatives. It is chosen after consideration of the consequences of the alternatives. It is something that I am happy with and as such celebrate. It is something that I am willing to state publicly. Finally, it is something that I have acted on recently and acted on repeatedly in my behavioral patterns.

In this chapter we have been talking about priorities. We now, in conclusion, want to talk about priorities as value ranking. The more our lists of priorities are chosen values, the more conscious I am of my direction and identity, the more free I am in the sense that I am at least choosing the alternatives that I am aware of. *Value ranking is a list of chosen priorities, chosen from alternatives, after consideration of the consequences, which I am happy with and will state publicly, and which I will act on repeatedly as a part of my behavioral pattern.*

Being Myself; Freeing Others To Be Themselves

To move toward the freeing of myself as a person, it is more important that my priorities be chosen according to the seven criteria listed above than it is that I become aware of choosing particular values.

Certainly to choose values according to the criteria and to act in my priorities from the criteria would be not only helpful, but very productive in terms of life development and identity. It is toward this end then that we should move young people and children in the educational process—not only to teach them how to value things through choosing, through seeing alternatives, through acting upon them, but to be able to see their priorities and to choose from alternatives the ranking of their priorities and to act on them accordingly.

The point here is that a person will not only choose his priorities from a list of alternatives, but he will also be able to reflect on the different effects which will appear in his behavior. That is to say, a person who ranks institutions first and people second will in fact behave differently than a person who ranks people first and institutions second. Educators need to be aware not only of the process whereby people rank their priorities, but also of the behavioral differences that come about due to the rankings.

As we remarked earlier in the chapter under primary values, it needs to be noted that there are certain values which we call primary that need to be included in any over-all life value rankings. The values we listed were self-worth and the worth of others. In any list of priorities or rankings, these two values need to be high on the list. At this point, of course, I am stating a biased presupposition which we have already noted. It is a presupposition that the reader may reflect on before accepting it.

We are stating at this point, then, that the way in which a person chooses his priorities is itself the valuing process, and secondly that in choosing the priorities there are one or two primary values that need to be there in order for the full development of the human being to be creative and authentic.

Finally, we need to see the freeing environment as a society, a group of persons, or a family that lives together in such a

way that the given priorities of each person may be maximized creatively in relationship to the other person's. If I am living with two other people, my priorities should not be such that they impose on the two other people. The idea is that we should be able to live together in such a way that the priorities of all three people would not be imposed upon any of the other two persons. The life-style will be structured as a "free environment." This structure would permit the maximum amount of freedom of all three persons as they act their values through their priority lists.

Let us try to give a simple example of this. Let us suppose that three persons, Person 1, Person 2, and Person 3, had the following lists of priorities:

Person 1	Person 2	Person 3
Self-Worth	Friends	Leisure
Work	Work	Self-Worth
Leisure	Leisure	Friends
Friends	Self-Worth	Work

We might say that those three people would have a lot of difficulty in living together since their priorities are different. Let us offer some clues to what their life-style might be, assuming that they were three persons living in one apartment, for example. Now for Person 1 and Person 3, self-worth seems to be very high. You might ask what this means. If it should mean that they need a lot of affirmation, then the three of them should set up a process whereby this could happen. Perhaps the three would have to sit down for an hour each week together and listen to each other's feelings or hopes or aspirations or the difficulties they have had at work, etc., and then try to point out to those who need affirmation their positive attributes. This then would be an example of a freeing structure in the area of self-worth.

Work was high for two people. A time should perhaps be allowed for people to share what their work is, or maybe tolerance given to study or whatever it is they might do alone to improve their work. But because it is a high priority it would have to be a part of this freeing relationship.

The place of leisure is important in these rankings. Perhaps for these people they have difficulty with it. In such a structure, in order that it would not be a difficulty, what leisure is would have to be clarified and then some provision made for it to enable the persons to have sufficient leisure.

The freeing environment here would be one dealing with all these priorities in such a way as to make sure that the "scarcity of time" did not manipulate them in such a way that they could not live their priorities and the identity that they had chosen.

Imposition of values through society on persons and on myself is a major problem. The freeing environment concept is one that moves to helping people live in structures, in societies, which will enable maximum non-imposition on the one hand and maximum freedom to choose one's identity on the other hand.

Hitler's Third Reich is a good example. As William Shirer has written:

> "*Danzig is not the subject of the dispute at all. It is a question of expanding our living space in the East, of securing our food supplies and also of solving the problem of the Baltic States. There is no other possibility in Europe. If fate forces us into a showdown with the West, it is invaluable to possess a large area in the East. In wartime we shall be even less able to rely on record harvests than in peacetime.*
> "*Besides, Hitler adds, the population of non-German territories in the East will be available as a source of labor*" (The Rise and Fall of the Third Reich, p. 649).

Man has continually tried to impose upon man. We must try to find new ways of freeing ourselves so that we can free our fellow man in the total environment. We must look for creative structures; we must discover the freeing environment. Teilhard de Chardin alludes to this position as follows:

> "*The very fact of our becoming aware of this profound ordering of things will enable human collectivisation to pass beyond the enforced phase, where it now is, into the free phase: that in which (men having at last understood that they are inseparably joined elements of a converging Whole, and having learned in consequence to love the preordained forces that unite them) a natural union of affinity and sympathy will supersede the forces of compulsion*" (The Future of Man, p. 125).

So spoke Teilhard de Chardin in *The Future of Man*. His vision was then one of where man would move finally into some new state of awareness, which might be a futuristic way of looking at the freeing environment. The freeing environment then would be a world where society was described as a place where imposition of values became minimal and a creative freeing environment became maximal.

When man imposes his values on another, he does so usually because his priorities are different. A teacher may impose the order of church, work, home and recreation on his peers. Another teacher may be in conflict with his fellow teacher with the following: home, recreation, work, church, for example. What we see is conflict, but the irony is that the divergent points of view also give the greater possibility of creative team cooperation. This would mean an acceptance of each other's priorities and working together with the new priorities (two instead of one). This would be the freeing environment.

This ends Part I of the book. Part II will deal in greater detail with particular aspects of man in relationship to time and space with their value implications. The second half of the book will try to see values much more in the area of priorities than individual values, the reason being that man lives with priorities and seldom with individual values alone. Therefore the question of value ranking is a question of the relationships of man as he relates to others in society.

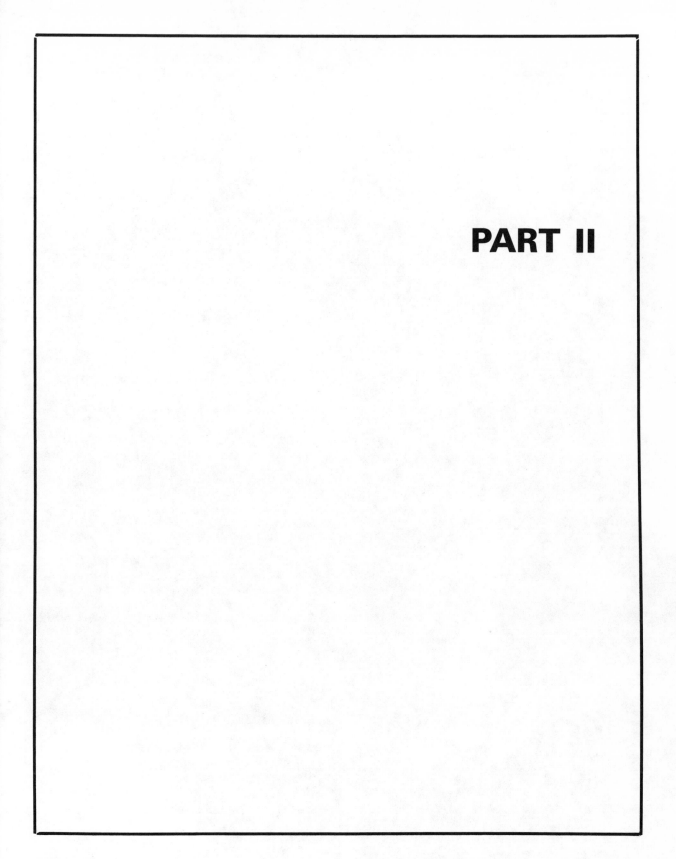

PART II

5.

Guilt As Limitation:
A Celebration of The Past

"Indeed the future has already broken into the present. We each
live in many times. The present of one is the past of another,
and the future of yet another. We are called to live, knowing
and showing that the future exists and that each one of us can
call it end, when we are willing to redress the balance of the
past."   Ivan Illich, Celebration of Awareness

INTRODUCTION

The focus in Part II will be on the relationship between values and priorities. The discussion will be primarily on value ranking.

Man can reflect upon his values and their ranking in many ways as he reflects on various time spans—as he remembers, or dreams, or is. In other words, conscious reflection can turn to the past, or the future, or the present. These subsequent chapters will merely be reflections in each of these time spans, looking for the potential "windows" through which a man may examine his values. This chapter deals with time as past. We will deal with memory. It is in the memory that we find the history of the race as well as our own personal history. Guilt resides in the past as a confrontation with priorities we are ashamed of. This chapter will also deal with guilt as confronting us with our limitations which we need to celebrate. Through celebration we can make the past a freeing experience.

PAST AS MEMORY

The past for the human being is in the memory. It is in the memory that we have things that we are happy about as well as things which bring us shame. The memory contains events that we acted on and which we learned from. From the past choices that we made, and the actions resulting from those choices, we have learned patterns of success and failure as we related to others in society. However, it is Bruno Bettelheim who has pointed out that people learn from their mistakes rather than from their successes, and it is precisely these mistakes that prompt feelings of guilt in us. So, to examine our guilt is an educational process. Mistakes are only one source of learning from the past; we also learn from successes and harmony and things we feel good about in the past.

However, we want to concentrate on the guilt areas for four reasons:

1. Attitudinal and value change occurs when there is a felt difficulty or disharmony. For instance, we say that we hold a value, but we see in our past that we have acted differently.

2. Modern man more easily remembers occasions of guilt than those of joy, if for no other reason than we're conditioned to do so. Therefore, working with guilt is easier and the data are more "retrievable" than occasions of joy.

3. Authentic growth and increased self-value results from coming to grips with the feelings of guilt and turning them into a celebration of limitations, and this chapter is about the process of doing this.

4. Modern psychology teaches us that if we are to grow, we must accept who we are with our limitations right now.

None of this is a denial that a man might be able to learn

about his values and their ranking from recalling positive feelings about the past. It simply means that, educationally and therapeutically, a reflection on the negative feelings of the past is more beneficial for our purposes, and the goal of this book for educators.

An important part of education in any civilization has always been its history. In the more primitive societies, it has often been in the form of religious myths passed down from generation to generation. These myths and stories have been very important in the formation of the identity of the people. They help persons to make sense out of their "contingencies" as they face the fears of sickness, death, and life itself.

In our society, history is of primary importance as young and old seek identity. There have been more than a few bitter arguments between father and son, in recent years, over the place of American heritage in our lives. To be proud to be an American is an historical *statement*. To object to what we have done in the Far East is an historical *judgment*. The young man who fears the draft is only too aware of the history of his country as it confronts him with the possibilities of his future. History, then, is important to us.

Reviewing the Past for a Creative Future

Like nations, it is good for individuals to often review their past, to review their past choices. This confronts us with our choice pattern in the present and helps us to act creatively for the future. As we review the past, we become aware of what our values have been, and this puts us in the free position of choosing how we want to root our values now.

The Diary: Chronicler of Change

Several devices may be used to help a person do this. One, which several writers suggest, is the keeping of a diary. The idea is to keep a daily diary over a period of a year of all the major events that happen during each day of a person's life. The importance of such a diary is in its review. As we look back over the past year at ourselves in detail, we can see how we have changed and evaluate that change.

The questions that should be asked in such a review might be as follows:

1. How did I use my time? Was my time well spent and could I start thinking about using it differently?

2. What kinds of values are indicated by my use of the time?

3. What choices did I make that I was most happy with and acted on?

4. Could I list some of the priorities that are evident in my diary and evaluate them in the light of my present experience and direction?

5. Am I proud of my priorities and the values indicated in my diary?

If keeping a daily diary doesn't fit your life-style, then try summary reviews at special times during the year. Take time at the bigger holidays to review your life.

Another use of the diary which some find very useful is to

report only certain things daily.

1. The bad things that happened to me during the day.
2. The good things that happened to me during the day.
3. The dreams that I had, if any.

The area of dreams includes:

1. Daydreams—those fantasies and thoughts that I have about my future, about sex, or about whatever it is that I fantasize about.

2. Actual dreams that I have at night. Dreams are considered by most counselors and by many religious leaders as being very important symbolic indicators of the deepest part of our nature. I would refer the reader who is interested to the writings of Morton Kelsey. As indicators of our deepest self, they are very valuable in helping us to understand what our values are. Dream interpretation is not always as complicated as one might imagine. The meaning of a dream is often self-evident, especially when a person reviews a whole series of dreams as recorded in a diary. Such a diary can be evaluated by asking the same questions as mentioned above.

Keeping Dreams in the Diary

The following are dreams recorded by a friend after keeping a diary for approximately one year.

SELECTION I

I am in a huge office complex, where each office is partitioned off with oak paneling. I suppose the room would be over a hundred yards square, very tall, with large marble columns. The ceiling is of the decorated type with large hanging chandeliers. It reminds me of a large bank building.

I am in my office doing something. All the offices have walls about four feet high, so there is only so much privacy. I am one of many workers. I do my work very well, but I am bored and unsatisfied. I have a feeling that I want to succeed and do better.

SELECTION II

Suddenly, I find myself in a larger office on the same floor. There is a carpet on my floor. I have a larger desk with a large bronze lamp on it. I have succeeded. I noticed that I am at the top right-hand end of the marble columned room. Am I successful now? It would seem that I am successful, but I am so bored and unsatisfied. I have a feeling that I want to succeed.

SELECTION III

The room is different. I know that I am in the same building. I am on the top floor. My office has walls to the ceiling and is paneled with oak all the way around. It is an old office and I have a feeling of tradition. I have bookshelves with old books on them. The door is of frosted glass and my name is on the door. I am successful, yet I still feel bored and unsatisfied.

SELECTION IV: CONCLUSION

What is this place? I know it is on the same floor. There are no frosted glass windows, but oak library walls, covered with many colored books. Most of the books have leather covers. They look used. There is a sense of history that resides in this room. But, why am I here? Is this my new office, is this the last place? Am I now successful?

Sunlight is flooding the room from the east wall, which is a huge window. Through the window I see huge networks of railway lines moving to a dock. On the dock are several ships from different parts of the world. Beyond the dock are huge oceans.

Then, suddenly, by the window I see an old man. He seems very wise and is looking at me and pointing out the window. He says, "You have succeeded and from this window you can see the ships moving to your dominions throughout the total world." I told him that I was bored and unsatisfied. He said, "Success and satisfaction are not found on the outside."

The above dream was discussed in a group setting with some friends who were evaluating their life-styles through the use of a diary. The above dream was one that came after a period of six months of record-keeping in a diary. The person in question was able to point out that the dream indicated his own history in business life. He began to relate how all his life he had had a compulsion to succeed. He related how he had been successful. As he became more successful, he said he became more and more aware of a lack of satisfaction.

The conclusion of the dream was not simply a conclusion of his history, but rather a confrontation with his values. He noted that he did feel more satisfied with the conclusion of the dream because he had begun to revise his priorities. Rather than constantly seeking success, he had begun to relax more with his family and children. The dream took him to the ultimate of success. Satisfaction, the dream suggested, was found in the man, not in outward success. This dream was a value indicator for him, confirming his impression that his priorities had been in the wrong order. He changed his priorities from work first and family second, to family first and work second.

From the above we see that the past can give us an implication of what our values have been and helps us to rank our values now. In the next section, we will discuss an important element of the past—our feelings of guilt.

GUILT AND THE PAST

Guilt is something that is always found in the past. Guilt has to do with past memory. It is related to the present as a feeling—to presently feeling guilty about a past event.

What then is guilt? Thomas C. Oden sees guilt as an act which is contrary to what we believe is a self-actualizing value. He defines guilt as follows:

*"The core of our definition of guilt, in its most elemental sense, is precisely **the awareness of irresponsible value negation.** Guilt is a form of awareness in which we are painfully conscious that we have said a tragic no to some valued relationship amid the process of attempting to say a self-actualizing yes to some other valued relationship.*

"That which makes a certain person feel guilty thus depends entirely upon his own unique ethical frame of refer-

ence. A thief might feel guilty that he cannot steal successfully. An anarchist might feel the burden of guilt simply by living in an ordered society. A pusher of dope might feel guilty that he could not make a sale to an innocent teenager. Whatever form guilt takes, however, it is always shaped by the contextual values at stake. Its essential definition is the awareness that one has failed to actualize a value considered necessary for his existence" (The Structure of Awareness, p. 47).

Guilt: Result of Choice and Action

What Oden calls a self-actualizing value is what we earlier said about values, that the value must be chosen from alternatives and work toward the creative integration of the personality. What Oden is saying, then, is that guilt is a conscious act to not choose a value one thought one should have chosen.

If we look at this a little more closely and remember our earlier chapter about existential value formers, we see that guilt is a result of choice and action. Every time I make a choice, it must be from a range of alternatives if it is to be free choice. This kind of choice is a part of a valuing process. If I have several alternatives to choose from, then happiness means choosing the right alternatives. Equally, I may fail to choose the right alternatives. Nobody is perfect. And sometimes we are caught in binds we can't do anything about. We are bound to choose the wrong alternatives many, many times. The consequence is guilt.

Guilt, then, is the failure of man to choose the alternatives that will bring genuine growth and healthy contentment. The degree of guilt usually relates to the degree of negative consequences.

An example: You have an important business engagement—an appointment to meet with an executive of X-brand dog food at three o'clock this afternoon. It may bring about some important sales. A few hours before the meeting, your wife calls up to say that a friend who is very important to you and whom you have not seen for a year and a half, called from the airport to say that he had arrived for a few hours and asked if you would pick him up. Your son has a bad cold, with the consequence that your wife cannot possibly leave the house.

If you do not go and pick up your friend, he will think that you do not care about him, since you have no way of communicating with him. If you miss your business appointment, you will feel bad about that. Yes, it is true that there may be many other alternatives, but how often have you been in such a bind? Think of the times you have been caught on the horns of a dilemma, knowing that you are going to feel guilty no matter what you choose.

Guilt as a Problem of Value Ranking

Guilt, then, has to do with choices we have made and acted on which resulted in the choosing of poor alternatives. Often we do not realize that the alternatives were bad. Since man is limited, he cannot know all the alternatives. *Therefore, the conclusion that I make is that guilt is basically a problem of value ranking and is, as such, social in its dimension.*

When I feel guilty, I do so because of a way in which I

behaved and the effects of this choice on myself and others. I chose a value ranking which I acted on and which I was probably happy with at the time. Guilt came about when I realized that I should have chosen some other value ranking which would have been more beneficial to myself and others. More often than not, the value ranking I should have chosen is the opposite to the one I did choose.

The importance of seeing guilt as value ranking rather than only a single value negation is that it puts us into a social context. Value ranking is, for the most part, something that almost always relates to other dimensions of space other than self. Guilt then may be seen as the failure of a person to choose the right alternatives.

The question then is: Should a person feel guilty? Is he, in fact, responsible if he does not see all the objectives? Often I think that a person is not responsible objectively. That is to say, a small child cannot be responsible for the death of his father who died of a heart attack, but he may feel guilty.

This brings in all the problems of guilt as related to psycho-social development and the problem of emotional illness. We are limited in what we can deal with, and so we will not be dealing with the problem of emotional illness in this book. We are concerned more with guilt as it afflicts most people and as it relates to our social awareness.

Definition of Guilt

Guilt is a problem of value ranking and is, as such, social in its dimension. Guilt is a past priority ranking, acted upon, contrary to the self-actualizing value ranking that I feel I should have chosen.

Various Ethical Levels: Or Different Guilt for Different Folks

As we have defined guilt, it might be helpful to mention that there is a complicating dimension which we should reflect upon. One person's guilt, defined in his terms, centered upon his issues, is simply not the same as another person's guilt, or terms, or issues. In addition, this is true not only because ethical judgments and moral codes differ, but also because *individuals operate on various ethical levels in general.* Each level brings with it certain priorities and concerns which are even more basic and general than the proclamation of any religious, cultural, or social ethical code.

Recent research and thought has considered this problem extensively. For the sake of simplicity, we will be using the considerations of Lawrence Kohlberg of the Harvard Graduate School of Education. However, philosophical, ethical, and educational research of the past century presents many other models of analysis which would serve equally as well.

Kohlberg states that there are at least six stages of moral growth open to an individual. Each stage will naturally have its own area of priority (value ranking process), and its own definition of guilt, regardless of the issue at hand. He delineates the stages in the following manner:

1. *Stage One:* A person is primarily motivated by the desire to avoid punishment from a superior power. Priority items and judgments: I am in danger, insecurity, the power of the pun-

isher, I am of less value, the punisher of more value. Guilt is the feeling of danger which occurs when I am liable to punishment due to an act committed in conflict with *his* (the punisher's) value rankings.

2. *Stage Two:* A person is primarily motivated by the desire to satisfy his own quasi-physical needs. Priority items and judgments: I am in need. What do I need to satisfy myself? How do others serve my needs? Guilt is defined as the feeling which results when I realize that I have blocked the fulfillment of my needs by another through any act which hampers the other from responding to my needs.

3. *Stage Three:* A person is primarily motivated by the desire to "be accepted" by another *individual* by fulfilling his expectations of me and acting within the role he prescribes for me. Priority items and judgments: I need his approval to survive; what does he expect? What are normal roles which I can play? Guilt: the awareness which comes from an act which does not fulfill the role expectations of another individual and blocks my acceptance by him.

4. *Stage Four:* A person is primarily motivated by the desire to "be accepted" by the institutions which others approve, by fulfilling the institutional expectations and roles. Priority items and judgments: What is my duty in this act? What does authority say? What is the institutional code? How can I survive in this institution? Guilt: the awareness that my choice took me outside the general norms and expectations and roles which duty and authority prescribe.

5. *Stage Five:* A person is primarily motivated by the variable and conditioned contracts and conventions which he has deliberately entered into for his own benefit and the benefit of others. Priority items and judgments: What is my present commitment? What is the need of the majority? How can or should commitments change? How do I share my values with others in dialogue rather than imposition or rejection? Guilt: the awareness that my choice violated pre-chosen and shared commitments to myself, others, and the majority.

6. *Stage Six:* A person primarily motivated by his own conscience and judgment seeks to apply that with consistency and respect for others. Priority items and judgments: How do I reconcile my action with my convictions, regardless of cultural forces? How can I be authentic? How can I express my respect for others? How can I be faithful to the intrinsic, personal authenticity which I possess? Guilt: the awareness of an inauthentic action, a non-free decision, a non-respectful direction.

Implications of Kohlberg's Model of Moral Growth

Obviously, such a model of moral growth has great implications in any reflection on guilt. Just a few of the implications could be:

1. The issue of guilt is not simply an issue of what is right or wrong, but rather what people perceive as right or wrong.

2. The issue of what people perceive as right or wrong is not simply a decision about any specific issue, whether it be abortion, pre-marital sex, racism, war, etc., but rather a conscious or

unconscious decision concerning the level of ethical consideration operative at that moment.

3. Finally, if Kohlberg is correct in his analysis, it becomes evident that as a person progresses through these stages, some of his guilt feelings might simply be present as he "frees" himself from one stage to proceed to the next. As such, it is a sign of growth. For example, someone going from Stage Three to Stage Four might experience a depth of guilt and insecurity as he transfers his allegiance from the expectations of another individual to an allegiance to "duty."

Another Thought

For public school teachers, it would seem within their realm to aid students to progress through these stages, and this could be done without entering into a consideration of any controversial ethical decision on any specific issue.

Responsibility for Guilt Essential

One of the implications of our definition of guilt is that responsibility for guilt is essential. It is only as we personally become responsible for our value choices that we are able to choose our own identity. Responsibility for choice is a part of growth in maturity. Guilt, therefore, may be seen as a very productive side of man which helps him and educates him into creative choosing rather than destructive choosing.

As a person grows, he moves through a process from "I ought to do something" to "I know what I should do." It is when I realize "I ought to have done but instead did" that we are confronted with guilt. The realization of guilt is an educator. To help a student reflect on what he ought to have done so that he comes to his own conclusions, understanding his own priority negation, is a very helpful process.

One of the basic reasons why we are considering guilt and its experience in our lives is to examine the positive potential of these experiences in terms of our growth. That is necessary for each of us individually; it is also necessary if we are to aid others in their own efforts toward maturity.

Guilt is tied to our conscious acts of choice; it is also tied to our personality and developed sense of responsibility. As such, it is intimately connected to our whole process of maturity. If we can continue to keep that in mind, then a consideration of guilt is not merely an exercise of self-flagellation; it becomes a creative opportunity to consider our life and choices and direction for the future. As such, it is a creative exercise and not a self-destructive one. There is a unique insight into our self-direction which can result from coming to grips with the occasions of guilt which are part of all of our lives.

Rogers on Man Becoming Self-Directive

Carl Rogers in his book *Freedom To Learn* describes the process of a man coming to self-direction in terms which parallel Kohlberg's analysis. In addition, he describes the various "oughts" and priorities which a man has in the midst of that process. These are pseudo-oughts with the accompanying feeling of guilt because we have not followed the authority of others. Whenever we have a challenge of an "ought" or the revision of a priority, or a choice which militates against such a priority, we have guilt. As we read Rogers' description, it might be beneficial to ask ourselves a series of questions:

1. Do I personally agree with Rogers' *theory* of the direction of maturity of thought and deed?

2. At what stage of this realization am I?

3. What are the issues of "guilt" found in each stage and how do they apply to me at this moment?

Rogers spells out the valuing process as follows:

> "Let me indicate a few of these value directions as I see them in my clients as they move in the direction of personal growth and maturity.
>
> "They attempt to move away from facades. Pretense, defensiveness, putting up a front, tend to be negatively valued.
>
> "They tend to move away from 'oughts.' The compelling feeling of 'I ought to do or be thus and so' is negatively valued. The client moves away from being what he 'ought to be,' no matter who has set that imperative.
>
> "They tend to move away from meeting the expectations of others. Pleasing others, as a goal in itself, is negatively valued.
>
> "Being real is positively valued. The client tends to move toward being himself, being his real feelings, being what he is. This seems to be a very deep preference.
>
> "Self-direction is positively valued. The client discovers an increasing pride and confidence in making his own choices, guiding his own life.
>
> "One's self, one's own feelings, come to be positively valued. From a point where he looks upon himself with contempt and despair, the client comes to value himself and his reactions as being of worth.
>
> "Being in process is positively valued. From desiring some fixed goal, clients come to prefer the excitement of being a process of potentialities being born.
>
> "Perhaps more than all else, the client comes to value an openness to all of his inner and outer experience. To be open to and sensitive to his own inner reactions and feelings, the reactions and feelings of others, and the realities of the objective world—this is a direction which he clearly prefers. This openness becomes the client's most valued resource.
>
> "Sensitivity to others and acceptance of others is positively valued. The client comes to appreciate others for what they are, just as he has come to appreciate himself for what he is.
>
> "Finally, deep relationships are positively valued. To achieve a close, intimate, real, fully communicative relationship with another person seems to meet a deep need in every individual, and is very highly valued" (Freedom to Learn, pp. 253-254).

Guilt: The Failure To Be Yourself

What Rogers has just said is very close to what Paul Tournier in the book called *Guilt and Grace* defines as his understanding of guilt. Guilt, says Tournier, is the failure to be oneself. The process that Rogers outlines above is exactly the process of becoming oneself. Failure to do this, choices that negate this, are choices that cause guilt.

Rogers talks a great deal about becoming oneself. He talks about choosing and self-direction. He talks, in fact, about the valuing process. However, there is one point that needs to be built upon which, although present, may not be self-evident to some. He says that a person moves from looking upon himself with contempt to valuing himself as of worth. What is so important about this is that it is a movement from value negation to the position of recognizing one's own limitations.

To confront a person with his or her limitations is, as such, a positive value indicator. Finally, Rogers' analysis is social in its dimension. Guilt, therefore, is always in relationship to other people. This is clearly indicated by his use of the word "expectations"—the problem of feeling guilty because I am not living up to the expectations of another. As I grow in self-value, so I disregard the expectations of others as guilt imposition and incorporate them into my being as one alternative among others as I move toward self-chosen, positive, creative life direction.

Value Indicators and Guilt Clarification

Let us now explore some examples. The following diagram called "Value Indicators" is a guilt clarification sheet that I have used often in group discussions. Take the time to study this process carefully. It is best if you try it yourself once you understand what to do.

In the first column, called "My Guilt," a person places some things that he feels guilty about. In the next two columns we have one column called "Behavior" and the other called "Ought To and Should Have Feelings." The point is that guilt is seen here as a past event consisting of the ranking of at least two values. The first value which was placed as number one in priority was the one that I acted upon, in fact. The second value was one that I felt I should have acted on. If we could follow through on a couple of examples, we would then end up with the value rankings for what was "done" and what I ought to have done.

154

VALUE INDICATORS

My Guilt	1. Behavior (What I Did)	2. Ought To and Should Have Feelings (What I Should Have Done)	Values and Ranking

It will become evident to the reader that this process can be an in-depth process. The kinds of questions that a person asks in order to clarify the guilt are called value clarifying questions. Often value clarifying questions are a part of the counseling process. They can also be seen for different reasons and different intentions as a part of the education process. The point in using this method is not to inquire into a person's guilt, but only to help a person discover his value priorities. This needs to be a non-judgmental, non-critical procedure.

In order that the process can truly give us new insight into ourselves, it is necessary to become more specific, more explicit as we move across the page. To say simply that I feel guilty about never cleaning my desk because I never clean my desk and I should clean my desk gets us nowhere. Rather, the general feeling of guilt should be concretized to a specific incident which then is analyzed to see precisely what got in the way of accomplishing the behavior which we think we should have accomplished; this then is analyzed to the point where we know clearly why we *should* have done what we did not do. It is in the probing and clarifying that the rivalry of priorities finally gets clarified.

Example I. We will look at the following example on two levels—first, the simple educational level and then a second level for those people who feel that they are competent in counseling. Let us take the example of the person who wrote in the first column the following guilt:

> *My Guilt*
> I spend too much
> time at the
> office and leave
> my wife and
> children at home
> alone.

The dialogue of value-clarifying questions might go as follows:

Educator: George, you have written your guilt as "I spend too much time at the office and not enough time with my wife and children who are left alone." Do you mean by this that you spend a lot of time at work and that your wife is left at home alone?

George: Yes, that is what I mean.

Educator: In the first column, which we have called "Behavior," we need to ask the question: What particular incident do you have in mind? That is to say, George, we must nail down a particular time that you feel guilty about, not just a whole series. Can you think of a particular instance?

George: Yes, I can. Just last night, I spent two hours working in the office when I could have been at home with my

VALUE INDICATORS

My Guilt	1. Behavior	2. Ought To and Should Have Feelings	Values and Ranking
Example I I spend too much time working. I leave my family at home alone.	Work is important to me.	Wife and children are important.	Work Wife Children vs. Wife Children Work

wife and children.

Educator: Your actual behavior, then, was that you did spend more time at the office?

George: Yes.

Educator: Then, in the first column, we place the value "Work Is Important to Me." Do you agree?

George: Yes, indeed, it is very important to me.

Educator: In the third column we have "Ought To and Should Have Feelings." What do you think you should have done? That is to say, what did you feel guilty about?

George: Well, as I said, I should have been home with my wife and children.

Educator: In the third column, then, we can place "Wife and Children Are Important."

George: Well, of course.

Educator: Then your guilt is over your priorities.

George: I am not sure I understand.

Educator: In your behavior you ranked work first and wife and children last. The conflict over these two priorities caused the guilt.

George: Then what I need to do is sort out and come to grips with my priorities.

Establish the Priorities, Then Explore the Problem

Once a person has his priorities straight, he is then able to explore what he can do about the problem. In the case example I have outlined, George was able to confront the fact that he often needs to work overtime. His difficulty was that he would keep promising his children and wife that he would be home without facing the reality that he would have to work. By listing his priorities, he was able to make some behavioral changes by choosing to act on the following:

Wife
Children
Work

He was also able to confront the fact that the limitation of his work altered this at times. However, he said he would make it a value of priorities, a value ranking, by not only acting on it but by telling his children and wife the situation when he could not avoid working overtime. By acting, he made the priorities a value ranking. So often what happens is that we live with these priorities that make us feel guilty without looking at them and acting on them. The above was used in an adult education group.

Often further guidance is needed that takes particular competence in the area of value clarification and counseling.

If we are treating the areas of guilt in a person's life, it is possible to deal with the guilt feeling at a deeper level than the one just described. A greater degree of training and sensitivity is needed if we are to prompt and facilitate a deeper analysis. In the case of George, just such a deeper analysis continued, following the group session described above. As you will notice, the same ground rules continued to operate:

1. The attitude of the clarifier must continuously be non-judgmental.

2. Every interpretation must be checked out with the one being interviewed and must be accepted by him.

3. The questions are meant to allow the opportunity to probe a bit deeper, but never more deeply than the interviewee can handle.

4. The questioning will center more closely upon the issues of self-value and expectations.

A further interview with George continued as follows:

Deeper Analysis of the Problem through Greater Sensitivity

George: *I have difficulty in knowing why I feel so guilty when I am not at work, even when I know everything is all right.*

Educator: *In terms of your behavior, work seems to be very important to you.*

George: *You bet it is. I often feel that if you don't do a job yourself, it will never get done.*

Educator: *This is true of those you work with?*

George: (Hesitating) *No, it isn't really. I wonder what's the matter.*

Educator: *What are you afraid might happen if you are not at work? That is to say, why should you be there?*

George: *I worry if I am not at work. You are right, I guess. I am afraid something might happen. After all, I have worked hard for this business. It is my bread and butter, although I don't need the money so much now.*

Educator: *It sounds to me as if work and success were at one time very important to you.*

George: *Boy, could I tell you some stories. It seems that at one time success was everything to me. Now I don't feel that way. My family is more important.*

Educator: *Are you feeling guilty again?*

George: *Yes, I guess I am. I guess I have needed to succeed* too much. It seems I needed to look after all the details, to be there all the time.

Educator: You felt you did not want to make a mistake?

George: (Clenching his hands) Yes, I never want to make a mistake. It seems I get very angry at the children when they spill their food or whatever or get bad marks at school. Yet, they are only kids. Of course, they can't be perfect.

Educator: A value for you, then, has been to be perfect?

George: Yes, indeed. (Becomes enthusiastic) I was going to be a minister and I guess to be perfect was one of my goals.

Educator: A clarification, George. It seems that you have defined being perfect as not making mistakes.

George: Yes, I have. Indeed, I have. You know, that does not seem right. We have to make mistakes. After all, I am human.

Educator: You are right, George. You have confused being perfect with perfectionism. To be perfect means to be the best human being that I, George, can be with my limits. It does not mean to be an angel, for heavens sake! No human being can live without making mistakes. In your original list of priorities with work first and wife second, which you want to change to wife first and work second, you need to confront your limitations. Perhaps in doing this, you need to laugh a little more at your mistakes and work at being a person who is not anxious about slipping up occasionally or about other people slipping up occasionally.

The new ranking that George may have come up with could have been as follows:

Self (to be perfect as limited)
Wife and children
Work

This new ranking would see self as being the best human being that I can be. This would mean that George would constantly evaluate his priorities and limitations. This would help him to confront and keep in order the ranking of self, wife, and children.

Another Example

Example II. In this example, we'll call our subject Mary. The guilt that she felt she wanted to deal with was: "I cannot seem to keep my desk tidy in the house." This will then be placed in the first column under "My Guilt."

My Guilt
I cannot keep my
desk tidy.

The beginning of the clarification took place as follows:

Educator: You are saying that you feel guilty when you do not keep your desk tidy in your house?

Mary: Yes. It is really more than that. I feel I should write letters to my parents and all sorts of other people, but it never seems to get done either.

Is Interviewer Comfortable with Interpretation?

Educator: Are you saying that the real issue is that you feel guilty about not writing letters?

Mary: No. It is really both. I really feel that I should write letters, but my desk is so untidy that I feel I should do that first. But I never seem to get around to it.

Educator: I see. Then, what prevents you from tidying your desk?

Mary: Well, I always seem to have other things to do. No, that's not right either, because the whole house is often untidy. Not that untidy, you understand, but untidy. (She smiles)

Educator: In value clarification you must always pick a particular incident or event if we are going to nail down exactly what the guilt is. Can you think of a particular time when you felt guilty about your desk and your letters?

Mary: Why, yes I can. A week ago was my mother's birthday. She lives in Pennsylvania. I sent her a letter, but I sent it two days late. I remember I was going to write it the day before her birthday and send it special delivery, but then—(period of silence).

Educator: What happened?

Hint to Contrasting Priorities

Mary: Well (looking guilty), my neighbor came in and we had a cup of tea and talked. She had some things that were bothering her, and, hell, I like to talk to people. Then we went shopping and had dinner together. I mean, what is the matter with that?

Educator: I don't know that there is anything the matter with that. Let us look at it a little closer. (Mary nods) It seems to me that you are saying in terms of the second column under Behavior that you have a positive value in your conflict over letters and a messy desk.

Mary: There was? I would like to know what it was.

Educator: Well, your behavior said that your neighbor, your friend, and personal interaction with her is a value and important to you.

Mary: Well, yes it is. You know, I should not feel guilty about that.

Educator: Now if we look at the third column, or what you ought to have done, it would seem that you are saying that you ought to have (1) ordered your desk; (2) written a letter to your mother.

Mary: Well, yes, I think so. Although my mother is more important than that. I think the letters are more important than getting my desk done, really.

Educator: All right then, it would seem that in the first column *under Behavior you have "People Are Important to Me." In the next column under what you ought to have done, it would seem that you had Mother, perhaps Order, and finally Letters. Or perhaps, Mother, Letters, and then Order?*

Mary: *I think you are right. I think that the way I have been acting I have had Mother first, then Order, then Letters.*

Educator: *Your guilt, then, is over your priorities. Your priorities seem to be: Mother, Order, Letters, People, over against: People, Mother, Letters, Order.*

This is how it would look:

My Guilt	1. Behavior	2. Ought To and Should Have Feelings	Values and Ranking		
I cannot keep my desk tidy.	People are important to me.	Letter writing and order is important to me. Writing to mother is important.	Mother Order Letters People	vs.	People Mother Order Letters

Identifying Conflict

To spell out these priorities was very important to Mary, for she was then able to choose the priority listing that she wanted. She chose the following:

People (interaction)
Mother (letter-writing)
Order (of desk)
Letters (in general)

The next stage in aiding Mary was helping her to rank these four in time. She was then asked to take that particular incident and rank how much time she spent on each and how much time she would like to spend. In the case of this ranking, Mary was doing what she wanted to do, but because she had not clarified what she was doing, she felt guilty about it.

Identifying Conflict and Value Ranking

By clarifying her value ranking, she was able to look at what she was doing and order her time in order to take care of her desk and her letters and her letters to her mother. Not ordering and clarifying her values resulted in all sorts of confusion—for example, confusing letter writing with writing a letter to her mother. What she finally was able to do was write once a week to her mother, spend some time ordering her desk, and then worry about the other letters. The problem of guilt, then, is the problem of priorities and the problem of coming to grips with, dealing with, and acting on my limitations.

In the value clarifying method used above, several points are noted:

1. When the person is asked to state what he feels guilty about, it must be a specific event in time, with a time span.

2. The first set of clarifying questions seeks to discover precisely the behavior acted on. The expression of the behavior is the indication of a value or value ranking.

3. The second set of questions seeks to ask precisely what the person thinks he "ought" to have done. This will give the second value which will be ranked as second.

4. The process continues by helping the person take all the values delineated and asking him how they were originally ranked and what other ranking would make them more comfortable.

5. If the new priority is to become a value ranking which will deal with a person's guilt, it must be acted on behaviorally.

The issue of guilt is a great motivator of our behavior. We tend to do things to avoid feeling guilty, and when "mistakes" are made or pointed out to us, we tend to adjust our behavior accordingly. Once you have become conscious of that process, you are able to more intelligently assess the influences which tend to tell you under the table that you have made mistakes and thereby prompt you to adjust your actions. Madison Avenue and the advertising media are masters at using this motivation, and a few examples of their efforts might be enlightening in considering the whole issue of guilt.

"WHAT HAVE YOU DONE TO YOUR COUNTRY LATELY?
Cigarette butts. Gum wrappers. Candy paper. Don't drop them in all the wrong places. Like a sidewalk. Or the highway. Or on somebody's lawn. Or in the gutter.
Every once in a while make a deposit in a waste can at your Shell station. It's a great way to save—the landscape."

This was a Shell Oil advertisement. What it was saying, in fact, was that people should have a priority of values that might be represented as follows:

Other People
Clean Environment
Self

The point is that this value ranking being suggested is one that we should have in relationship to the environment. It is suggesting that people should feel guilty for having no ranking or priorities except self.

Shell, in its advertising, is suggesting a value ranking which places the concern for others and our environment above our concern for ourselves. If we "buy" the ad, we will feel guilty if we have no priority but ourselves. No matter how we finally rank these priorities, we have been influenced by the advertising to reject destructive, contaminating behavior; we have been influenced to make some decisions about future behavior. This has been done because the advertisers have chosen to raise the issue of guilt, and that is a methodology which is often employed.

A very common series of advertisements along this line has been put out by the Cancer and Heart Societies. There is one in particular which shows a man smoking a cigarette who is talking about how he is going to spend time with his wife and children, and what he is going to do when he retires. The implication of the advertisement is that if he smokes, he is, in fact, putting his wife and children after his cigarette smoking. The priorities here might be listed as follows:

Smoking
Wife and Children
Health

The advertisement is suggesting that self and his health should come first, wife and children second, and smoking eliminated altogether. It soon becomes evident that what the priorities are in the advertisement is partly to be determined by the viewer.

Why don't you look at some advertisements and see if you can guess what the priorities are? The priorities that I came up with above are just examples to help clarify what the situation is. Maybe you have slightly different variations. One way or another, the implications are as follows: If you mess up your environment or your health, you are going against values that you have or at least you should have. In this instance, guilt is being used as a value former and as a way to force people to look at themselves.

Other kinds of advertisements use guilt as a sales pitch. It is a subtle imposition of values—for example, the advertisement that says: "Buy a new Chevrolet; you owe it to yourself." The point here is: "Don't feel guilty about your finances. Buy what you really want." The values here are self first and others second. Other kinds of advertisements try to make you buy dog meat for your dog. If you don't buy Brand-X dog meat, you are not really treating your animal well! The use of such advertisements indicates the presence of guilt in so many people that Madison Avenue can capitalize on it.

Dealing with Self-Limitations: Dealing with Guilt

Guilt, says Tournier, is the failure to be oneself and to face one's limitations. Guilt normally arises when we consciously or unconsciously feel that we have not been ourselves—not the perfect "ourselves" but the best "ourselves" that we can be with all of the limitations which are just part of being ourselves. It means that to come to grips with guilt is to come to grips with all those limitations that make me "me." Carl Rogers, in *Freedom To Learn*, describes a number of examples of this coming to grips process.

"The individual in therapy looks back and realizes 'that I enjoyed pulling my sister's hair—and that doesn't make me a bad person.'

"The student failing chemistry realizes, as he gets close to his own experiencing—'I don't value being a doctor even though my parents do; I don't like chemistry; I don't like taking

steps toward being a doctor; and I am not a failure for having these feelings.'

"The adult recognizes that sexual desires and behavior may be ritually satisfying and permanently enriching in their consequences, or shallow and temporary and less than satisfying. He goes by his own experiencing, which does not always coincide with the social norms.

"He considers art from a new value approach. He says, 'This picture moves me deeply, means a great deal to me. It also happens to be an abstraction, but that is not the basis for my valuing it.'

"He recognizes freely that this Communist book or person has attitudes and goals which he shares, as well as ideas and values which he does not share.

"He realizes that at times he experiences cooperation as meaningful and valuable to him, and that at other times he wishes to be alone and act alone" (Freedom To Learn, p. 248).

What Rogers says of the valuing process can be related to our discussion of values and guilt. From Rogers we see two major sources of guilt feelings. The first is that, choosing from a series of alternatives, I failed to make the right choice. As such, I may be living by certain priorities that I think should be in a different order.

Secondly, we have feelings of guilt when we think that what we have done is contrary to social norms, that is to say, that some other person or body of persons will reject me if they know what I am thinking. In the latter example, Rogers points out that human growth and valuing is moving from playing the role of someone for someone else's benefit to being and choosing myself.

I Am Who I Am and I Matter

Choosing myself is an act of reconciliation. It is the process of celebrating myself. It is the movement from "I am of value because others accept me in a particular role" to "I am of intrinsic worth no matter what anyone says." We are back then to the idea of primary values. The degree to which I do not understand that I have self-value is the degree to which I am open to feelings of guilt as I fail to live up to the expectations of other people. Often a person who remains in such immature dependence and then enters into a crisis which demands mature independence must seek counseling in order to grow as a person.

Beyond expectations there is the continued feeling of guilt that I have about any given past event. *Generally speaking, when I am guilty about a particular event, it is because I am still doing that which makes me feel guilty.* What this means is that the priorities that are making me feel guilty, the way in which they are ranked, probably have not been examined and are still priorities that I would repeat blindly if the situation were to repeat itself.

Reconciliation here would be the coming to grips with that guilt, discovering my limitations, and celebrating them by recognizing the limits. Next I would move to change my behavior in a more creative way by reordering actively my priorities. It may

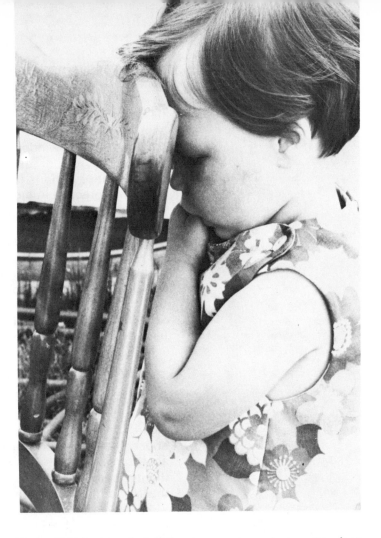

be that I will decide that my behavior does not need changing but only that I need to recognize what I had committed myself to—that is, to change what "I do" as unconscious priority to a value ranking. It is in this sense that we realize that all guilt is not bad. The irritating awareness that I have wrong priorities may be a constructive force in my authentic growth.

CELEBRATING GUILT

You might find this title for the remainder of the chapter puzzling, but it is the best way we have for describing "coming to grips" with our guilt. It means, simply, seeking to find the creative possibility for growth while reflecting upon our feelings of guilt in the past. The rest of this chapter is meant to be simply a montage of a number of elements which seem essential in this process:

1. No one can come to grips with his guilt unless significant people around him continuously affirm his essential worth and give him the courage to face the conflicts in his life.

2. One of the most essential techniques for coming to grips with guilt and limitations results from being able to take

myself and life itself a little less seriously than normal; it means being able to laugh at me; it means making a "festival of life."

3. Finally, every one of us must come to see, experientially, personally, that almost all of our limitations also point to some inherent qualities and talents which we also possess; that our limits are the windows to our richness.

The rest of the chapter will be spent trying to explore each of these notions in greater detail. If we are ever able to put them into practice in our life, we will be able to reflect on our guilt and begin to "celebrate guilt."

Since a great deal of guilt in modern man has to do with his failure to come up to the expectations of others, the idea of *acceptance* as a healing force is necessary in the social development of the human being. What a person should learn in counseling or in the classroom through the educational system is not that his value system or list of priorities is acceptable, but that he as a person is acceptable even though some of his past priorities have been out of balance.

AN ATMOSPHERE OF ACCEPTANCE

Value learning cannot take place as an idea, but as a living relationship. In the classroom we talk of a student learning about positive regard. In therapy people talk about empathy and acceptance. I must find myself in a relationship with a good authority which accepts and understands me as I struggle to find those priorities which are most creative for my development.

It is in the environment of acceptance that a person can truly learn to "be himself." A person must therefore be in the type of environment where he can examine alternatives and the consequences of various priorities. The classroom that dominates, that permits no dialogue, and allows no experimentation is one that ultimately for so many children is rejecting. Why? Because the child has no way of reconciling past mistakes by examining his limitations in an attitude of positive regard.

The teacher, the priest, the counselor, should be a mediator of acceptance of the human person as he struggles with his priorities in order to discover authentic existence. This, of course, cannot happen unless the teacher, educator, or counselor has felt acceptance in his own life. At this point we need to be reminded that not only students but teachers and counselors need as a part of their training the experience of affirmation, acceptance in an environment where they are seeking and experimenting with their own lists of priorities.

FESTIVAL AND GUILT

What we are suggesting then is that guilt confronts us with limitation which is a neuter state of my human reality, and, further, that reconciliation and growth come as I accept this reality of myself and grow. To accept the reality of myself in terms of values means: not only a matter of choice, but a matter of celebrating. It is something that I will act on, will be happy with, and state publicly. It is at this point we get on to the subject of festivity and celebration.

A festival generally is something that we take joy in and that relates to a past event concerned with our human development. We celebrate birthdays. We celebrate Christmas. We celebrate wedding anniversaries. In the Church people celebrate the feast days of saints. They are reminded of famous people who in turn remind us of the possibility of new life. Festivity is a part of "celebration."

Harvey Cox defines the ingredients of festivity as follows. He says that a festive occasion has three ingredients:

1. Conscious excess
2. Celebrated affirmation
3. Juxtaposition

By excess, he relates the word "festive" to revelry. It is a situation where we overdo it on purpose. We "live it up." He notes that in some cultures even conventional morality is relaxed. In this sense, to celebrate becomes a vacation from normal convention and is marked by an attitude of radical change.

By celebrated affirmation, he says that festivity always is a "saying yes to life." It is a sense of joy. It is a happiness.

He speaks of juxtaposition. This, he says, is related to the elements of excess. It is the idea that festivity shows contrast. It is different from everyday life.

Harvey Cox speaks of a medieval festival called the Feast of Fools, which was described as follows:

> "During the medieval era there flourished in parts of Europe a holiday known as the Feast of Fools. On that colorful occasion, usually celebrated about January first, even ordinarily pious priests and serious townsfolk donned bawdy masks, sang outrageous ditties, and generally kept the whole world awake with revelry and satire. Minor clerics painted their faces, strutted about in the robes of their superiors, and mocked the stately rituals of church and court. Sometimes a Lord of Misrule, a Mock King, or a Boy Bishop was elected to preside over the events. In some places the Boy Bishop even celebrated a parody Mass. During the Feast of Fools no custom or convention was immune to ridicule and even the highest personage of the realm could expect to be lampooned" (The Feast of Fools, p. 3).

Whatever we might think about such a feast or whatever we might feel about excess, there is no doubt that such festivals and attitudes toward festivities allowed man to look at his limitations. Undoubtedly, such a festival would be, for many, a freeing event. Why? Because the expectations of others would be dealt with in a moment. Free from the guilt of expectation, a person could laugh at the limitations which were being imposed on him.

Guilt: As It Relates to Society

Our goal is to deal with guilt as it relates to society. The problem of expectation, dealt with hilariously in *The Feast of Fools*, is one side, and a very powerful side, of the coin. The other side is that of choosing self-direction in one's own priorities and looking at the limits of one's own choices in the past. In an attempt to come to grips with the need to celebrate our limitations as good and as a starting point, I offer the following as a means of choosing and celebrating your own values:

1. To delight in my limitations as the reality of who I am. This would mean to go through, occasionally, a value clarification of my priorities, as in the guilt example above, and to see who I am as being a good thing. To look at my priorities and to laugh.

2. To delight in my limitations by not only clarifying my priorities but by choosing a new list of priorities, or rechoosing, from the variation of alternatives available to me.

3. To delight in who I am, my old and my new priorities, by sharing with a significant other person repeatedly in a spirit of

good humor. This is to prize and make public my celebration with persons whom I trust.

4. To delight in my limitations by seeing the comedy in my mistakes through continual re-evaluation on some ordered, repeated basis.

To relate this celebration directly to celebration in festival, we might for a moment fantasize on the possibilities in terms of our own Feast of Fools. In my own family, we make public our mistakes and laugh at them through the concept of a family council. My wife and I and our small children examine each other's errors and priorities each week. I personally find it very difficult at times to laugh at my own mistakes. If we moved this concept to the idea of a larger festival, for example, the area of a party, we might clarify a lot of things.

Celebration: Freedom To Be Yourself

It would be impossible to have a celebration or festival as an extension of business where business contacts are made. In Harvey Cox's terms, this would not offer juxtaposition or excess. I would not dare lower the facade with business associates whom I did not know and trust! *Integral, then, to celebration and festival is the value of "being free to be myself." Celebration, then, confronts me with myself in a freeing environment which reduces the expectations of others upon me in such a way that I can celebrate my limited being and grow authentically.*

Such a festival would need to be one with only people whom I trusted. It would need to be one where I would not only laugh at the politicians and express my opinions, laugh at the Church and express my true opinion, laugh at my friends in a spirit of creativity and express my opinion, but also be laughed at and laugh at myself.

There are many ways in which such a party can be conducted. Here are a couple of examples. One that has been popular all through the ages is the fancy dress ball. Dress up as the kind of person that you would like to be, that your priorities extended and developed. Be and dress up like the person you would like to be, but now discover you should not be. Dress up as another person, quite different, who has the kinds of elements and spirit of adventure that you would like to have.

We also have been to parties where people were able to paint and draw and even use charades and role plays as an expression of their own comedy of errors or their own delights in life and so on. They were able to express parts of themselves that others never knew of. They were able to be themselves in a new way.

It would also be possible to allow people to rearrange rooms in their houses and even decorate them in a way which expresses their own views and attitudes toward life. These "festivals" should not be group education sessions! God forbid! Just the doing and the being allows people to experience freeing environments. We live in a society where limitation is often seen as bad rather than as a celebration of human life.

LIMITATION AND RICHNESS

An exercise that is helpful in this regard which you may do with a friend, in your family, or in a small group is to look at the question of Talents and Limitations. The idea is to make up a sheet like the following diagram.

TALENTS	LIMITATIONS

The next point is to list for yourself, if possible with another person, what you think your talents are in the area of human relationships. You might choose human relationships at work or in your family. You might choose them in your class as a student. List down the one side what you think your talents are and on the other side what your limitations are. In the following diagram, we have an example.

TALENTS	LIMITATIONS
I am always on time at school.	I am untidy in the morning.
I relate well to the children individually.	I am bored with school board meetings.
I am a good cook.	I get depressed occasionally.
I am very concerned and care deeply for my family.	I fail to get dinner on time occasionally.
I support my husband so that he can go to graduate school.	

The above list was a list made by a woman who was teaching in grammar school while at the same time supporting her husband's graduate training. The next problem, given the theory that limitations are not negative, but rather statements of where I am in life, is to try now to place each limitation that you have into positive terminology, that is, to give a positive side to the limitations stated. The school teacher's above limitations were put into a positive framework as follows:

LIMITATIONS	POSITIVE SIDE OF LIMITATION
I am untidy in the morning.	I wait up late at night for my husband.
I am bored at school board meetings.	I like more intimate relationships.
I get depressed occasionally.	I am very conscientious.
I fail to get dinner on time occasionally.	I work very hard.

As we look at the list of positive statements from the teacher's notations, we see immediately that they are very personal and particular to her situation, that is, putting limitations in a positive statement particular to her. Let's take the examples above.

The first one was: "I am untidy in the morning." Her positive statement was: "I wait up late at night for my husband." The point was that this, like most of these situations, is a question of coming to grips with one's limitations. When the teacher was asked why she was untidy in the morning, she replied, "I am tired because I go to bed late at night." When she was asked why she went to bed late, she replied, "I wait up for my husband." The latter, then, was a positive thing that she did. The question is coming to grips with my limitations. Waiting up late meant being untidy in the morning.

The next limitation was that she was bored at school board meetings. When she was asked why, she replied that they were so impersonal. Her positive statement of her limitation was that she liked more personal relationships. She gets depressed occasionally because she works very hard and just gets tired. That she is very conscientious is the positive aspect of her depression. Finally, she fails to get dinner on time occasionally. These statements of limitation, then, have a very positive side. See now if you can put your limitations into positive statements.

The original list had talents and limitations. My limitation is a statement of where I am, something that I should celebrate.

To celebrate it does not mean to ignore its negative aspects. It means to realize that I can only do so much from where I stand. It means that a positive stand always has its limits.

Because this teacher is a person who emphasizes intimate rather than impersonal relationships, she tends to get bored at meetings. But life has to go on and we do need people who can function well at meetings. Perhaps other people can do better than she does at meetings. She was limited in this way. Was this bad? No! It was simply a statement of where she was.

A good way to finish the exercise is to review all the positive limitations and their negative expression and think about them. Then ask the question, "If I were to extend my talents and really come to grips with and work with my limitations, what is the best kind of person I could become in the next year?" A dreamy question, perhaps. Have your partner dream for you and see if your perception of yourself and your perception of the possibilities of another are the same.

EXTENSIONS

The valuing process then asks us to look at the past as a gentle confrontation with the reality of who we are. By learning from the past, whether it be history, or our own personal history in the form of a diary, or in clarifying our values through guilt, we come to know who we are and, as such, are able to celebrate this reality. Such a celebration need not be confined in the realm of the self, nor need it be confined to the reality of our friends or those we trust. Its truest reality would be in its use as a celebrated confrontation with society itself. Let us take one or two examples of this.

The first example is from a business executive in the area of management development. *Up the Organization or How To Stop the Corporation from Stifling People and Strangling Profits* by Robert Townsend has a title which is fascinating. The organization, the title suggests, should not stifle people and, at the same time, should be aware of its profits. In terms of big business, this would be: Look at the limitations of the business, but don't trap and impose values on people! Free them. Look at the following quotation:

> *"G. Geography, respect for*
> *"If your business is in Cleveland, start to acquire an operation in Santa Barbara at your peril. Absentee management is fatal.*
> *"And the disaster potential is equal to the square of the distance—measured in hours—between your home base and the new plant. No matter how determined you are to visit it frequently, you'll discover that your capacity to find last-minute reasons not to go is unlimited"* (Up the Organization).

His book is full of challenges such as this. Repeatedly he is stating, "For heaven's sake, know your limits, and consider your priorities before you make a move." Consider priorities such as home as well as where you work if you are to be a happy executive. Here is another example that he writes on firing people:

"Firing people is unpleasant, but it really has to be done occasionally. It's a neglected art in most organizations. If a guy isn't producing after a year (two at most), admit that you were wrong about him. Keeping him is unfair to other people who must make up for his failure and untangle his mess. And it's unfair to him. He might do well in another company of industry."

Again he is saying, for the sake of others in business: Do not fool yourself. Know the limits of business and know your own personal limits. He is also pointing to the reality that to fire somebody, to confront him with his limitations, might be a very positive contribution to his further development. It might force him to think, to get a better job, to find his real place. There is a real element in this book of seeing limits and celebration.

Are We More Concerned with Guilt than with Happiness?

It is interesting that there is more literature on guilt and the presence of sin and corruption in our society than on the idea of celebration of our limits and positive growth. If you want to read the negative side of alienation and deprivation, there is much more material available. Erik Fromm writes the following on this matter:

"What could be the cause of so much guilt feeling? It seems that there are two main sources which, though entirely different in themselves, lead to the same results. The one source is the same as that from which the feelings of inferiority spring. Not to be like the rest, not to be totally adjusted, makes one feel guilty toward the commands of the great It. The other source of guilt feelings is man's own conscience: his sense, his gifts or talents, his ability to love, to think, to laugh, to cry, to wonder and to create. He senses that his life is the one chance he is given, and if he loses this chance, he has lost everything. He lives in a world with more conflict and ease than his ancestors ever knew—yet he senses that, chasing after more comfort, his life runs through his fingers like sand. He cannot help feeling guilty for the waste, for the lost chance. This feeling of guilt is much less conscious than the first one, but one reinforces the other, the one often serving as a rationalization for the other. Thus, alienated man often feels guilty for being himself and for not being himself, for being alive and for being an automaton, for being a person and for being a thing" (The Sane Society, p. 182).

Why Does Man Feel So Guilty?

This paragraph certainly introduces us to the whole social area of the relationship of guilt—the relationship of man to himself and to creation itself as he misuses it, wastes it, and feels guilty for his existence in and among it. The question has to be raised, "What traps man that he feels so guilty? What is it that places him in an environment that tells him he is free, yet teaches him to live a way of life which is far from being authentic and more like a prison, a prison of the mind?"

For the answers to this, we shall have to move from guilt

to the question of imagination and the problem of anxiety. We will have to deal not only with the problem of failure to make the right choices as guilt, but with the problem of inability to choose because of a fear of the future. This brings us into a new dimension, a dimension of future as we confront it creatively. This does not mean to say that we have said all we can about limitation and guilt, but rather that we have to move into the area of time as future in order to get a more total perspective that can help us better understand the wider dimensions of the valuing process.

It is important to see that we are trapped in this prison of the mind not only because of the *past* experiences *(guilt)*, but because of our fear of the *future (anxiety)*. We will be exploring that topic of the future and anxiety in the next chapter so that we will be better able to understand the wide dimensions of the valuing process.

As we walk the bridge from the past to the future, it might be well to think of the words of Ivan Illich in *Celebration of Awareness:*

"We call you to join man's race to maturity, to work with us in inventing the future. We believe that a human adventure is just beginning; that mankind has so far been restricted in developing its innovative and creative powers because it was overwhelmed by toil. Now we are free to be as human as we will.

SPACE	TIME: PAST	TIME: PRE
	Memory	Ac
World | Others	History—Society | History—Self and Family	
Self | Others	Guilt | Value Ranking	
Self | World | Cosmic	Celebration | Reconciliation as Confronting Limitation	

"The celebration of man's humanity through joining together in the healing expression of one's relationship with others, and one's growing acceptance of one's own nature and needs, will clearly create major confrontation with existing values and systems. The expanding dignity of each man and each human relationship must necessarily challenge existing systems.

"The call is to live the future. Let us join together joyfully to celebrate our awareness that we can make our life today shape tomorrow's future" (Celebration of Awareness, p. 18).

6.
Freedom and The Excedrin Headache: A Look At The Future

> "Fantasy, of course, starts out with an advantage: arresting strangeness. But that advantage has been turned against it, and has contributed to its disrepute. Many people dislike being 'arrested.' They dislike any meddling with the primary world, or such small glimpses of it as are familiar to them. They, therefore, stupidly and even maliciously confound fantasy with dreaming, in which there is no art; and with mental disorders, in which there is not even control; with delusion and hallucination."
>
> J. R. R. Tolkein, The Tolkein Reader

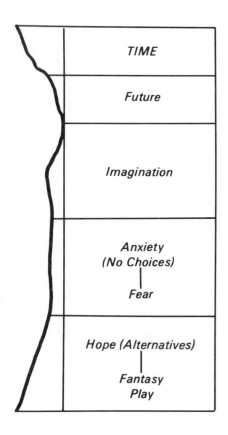

| TIME |
| Future |
| Imagination |
| Anxiety
(No Choices)
\|
Fear |
| Hope (Alternatives)
\|
Fantasy
Play |

INTRODUCTION

This chapter is going to deal with the future. That is to say, we are going to see the future as a value indicator. In the last chapter, we looked at the idea of the past as being memory, pointing to guilt and celebration. In this chapter, we are going to look at the future as imagination, pointing to anxiety and fantasy. Fantasy here is understood as creative use of the imagination.

Just as the past resides in the human personality as memory, so does future reside in us as our imagination. (Please see the diagram.) As we imagine any event, so it is that we look, in fact, to the future. That future, of course, simply is not as concrete as the past. For no matter how active our imagination is, no matter how much we guess what will happen or fantasize about some future event such as a holiday, we can never be sure that it will happen as our imagination dictates. We may pre-imagine it to a very large extent, but we may be totally wrong.

I may be worried about being fired from my present job. The act of worrying is in the imagination and, as such, deals with the future. I may be thinking about the baby that my wife is going to have. I may be looking forward to getting married. I may be having all sorts of fantasies about the marriage, about my success in the future as I work with my wife toward a new life. I may be thinking about what I can accomplish at school. I may be worrying about my examinations. I may be thinking about the holiday I am going to take next year. All these fantasies, images, thoughts, stories, and so on are my imaginations about the future and are also indicators of my values.

If one thinks about the dreams that we have had as a symbolic portrayal of my imagination, most of us will recognize that, generally speaking, there are pleasant dreams and unpleasant dreams. The latter we usually refer to as nightmares. That is to say, in our imagination reside symbols, images, some of which we like and some of which are frightening to us. Using this as an example, we might say that there reside in the imagination the presence of negative images which we call anxiety and fear, and positive images which become pleasant and creative experiences for us.

Since our imagination directly affects our behavior, its development is essential to understanding and developing human values. This chapter is designed to help us look at anxiety and see our own fears and worries. This chapter is also designed to help us look at the creative side of our imagination and see how it might be developed. Finally, this chapter is going to look at these elements as they affect human relationships and are present in society as a whole.

IMAGINATION, THE FUTURE, AND CONTROL

The future holds my hope in that it contains all that I will do that will be creative and successful. Also, the future holds all those things that are unpleasant that might happen to me. It holds the results of any choices and any acts that I might make. As such, it holds the perennial error of man himself, namely, to think that he can control the future.

Why would man want to control the future? Because in so doing, he guarantees his own security. Theologically, we say that man wants to be God. That is, man would like to control the future and so guarantee himself security. We see this in the whole system of life insurance and health insurance. I am not suggesting that life insurance and health insurance are bad. No, not at all. At the same·time, I am sure that most of us know people who worry excessively about insurance. Why is it an error to think we can control the future? Simply because man is limited, and, as such, cannot contain all the alternatives that are possible to him.

When man tries to control the future, he must, of necessity, become anxious. Manipulating the future represents a natural but futile attempt to gain absolute security. Such security can only be found in relationships that are present and meaningful, and not simply in the future. Therefore, while it is most important to activate the imagination, to dream about the future constructively and creatively, it must also be stressed that the dreaming should be realistic. Realistic dreaming means to be able to dream from where I am as a limited human being.

An excellent example of unrealistic dreaming was illustrated to me a number of years ago when I asked a group of people to cut pictures out of a magazine which would symbolize their future as a dream for themselves. One lady saw herself as being a great athlete. The lady in question was a terminal diabetic. As such, she had dreamed unrealistically, and she had used the dream to avoid facing her unfortunate and present limitations.

Tomorrow I Will Not Feel Anxious

Therefore, when we speak about dreaming and using the imagination in this chapter, our intention is to reflect on realistic dreaming, that is to say, dreaming of my potential starting with my limitations. If my limitations are not taken into consideration from the very beginning, my imagination becomes distorted and a source of anxiety.

The major source of anxiety in man is in his attempt to try to control the future. In recent years major examples of this have been over the many so-called "conservative" and "liberal" conflicts in our society. This is an over-simplification, but will serve to illustrate the point. Often the conservative, who is extreme in stance, will try to insist that all truths are eternal, that things should remain as they have always remained, placing a strong emphasis on the past as this particular person experienced it. This is evident in churches, in school systems, and, of course, in many businesses. I am talking here of the person who tends to do this in extreme. Such a person becomes very defensive and anxious when people start talking about changing the system. Why? Because unconsciously this person is trying to control the future. The person is trying to dictate the future by insisting that it be like the past has always been. Therefore, what appears to be a movement toward the past really is an attempt to control the future.

A similar trend is seen in the extreme—and note that I say the extreme—liberal. This person can get just as defensive as the "conservative" when people suggest that maybe something good is to be seen in the past and that we should not be so fast to change everything. Such a person will want to change the complete system now. He really is trying to impose his view of what the world should be like in the future. As a result, he is a very anxious person.

Whatever point of view a person may have when he tries to control the future, anxiety will always be present. The most common way in which this imposition appears is when people try to manipulate other people—when teachers try to manipulate children by not allowing them to express themselves in the classroom, when parents try to manipulate their teenagers by not giving them good sex education or allowing them to speak freely about their difficulties, but rather try to dictate to them what their behavior should be.

When these various forms of control appear, they are often the unconscious imposition of an adult's feeling of insecurity upon the child or student. That is to say, they are trying to dictate the future.

Control of the future in a person's behavior then is an attempt to gain security. The result always is an increase in a person's anxiety. What needs to be pointed out at this stage of our development is that anxiety is a natural phenomenon.

The reality is that the future increasingly presents us with a growing number of alternatives. As a child grows up, he enters realms of his existence which offer more and more alternatives from which he must choose. When he becomes a teenager, he is confronted with college, with marriage, with the draft, and so on. As he tries to tie up all the ends so that he can guarantee his future, he becomes more and more anxious. Why? Because the task is impossible.

This is a natural phenomenon, since we are all continually presented with growing numbers of alternatives. The anxiety is the result of the fact that our limitations usually cause us to make a lot of wrong choices as well as right choices.

How Will I Confront Anxiety?

The question, then, is not how to eradicate anxiety, but rather *how to confront and live with our anxiety*. The only guarantee for choosing better choices is in the kind of value system that we have. That value system will depend on how we tend to make choices. If I value certain priorities, then my life orientation will move in a given way.

If my value system is the same as that of my parents, then it will prove adequate if my parents' value system is still relevant to the stage and development of the culture in which I live. We will say more about this later. The point is that there are no guarantees, but there is a methodology.

The methodology is to teach children and adults how to choose alternatives creatively. Secondly, we need to teach people that when we do choose the wrong alternatives, it is not the end of the world, for there are more alternatives from which we can choose. That is to say, we need to learn how to choose alternatives, and we need to learn how to live with anxiety, with our limitations.

Anxiety and Fear

Finally, before we go on to the next section, we need simply to clear up the difference between anxiety and fear. Fear, like anxiety, resides in the future. Anxiety is the apprehension that something bad is going to happen to me. It is an apprehension of something, and, as such, I do not know what it is. I do not know why I feel this way. Fear, on the other hand, is not an apprehension, but rather an awareness of exactly what might happen to me.

We might illustrate it something like this. Imagine being locked in a dark room and knowing that there is some creature in the room that is dangerous. The room is dark; I cannot see the creature. I can only hear it clawing at the wall! I become very anxious. Why? Because I do not know what is in the room and what is going to happen to me. Fear, on the other hand, would be like turning on the lights and seeing that there was a lion in the room and knowing exactly what might happen to me. Fear and anxiety, then, are different, although they are very close in nature. Let us now move on and look at the question of anxiety a little closer.

WORRIED ABOUT YOUR VALUES?

Is the plumber late and the basement filling up? You do not have a headache, just simple nervous tension. Take a Compoz!

It is readily evident that a considerable portion of radio and television advertising is directed at soothing nervous tension and dissipating anxieties. Nor is this trend confined to the medical market.

Mother-in-law might approve of me more if I change to her brand of detergent. Or should I use a biodegradable detergent and keep in line with the anti-pollutionists?

Worried about your masculinity? Try Right Guard! Worried about your femininity? Buy FDS! All your anxieties will be put to rest.

What sense can we make of this? First of all, the companies involved would not be spending millions of dollars on this kind of advertising if it did not appeal to the self-interest of the viewer.

What precisely is the appeal? It is a fact that people are hurting and naturally do want relief from their pain—the pain of nervous tension, upset stomachs, headaches, etc. Nor is it even a matter of one brand of aspirin claiming that aspirin is good for headaches and everything else. Rather, St. Joseph's is in competition with Bayer's, Excedrin, and half a dozen others, each trying to convince us that its product is best. Thus, it has got to the point that the question is not whether we need tension-removing drugs, but which one shall we use? In other words, we have become comfortable with the drugs around; they are a natural part of our tense environment.

Psychiatrists and counselors for some time have accepted the idea of a direct relationship of tension, worry, and anxiety to physical symptoms such as ulcers, headaches, and worse. We are all aware of sweating hands and rapidly beating hearts when frightened. Most of us have blushed at some embarrassments. These are all physical manifestations of some moment of anxiety.

The word "anxiety" as used in this book describes the present underlying feeling, variously called worry, tension and nervousness. It can be described and is manifested by physical symptoms. What is clear is that there is an inverse relationship between a person's ability to tolerate anxiety and the appearance of physical symptoms.

I'm Anxious;
You're Anxious

The intense competition between anxiety-reducing drugs illustrates the increase in physical symptoms related to nervous disorders.

One might say that with the knowledge explosion and the general accelerated pace of life all over the world, we can expect people to be under more pressure and, as a result, experience more anxiety. The problem is that if there is an inverse relationship between physical symptoms and a person's ability to deal with anxiety, increased drug usage indicates that there are more and more people who cannot handle their anxiety. We are even at the point where some younger people advocate the use of drugs, such as hallucinogens, as a way of life.

We might ask: What is so wrong with anxiety anyway? Don't we all feel miserable at times?

The point I would like to make is that anxiety is not just a feeling, but a consequence of *who we are,* and, as such, relates to our whole *system of values.* For example, it inhibits our relationships with others.

In a popular Anacin commercial, we see a husband coming home with a "terrible headache" due to a tense day at the office. His wife has just finished a painting in art class and can't wait for her husband to see and admire it. He can't possibly look at it; after all, he is tense and has a headache. Anacin comes to the rescue and enables him now to be able to relate to his wife and her work of art.

If we are not fooled by the symptom, as the wife was, we see that he was not able to deal with his worries and tension sufficiently to be able to appreciate her at a time when she wanted to share her world with him.

The question, then, is not one of removing all the pain of anxiety, but rather of dealing with it in such a way that we can live creative and uninhibited lives. Anxiety is common to all, and is certainly not reserved for the emotionally ill. However, the more anxious I am, the more inhibited I will be, until I can no longer function socially. When this happens, the person is experiencing "exaggerated" anxiety.

We all know what this is. Think of the mother crying hysterically after her child was almost run down by a car. Some experience this type of anxiety when they have to face large bills. An emotionally ill person is one who experiences this exaggerated anxiety to such an extent that he cannot function normally in society, such as the man who drinks so much as to be unable to keep a job and support his family.

Anxiety traps us, inhibiting us both physically and socially. By dealing with it, we can become free to relate to the world of family, friends, and job more creatively. But what we must deal with are our own particular worries and tensions. We must then be able to look into ourselves, discover our own prison, so that we can become free.

The point is that we each have the key to *freedom* in our own creative potential. But before we can free ourselves from the tensions of our environment, we first have to examine our own anxiety, our own particular worries and tensions.

Things To Worry About
Take the time to write down what you worry about, e.g.: parents, job, family, home, old age, sickness, keeping up with the Joneses, car accident, being robbed, etc. Add your own unique worries to this list. Next take your list and rank them according to what you worry about 1. very often; 2. often; and, 3. occasionally.

Another way to discover your worries is by recalling what you dream about while asleep or what you daydream about while awake. For example, you may daydream about being a hero, meaning that you are worried about being successful or perhaps worried about being popular. Try to think about and list your night dreams and daydreams of the last month.

THE NATURE OF ANXIETY

It is important to realize and to accept anxiety as a part of our natural condition. It arises out of the natural circumstances in which man finds himself. We all have anxieties and worries, and this is a natural consequence of what it means to be human. The difference between mature people who are growing and immature people who are stifled is often in how each confronts and deals with his anxieties. Let us look first at some of the elements in our natural condition. They are as follows:

First: *Man is limited.* How are we limited? Well, we are vulnerable to illness, for example. We have only a limited life-span. As we grow older, our own particular abilities diminish. Each of us is talented in a special way; we are not all practical, not all artists, not all engineers. That is to say, we all have our own talents, and so also our own limitations. (Take a minute to think about some of your own limitations.)

Second: *We are all interdependent.* This is very closely allied to the idea of being limited, and results from the fact that

the human being is at one and the same time dependent upon others and alone within himself.

On the one hand, I recognize that I am alone and separate from others. No matter how much I am loved, supported, even physically held, there is the constant reality of being separate from others. I am alone.

At the same time that I am alone, however, I am also very dependent on others. Man is a social being. The newborn baby cannot survive without the mother, or at least a hospital nurse.

This dependency extends itself necessarily to the opposite sex. Everyone knows of the anxieties caused by extended living with persons of the same sex only, such as military life, incarceration, the celibate life, even research teams in the middle of the desert. Social limitations soon become evident in these circumstances.

Interdependence then means being alone, but at the same time being dependent upon others of both sexes to some degree. I am not suggesting that the single life is not a valid or healthy life-style, but only that socialization with the opposite sex is a natural and necessary part of the growth process.

Third: *We all have both the potential to act and the necessity of making choices.* I am pointing here to an underlying creative force which is basically good (i.e., not destructive) in nature, which needs to go out to love and value others. The underlying assumption here is that man is created good and has the ability to act.

The fact of choice presumes this potential and faces us with the question of how I should behave now in the world in which I live. My behavior can be defined as the sum of the choices I make and act on.

Now reflect on the anxieties arising from this natural condition.

1. The anxiety that arises from *being limited* ultimately is the fear of death and loss of control. (How did you score on your test in regard to these?) Facing any human limitation is always in some sense facing death, as man's final limitation. Hence, fears about loss of control, getting older, being ill, or failure are all facets of the same anxiety.

2. The anxiety that arises from being *interdependent* is the fear of being alone. Loneliness is a horror to many people. I often find that a person is unable to recognize "being alone" in these terms, but will understand fears of retirement, or the children growing up and leaving home, or the feelings of apprehension about moving to a new neighborhood or job. All these events are moving from the familiar to the new and unknown. It is loneliness.

This "being alone" is closely allied to being limited. When I am alone, I am alone with my limitations, with my fears of failure and rejection. When I retire, will I be a useless old man? When I move, will my friends forget me? Maybe I will fail at my new job!

What about the poor immigrant coming to our country, with all the limitations of language and economics? What about the divorcee getting married for the second time with all her fears of failure? In my own experience, the anxiety of a dying man is more often over the separation from loved ones, over being alone, than it is over the fear of physical death.

3. The anxiety that arises from my potential to act and the fact of choice is the fear of condemnation, failure, and even possibly guilt through the remembrance of a past bad choice. I want to act and to be creative, but what if I do not make the right choice? Once I know that I have creative potential, I am stuck with the responsibility of using it properly.

"Did I study hard enough for that exam?" "Am I really a conscientious objector?" "Do I really think I should break the engagement, or am I afraid of the responsibility?" Every question of this type brings with it the need to choose and its natural consequence—anxiety. If I now choose, I can succeed or fail. If I fail consistently, then life might well become meaningless and absurd. Many people will not be aware of these extremes, but many others are.

Fear of the future, of possible failure, and the feelings of meaninglessness, hopelessness, or even boredom are signs of one's inability to make choices. This inability can well be an inner problem of overwhelming anxiety.

Sometimes this inability is imposed from without, but it still results in the same feelings. For instance, the dictatorial parent who allows no one else in the family to take part in the decision-making process may find that his family finds life meaningless, no matter what their degree of material security may be. Thousands who live in ghetto conditions with no choice about their living conditions are hardly likely to be hopeful. These are types of imposed anxiety, and it is natural to find them in such circumstances.

EXAGGERATED ANXIETY

What needs to be pointed out is that the fears about choosing, being limited, being interdependent, are of themselves natural anxieties, and as such need to be faced as a part of our human condition. But when we ignore them, fail to face them or recognize them, deny we have them, then we deny a part of our humanity and alienate ourselves from others. When we do this, what had been a natural anxiety becomes exaggerated and can cause severe problems. We will illustrate this with two examples.

Example I: Joe and Helen had been married seven years, with two small children. When they came to me for counseling, they were on the brink of a "trial separation."

Joe had come from a success-oriented family, and had tried to follow in his father's footsteps in engineering. When he was unable to master the necessary mathematics, he went into a general liberal arts course, and ended up teaching at a high school where he liked neither the principal nor his assigned courses.

Life at home was not very pleasant. Helen complained that Joe kept the family tense by spending most of his time preparing his classes and not allowing much of the banter of an ordinary family. He was impatient with the children and would not listen to suggestions from the family. Soon Helen came to think of life as meaningless and useless, and at this point they finally agreed to seek counseling.

Several things became evident after a few weeks. First, Joe had accepted from his family not only that success is good, but that failure—any particular failure—was bad. He began to make the mistake of identifying a given failure with "I am a failure." With the remembrance of his college "failure" on his mind, Joe became a perfectionist by rigidly controlling his total environment.

This included not only his family, but also his students, who were not allowed to voice their opinions and soon found Joe's classes boring. Joe was becoming a classic case of one who is anxious because he could not accept his own limitations, and once he saw this, it was possible to do some effective counseling.

When we began to evaluate Joe and Helen, we came up with several key points that had prevented them from solving their problems. Note that our emphasis is not on cause, but on moving ahead to solve the problem:

1. Joe felt that his fear of failing was really his inability to accept the fact that he was a limited human being. To be human means to be limited, and therefore the injunction to be perfect really means to be the best human I can, with all the mistakes and limitations I have to live with.

Church was a problem for Joe because it kept talking about sin and death. That is, it kept talking about human limitations, and, as Joe put it, "It kept imposing a feeling of guilt on me." Then Joe transferred this insight to his children and students by reminding himself that we learn by our mistakes, not by doing things right! Joe could finally begin to laugh about his mistakes instead of trying to tell everyone that he had made no error in the first place.

2. The consequence of Joe's trying to avoid failure was his controlling nature. By staying away from home he could keep from doing anything wrong there. By controlling his wife and children through shouting at them, he could keep them from contradicting or criticizing anything he did or said. By not allowing his students to question his material or discuss openly, he could keep them from saying anything he was unable to handle.

By acting this way, Joe felt that his imperfection wouldn't be noticed. Of course what was really happening was that he was alienating people by controlling them. He had made them feel like puppets. Now he began to avoid the anxiety of pride, of being perfect, by stating whenever he could, "I don't know the answer. Why don't we look for it together?"

3. Another consequence of his previous behavior was loneliness. As a result, Joe's anxiety increased as did his need to control. Naturally, he was not able to trust his school principal enough to ask him for a change of class. Thus he ended up feeling trapped by his own anxiety, unable to make any new choices.

He became ruled by this vague threat of failure, which was largely his inability to accept his own limitations. His inability to relax, to take leisure seriously, was caused by his need not to be unprepared for school. He had to appear perfect.

One day Joe and Helen walked into the office with big smiles. It seems that Helen had been talking with the mother of one of Joe's students, who told her how much he enjoyed himself in Joe's class, now that he felt free to express himself. He had said, "Now I feel that I am trusted with my ideas, even when they may be wrong." The same situation was also evident at home, where goofs were something to be laughed at and talked through.

The example of Joe points out that the fears about choosing, being limited, being alone, are natural anxieties, and as such need to be faced as a part of our human condition.

But when we ignore them, fail to face them, say we do not have them, then we deny a part of our humanity and alienate ourselves from others. When we do this, our natural anxieties become exaggerated.

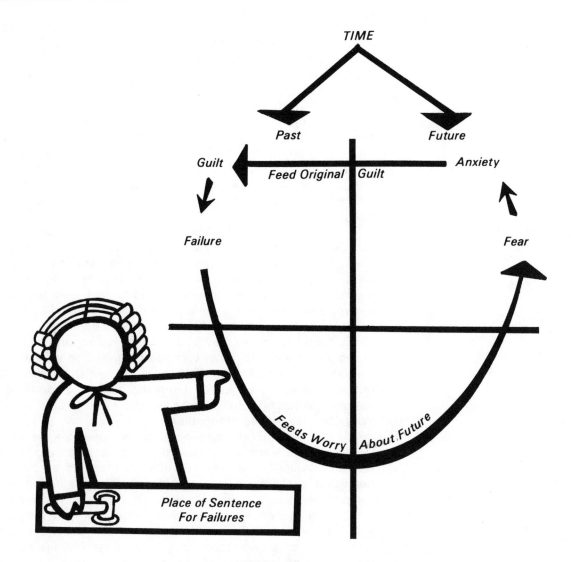

Exaggerated anxiety is one that overwhelms us, and dominates or even possesses us. Natural anxiety is creative in that it pricks us to make decisions and choices. Exaggerated anxiety, on the other hand, freezes us, makes us extremely up-tight, and renders creative decision impossible.

Example II: Dorothy was a social worker who came to me with the complaint that every time she had her weekly conference with her supervisor, she had feelings of physical sickness, and as a result often had to leave the conference.

At first she felt that she was run down and needed to get away. However, she found that while on vacation she couldn't rest and was becoming increasingly anxious. The crisis came

when she herself was made a supervisor over a staff of six case-workers. She became very angry and physically ill, to the extent that she was unable to continue her work. We could say that her anxiety overwhelmed her, that she was literally unable to act.

Like Joe in the previous example, Dorothy had confused being perfect with not making mistakes. Not making mistakes meant doing what social workers are supposed to do. For her this meant: "Keep your troubles to yourself; you are a woman for others." It meant to wear serious clothes as a sign of dedication, and never to laugh, since it is considered frivolous. Dorothy was playing a role of what she felt "social worker" meant, but her humanity within was rebelling.

As she faced the future, Dorothy felt lonelier. She wanted someone to listen to her troubles. When she was made supervisor, she saw her inner hopes disappear as she felt even more the pressure to "be for others" and not to be herself. She was not being herself; she was playing the role.

Suddenly her need to be herself and her loneliness became an increasing threat. Why a threat? Because for Dorothy, to admit that she needed help, to admit that she wanted more freedom, in her mind would not be acceptable to her social agency and her friends.

In other words, Dorothy was living a role that she felt others expected her to play, and she feared the ultimate rejection of all her friends if she admitted her limitations and loneliness. She felt she could not choose, but dared not admit it, because she felt that this would deny her role as a social worker as she thought her agency, staff, and clients viewed it.

She had, of course, confused dedication to a role with dependence on her agency. She was not herself; she was becoming her agency.

Dedication is openness to another. It is being oneself such that the appropriate creative choices open to one become evident. Unfortunately, too often in business, professional life, and schools, as well as in religious life, obedience and dedication are confused with neurotic dependence.

In Dorothy's case, the fear of rejection or anxiety about interdependence or loneliness—even to the extent of physical disability—dominated her and rendered her choiceless. Again we see the exaggerated form of a natural anxiety. Denial of her real self brought about feelings of guilt, and her fear of making the wrong choice also became exaggerated. Thus she was dominated by the fear of choosing, and life became absurd and meaningless to her.

It should be noted also that an important result of Dorothy's dependence on her role was that it provided her an excuse for avoiding any intimacy with others. Thus it trapped her, giving her both the excuse and the resulting loneliness.

This example is common in groups of any kind. So often a young person is afraid to cut his hair, even when he wants to, because he feels that his peer group will reject him. So often a young person will smoke pot or drop acid because his friends do; he plays a role to suit them.

This is a carry-over of the keeping-up-with-the-Joneses routine: Let's not admit who we are. The labels "preacher's kid," "nigger," "Polack," "divorcee," etc., are roles we are forced into and perpetuate in turn. At this point we give in to the pressure and perpetuate the roles, as did Joe and Dorothy. Then we are dealing with exaggerated anxiety.

ANXIETY, GUILT, BOREDOM

Man's situation is such that he is aware of an infinite number of possibilities. Man is free in that he has a choice in any given situation, even though within certain limitations set by himself, his environment, and his very nature. It is the confrontation with these possibilities that causes him anxiety.

In counseling, when anxiety is located in a particular fear, the job is half done. The fact is that when I know what it is I fear, I stand a chance at least of doing something about it. When the fear is unknown in the form of anxiety, I can only imagine what might happen, and tremble in anticipation.

Dorothy was paralyzed by her anxiety, which was indeed exaggerated, but when she was able to locate her fear ("I fear my agency will reject me"), she was able to do something about it. Anxiety then is an apprehension of some *unknown* future disaster. It is also a feeling in the present of being trapped or smothered.

Thomas C. Oden in *The Structures of Awareness* defines anxiety as my response to some future possibility felt as a threat to some value regarded as necessary to my existence.

The more creative a person is, the larger is the span of possibilities of disaster as well as of success. Exaggerated anxiety comes when the gap between what a person sees as possible and what in reality is possible cannot be brought together.

Anxiety is seen as a future negative possibility, but the feeling of being anxious is in the present. I feel anxious now. What is it that I am doing now that causes me to be so anxious? It is surely the use of my imagination (conscious and unconscious). Anxiety then is the imagined possibility of disaster which threatens my existence. The more exaggerated it is, the more do I feel my existence being threatened.

As anxiety is concerned with the future, guilt is similarly concerned with the past (see diagram).

Guilt involves remembering a past event in which I acted irresponsibly. That is, guilt involves my awareness of having done something contrary to my own value system. The remembrance of this becomes a constant threat to the vulnerability of my value system. It is here that guilt and anxiety interlock.

If guilt is a reminder of my vulnerability or limitedness, an increased amount of guilt undermines my confidence and my ability to act.

Dorothy felt continually guilty that she felt unloved. This undermined her own image of herself and increased her fear of failure, which, as we noted earlier, rendered her unable to function in her work as well as socially.

I feel that it is this last sentence that gives us a key to understanding anxiety and how we might avoid its exaggerated form. Although anxiety is defined as anticipation of the future disaster, it is an experience felt in the present. We might describe it as a feeling of being trapped. However, we can also ask what it does to us.

We have seen above that natural anxiety pushes us into making creative choices. Exaggerated anxiety, on the other hand, renders us powerless. It takes the creative visions and possible alternatives away, and leaves only one alternative: disaster. In other

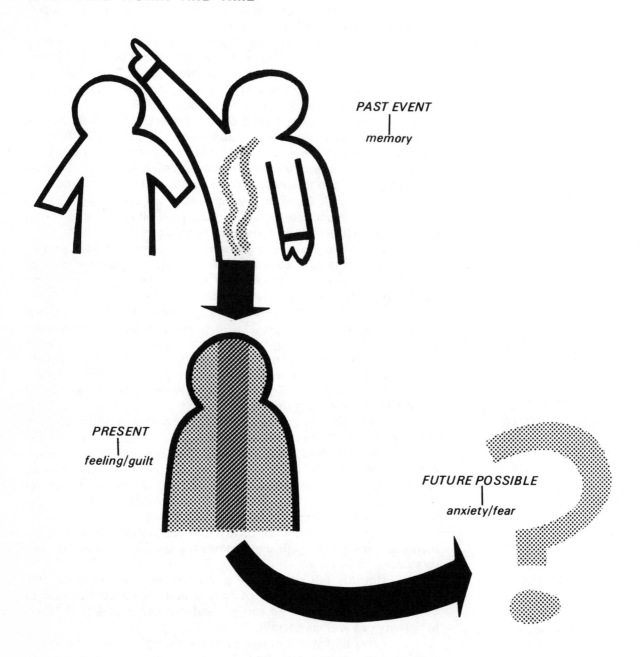

PAST EVENT
memory

PRESENT
feeling/guilt

FUTURE POSSIBLE
anxiety/fear

words, the more exaggerated the anxiety, the less able we are to choose.

We can define anxiety, then, as my response, through my imagination, to some future possibility seen as a threat to some value regarded as necessary. The feeling in the present can be either that of the pressure of making a creative decision (natural anxiety), or of being trapped, of seeing no alternatives (exaggerated anxiety).

192

If I am overwhelmed by anxiety, I am unable to make any decisions, as was Dorothy. The less I am able to decide, the less I am being creative.

An extreme fear of this results in a feeling of meaninglessness and *boredom.* One definition of boredom is the inability to fulfill those hopes and aspirations which I value as necessary to my existence. If I am unable to choose, if I feel consistently trapped, boredom begins to set in. It happens whenever I feel myself controlled or live too much in the future (anxiety) or in the past (guilt).

ANXIETY, EXPECTATION, AND CULTURAL INTERFACE

Definition of Anxiety

We have said repeatedly that the most important issue in value clarification is the priority of values that I decide on. For this reason, we might expand the definition of anxiety given in the previous section to the following: *Anxiety is the response of the*

*person, through the imagination, to some future possibility seen
as a threat to his values and the way they are ranked.*

Anxiety can be a threat to a person's priorities or his value ranking. The anxiety then may not be over the particular value as such, but over the way in which it is listed as a priority.

Up until this point we have seen anxiety very much as a personal thing that affects our relationships. The emphasis, it could be argued, has been on anxiety as the problem of a particular person. This is particularly true when we look at "exaggerated anxiety," as in the example of Joe and Dorothy. However, it needs to be noted that this anxiety has a much wider dimension than that of the individual as he relates to others. It can be seen as a cultural problem. Rollo May states:

> *"The problem of anxiety and culture may be broken down into two phases. First, the kinds (forms, occasions) of anxiety experienced by a given individual are culturally conditioned because his existence as a personality is largely due to cultural products. Second, the quantities of anxiety experienced by a given individual are conditioned by the degree of unity and stability in his culture. If the culture is relatively unified and stable, the individual will be able to orientate himself (whether he is in accord with cultural mores or not) and his experience of anxiety will be relatively less frequent and less intense. If, as in the case of contemporaneous period, the culture is in a state of disunity and traumatic change, not only will the individual reflect this disunity in his own psychological life, but his orientation to his changing culture will be proportionately more difficult. Hence, his anxiety will be more frequent and more intense"* (The Meaning of Anxiety, p. 216).

This cultural definition of values by Rollo May speaks very much to our present upheavals in society. Since the society is in a rapid state of change, the problem of increased mental illness of course is a natural by-product. In our original look at anxiety, we saw that it was the result of a person's value system being threatened. This threat could come from the inside as a person considers options for the future and fears all sorts of risks in whatever choices he may take. In this day and age, it is more likely that a person's anxiety will rise from the threat to his priorities by the society in which he is living.

To illustrate this point, Jean-Francois Revel, in a book called *Without Marx or Jesus: The New American Revolution Has Begun*, states that the revolution of the twentieth century will take place in the United States. He also states that this revolution has begun. Elaborating on this theme, he points to five conditions, prerequisites for revolution, which are developing in our present culture:

> *"1. There must be a critique of the injustice existing in economic, social, and racial relationships.*
>
> *"2. There must be a critique of management, directed against the waste of material and human resources. This is related to the preceding critique, since it demonstrates that in-*

justice results in inefficiency, and thus in counterproductivity and in the ruin of a nation's resources. It also calls into question the orientation of technological progress toward goals that are either useless or harmful to man.

"3. There must be a critique of political power, directed against its sources and principles as well as against its exercise, the conditions in which it is exercised, distributed, or monopolized, the localization of decision-making powers, the relationship between the consequences of these decisions for the people and the difficulty (or the impossibility) for the people of participating in these decisions.

"4. There must be a critique of culture: of morality, religion, accepted beliefs, customs, philosophy, literature, art; of the ideological attitudes which underlie these things; of the function of culture and of intellectuals in society; and of the distribution of that culture (education, communication, information).

"5. There must be a critique of the old civilization-as-sanction or a vindication of individual freedom. This critique is aimed at the relations between society and the individual. In it, the individual is considered as a sensitive and original being, rather than as a citizen; and society is regarded as a means either of developing or distorting the proper worth of each individual. Such a critique measures, for example, the failure of a society to deal with poverty and the sterility of the human relations it establishes (brotherhood versus aggressiveness); with the uniformity of the human types it engenders (conformity); in general, with the restraints with which it burdens its people, and the obstacles which it places in the way of the development of individual potential and self-identity. In this context, revolution is seen as the liberation of the creative personality and the awakening of personal initiative, as opposed to the "closed horizons," the climate of frustration and despair, which prevail in repressive societies" (Without Marx or Jesus, pp. 11-12).

If we look at the various definitions of anxiety that we have and look at the statement of where our society is according to Revel above, we can understand that many people should have a great deal of anxiety at this time. The importance of this is to help us understand that people's lives do have meaning, that as I become anxious in a given situation or as I perceive someone else becoming anxious and controlling, I know strangely enough that their life has meaning because a set of values is being threatened. It is the values and the priorities that give life meaning.

It is, therefore, as we have said before, extremely important that we clarify our values so that we understand the nature of a threat when we are confronted with it. An answer to anxiety always has to come in terms of my ability to make conscious choices. Unfortunately when I am threatened, my choices are restricted because I become anxious. *The degree to which I feel anxious is the degree to which my ability to make choices is restricted.* Both fear and anxiety restrict my ability to see alternatives and render choice often impossible, if not very difficult.

The point is, then, that anxiety most easily appears in its

exaggerated form when I am not aware of my priorities. When I know what my values are and what those priorities are, then I have alternatives from which I can choose. Value clarification, then, as clarifying what my priorities are, is itself an enemy to my anxiety. That is to say, it can turn exaggerated anxiety into the kind of anxiety that helps me to choose creative alternatives.

As Rollo May has pointed out, *anxiety is that which helps a person to be creative*. Anxiety is not all bad. It is only bad in its exaggerated form.

If we look at many of the words that Revel chooses above, we see many, many values. Let us look at a few: human relationships, justice, political power, culture, morality, religion, literature. All these words which have just been mentioned and which are being examined often pose a threat, not so much as words which are values to individuals, but to the priorities in which they are held.

If we were to believe most of the values of advertising and of the majority of our society, we would see that functioning well and work have a major priority. We might list some of the words that would indicate this from Revel's list: management, technology, political power, intellect. Now, some of the values that have been seen as being exclusive to those who have time (in terms of this old value system) might be seen as follows: literature, philosophy, religion, culture.

It is interesting that I have known many young people who have had severe conflicts with their parents for placing some of the words in the latter list as their primary priorities and some of the words from the former list as being of least importance, whereas their parents emphasize the former list and de-emphasize the cultural words in the second list. One way of looking at this, perhaps an over-simplification but maybe a help to illustrate the point, would be as follows. Some people put their priorities as follows:

Work
Leisure

Such people then are often in conflict with people who put the above as follows:

Leisure
Work

It would seem to me that this is one of the growing conflicts in our society, where many young people, and more and more older people, are simply regarding work as being less important, giving up their jobs, and just traveling around the world or around the country on a shoestring, so to speak. What is important is not that the values have been dropped or that any values have been changed, but simply that they have been placed in different orders of priority.

GREAT EXPECTATIONS

When we compare individuals' different value rankings, we see that we are beginning to deal with the problem of culture. That is to say, a young person who disagrees with her parents will often appear to come from a different culture.

We talk about the "youth culture," but there also is the culture of the parents of the youth. Toffler has pointed out that as culture moves more rapidly, so year by year people form new cultures almost as quickly as they change their priorities. As such, a person could be moving or creating a new culture for himself week after week. As new cultures are formed, there is an increasing possibility of conflict as people confront each other's culture and its values.

As was pointed out earlier in the book, conflict comes about when people lack the imagination to be able to see alternatives, that is to say, when people impose their culture and impose their priorities on another person. Imposition takes place, however, when a person is anxious, because at such a time he does not see other alternatives.

Cultures within Culture

However, even though it is true that people form individual cultures as we change from day to day, it is also true that within society there are larger cultural groups. The problem is increased by the fact that large numbers of people seem to have similar value systems. We see this in professional groups or religious groups. We see it often as codes of ethics for, say, the medical profession. Charles C. Reich talks about the different consciousnesses in America—pioneer man, consumer man.

Revel has his own way of looking at it. He says instead that there are three nations in the United States: a black nation, a Woodstock nation, and a Wallace nation. The first one is self-explanatory. The second takes its name from the great political and musical convention held at Woodstock, New York, in 1969, which has been documented by the film *Woodstock:* It includes the hippies and radicals. The third nation is embodied in George Wallace of Alabama, and is composed of "lower middle-class whites" whose symbol is the hard hat worn by construction workers. Each of these nations has its own language, its own art forms, and its own customs. And each has a combat arm: the Black Panthers for the blacks, the Weathermen for Woodstock, and the Ku Klux Klan, and various civil organizations for Wallace.

Yes, this seems very much like an over-simplification. However, it does point to a reality and a problem. Cultures do exist within our society, that is to say, cultures which have their own values in the areas of confrontation, art, legislation, and so on. Each culture has certain common value systems and priorities which, when confronted, cause conflict and anxiety. When certain values are confronted within these cultures, then problems often ensue.

World Culture

To expand this culture to the world culture, we see that even nations can appear at least to have common sets of values.

On a recent television program called "Overkill," devoted to the continuing arms buildup of the United States and Russia, a man from the Pentagon stated that even though both countries had more arms than they needed, it was unlikely that the arms buildup could be stopped for some time as yet.

Whatever one's view of this might be, it would appear that countries like Russia, the United States, and China seem to have as their first value "security," that is, an incredible need to try to control the future, to try to prevent some disaster which maybe is mythical. I suppose if we were to push this further and look at the underlying reason for the need for security, we could probably again point to the whole question of organization and function. We might end up with a national value system for the United States which would look like this:

Security
Function as production
Democracy

PROBLEMS OF CULTURAL INTERFACE

One place that I have found this problem of culture and values to be particularly evident is in the conflict between persons in various professions—for example, the problem that teachers often have. I have a friend who teaches in the training department of a college of education, in charge of a class with about twenty students. The problem was that when his students went out to do their practice teaching, imbued with inductive and experiential learning-centered theories, they found themselves being supervised by teachers whose whole training background had been deductive and cognitive in approach.

Inductive vs. Deductive Learning: An Example of Cultural Interface

The students had assimilated a culture of the classroom from their professor that said that inductive learning was a value. They had come to believe that the student learns from experience, that one should allow the student to work in a very flexible environment with various creative processes through which the teacher could then help the student reflect and grow. The implicit value orientation was that values and knowledge are intrinsic to the child and that he will discover this knowledge out of the experience which he is living. Now whatever we may think about this, I am simply saying that this was a part of the culture of these young student teachers as they went into a training situation.

Their training supervisors in the local schools had been trained in a totally different way. Their situation and their culture dictated a different set of values. They felt that the student was more of a precious, but yet unformed, lump of clay. That is to say, they saw the student as being very important, as of great worth, but that his mind should be developed cognitively through tradition from the teacher to the student. Here, then, the culture said that intelligence and reason were the prime values.

If we try to list the priorities of the two cultures here

above, we might see them as follows. The young student teacher would list the values as follows:

> Child's feelings and imagination
> Child's ideas
> Open environment (child could move around the class-room)
> Teacher as a respected equal of the student

The teachers in the school system to which these students went, however, had another set of value priorities which *legitimately* came out of their culture:

> Teacher as authority
> Disciplined environment (child at desk ready to receive cognitive input)
> Child's feelings and imagination
> Child's ideas

Quite obviously, when these two cultures got together with their priorities as above, there was a great deal of anxiety on the part of both parties. Now a great deal could be said about what can be done in these situations. However, what is clear is that there would be not a resolution of anxiety unless the priorities of both parties were clarified. No matter how flexible the student trainee and the training teacher were, no matter how much they listened and were open to new views, they would still have conflict since they both came from different cultures.

No matter how open the teacher in the classroom would be, the underlying value that was basic in her priorities would be that knowledge and truth were given by the teacher, whereas the underlying value in the student teacher was that knowledge and truth were implicit in the student.

This is a cultural confrontation which would cause both persons a great deal of anxiety unless there was a great deal of clarification allowing each to maintain his own point of view.

I am not here advocating one point of view or the other, but simply saying that when two people of various cultures get together like this, there is no resolution without clarification. Quite obviously, many teachers who work in school systems have this same clash. It is a problem of culture. Each culture presents different value priorities.

Another Example of Cultural Interface

Another example of a culture clash became evident to me in speaking to a Roman Catholic nun who had been trained in counseling. This particular sister was about to receive a doctor's degree in counseling and had been trained in the fact that charging fees for counseling was related to the motivation of the patient in the whole therapeutic process.

She reflected on the fact that in her religious order they had an attitude toward money, conditioned by their vow of poverty, which said that money basically was to be seen very low on the list of priorities of concern of the sister. To charge fees, therefore, was to immediately place the sister in a cultural confrontation both with herself as a part of that religious order and with the religious order itself.

On the one hand the values of her profession placed money not as the first value but high on the list of values as a part of the therapeutic process; on the other hand, the religious order to which she belonged was telling her that money should be placed much lower in order of priority.

The fact here is that no matter how flexible a person is, no matter how much he has been trained to be open and honest, there will always remain a conflict. Why? Because two cultures would be in conflict in one human being. That is to say, the human being would be confronted with the expectation of the religious order, on the one hand, and of professional practice, on the other.

It is then the problem of expectation that is causing so much anxiety and pain for so many people. Expectation here means that the value priorities that other people expect of me are often in direct confrontation with my own value priorities, rendering me trapped and quite often unable to move because of the anxiety that it causes me. We will take a closer look at this problem as we examine expectation and poverty in the next chapter.

What is the answer to this? What is the other side of anxiety? Well, the reality is that anxiety and fear form only one part of the imagination, representing the fearful images. What about the good images? What about the whole area of creative fantasy and play?

IMAGINATION

At this point, in order to get into the subject of fantasy and imagination, we will develop the following experience which goes by various titles, such as "Directed Daydream" or "Visualization" or "Meditative Technique." This technique, which can be used as a means of meditation, is also one that is very helpful in developing the creative imagination. It is important for the reader to experience the meditation and not merely read about it.

What we are talking about is growing beyond anxiety to new realms of our own creativity. From this author's point of view, going beyond anxiety to creativity is what many religious writers would call the life of the spirit. The spirit is seen as a deep inner power associated with the idea of a creative and unifying force in man.

But to release this creative force in man, it is necessary that he be able to use his imagination creatively and actively, that is, to fantasize. The imagination is very much operative in the present to both produce and overcome anxiety. The positive use of the imagination, then, can be very effective in helping one find alternative ways of action when faced with anxiety.

The approach we are taking in the experience can be

called a meditative technique, and as such draws heavily on the imagination. The goal is to help one expand his ability to fantasize hopefully.

This type of exercise is not something new. Apart from its obvious roots in religious traditions, methods like this are being used in modern psychotherapeutic practice.

Please note that the exercise is not intended as an answer to problems. Rather it is a stage in development that helps to expand one's imaginative abilities in terms of discovering more hopeful (as against anxious) possibilities toward finding realistic solutions. Ultimately, then, I am not suggesting the dissolution of anxiety, but rather seeking more creative ways of dealing with it.

Meditative Techniques: Exercise 1

1. Before using each of the following five pictures, assume a relaxed position. Breathe in and out deeply four or five times. Sit still and be quiet; imagine yourself in the setting described by the picture.

On the following two pages you will see a picture of a rich grassy field, with the sun shining. Look at the picture for a moment; then close your eyes. Imagine yourself leaving the room where you are and entering the meadow.

Look around and notice what it is you see—flowers, people, or whatever. Take ten to fifteen minutes walking through the meadow before returning to your room. Before you open your eyes, move your limbs about to avoid becoming sleepy. Then open your eyes.

This exercise should be done several times until your ability to relax and visualize becomes more natural to you. Do not worry about the images you see or what they mean. The interpretation of the symbolic is a technology of its own. Much more important is the experience of your own inner creative world. You will notice how difficult, perhaps even impossible, it is to control the image.

The meadow is symbolic of Mother Nature, representing the blossoming of life which you seek. It is the world of the playful child.

The healthy person will experience the greenness of life, populated perhaps by children and other people you might meet. A sign of ill-health would be a barren place populated with frightening symbols, and such a person should seek further counsel with a trained person if such symbols persist.

PICTURE A

Exercise 2

2. After you have used picture A several times, move on to picture B. This time imagine the meadow with the mountain. Climb the mountain, enjoy the view and the things you see, the people you might meet. Finally, return to your room via the meadow as before.

In doing this exercise, some people have encountered a forest to walk through before climbing the mountain. Dark forests are often symbolic of the darker side of our nature, and are often symbolic also of our guilt.

It may be that you will have to do this exercise several times before you are able to climb the mountain to the top. Climbing is a symbol of movement, a striving after attainment to develop inner (and outer) freedom. It thus indicates a person's ability to succeed and grow.

PICTURE B

Exercise 3

3. After A and B have been completed, they should be used again in sequence. Imagine yourself walking through the meadow and climbing the mountain. Finally repeat the above sequence, but instead of returning to your room, open your eyes and look for a moment at picture C (a house or chapel), and imagine yourself returning to it rather than to your room.

The type of building you imagine is not important. What is important is that it be for you the building where you feel most at home. After you have been in this building for a while, return to your room and open your eyes as before.

The goal finally is to consider pictures A, B and C as a complete meditation each time. The house, chapel, or other familiar building is symbolic of one's innermost self. It is where one discovers the creative within. It is within this last sequence that the resolution of problems and insight begin to take place, or where resolutions for new life-directions and attitudes may be confronted.

Ira Progoff (see Appendix) has likened the material in the unconscious, whether in the daydream as above, or in night dreams, to material in a flowing river. Ill-health occurs when the river gets dammed up. The concept which underlies the above meditation is the maintenance of the flow of psychic energy as a means of emotional and spiritual growth.

It is therefore important not to avoid bad experiences in the meditation, but to try to relate to them. Anything that I encounter in the fantasy is a part of me, and therefore something that I need to examine if I am to grow. If I avoid anything, I am avoiding a part of myself. Very much like the previous experiences, this can teach something about myself that I need to know if I am to grow.

PICTURE C

Exercise 4

4. As has been mentioned, water is symbolic of emotional growth and movement. It has often been associated with cleansing and renewal. The use of water in the meditative sequence is therefore also suggested.

Picture D is for this purpose, and can be used separately, or between B and C.

PICTURE D

Exercise 5

5. The more practiced person may use the integrative symbols in picture E. These three symbols are archetypal symbols, common to all major religions and to the therapeutic techniques of the Jungian school. In the unconscious, they symbolize integration, transformation, and wholeness.

The triangle, for example, is symbolic of the unity of the Trinity in Christian thought. The cross symbolizes death and resurrection, or new life. The circle is a common symbol of wholeness.

These symbols can be used on their own, with the one who is fantasizing choosing his or her own preference. Alternatively they can be used to replace the building in picture C.

USE OF A GUIDE OR TEACHER

An excellent use of the above experience is to have a person (director) guide another person or persons through the sequence. I have practiced this with groups of up to ten persons. When this method is used, the person doing the meditation verbalizes continually what is seen, while the rest of the persons try to follow that person's image with their own. This usually takes about twenty minutes for a sequence like A-B-C, although a person should never worry about completing the sequence, but rather try to end each time back in the room.

The purpose of the guide is to help the meditator overcome symbolic blocks to the process, by giving that person verbal alternatives. For example, many times I find a person having difficulty climbing the mountain. He might enter a dark forest with no way out, or the mountain may become very steep and too difficult to climb.

In a case such as this, the guide can suggest a road appearing in the forest, or a ladder up the mountain. For more extreme cases I have had a large bird or even an angel carry the person up the mountain. These are introduced symbols of their own inner potential to choose alternatives. Another method is to introduce a saint or other supportive person whom they see as a help.

This approach of introducing alternatives has a very potent effect in helping a person choose and discover new alternatives which often expand into the day-to-day life experiences of choosing.

This expansion is really the goal of the experience. As we explore the hope of an individual and his ability to find hopeful alternatives in his life, we come face to face with the reality of the necessity for commitment and action to achieve real growth in society.

A person's motivation in striving after a goal and in overcoming exaggerated anxiety is dependent largely on his ability to feel that the goal is attainable. The very fact of a person's doing the exercise is to a large degree a sign of his commitment, and the doing of it can therefore increase his motivation in real life.

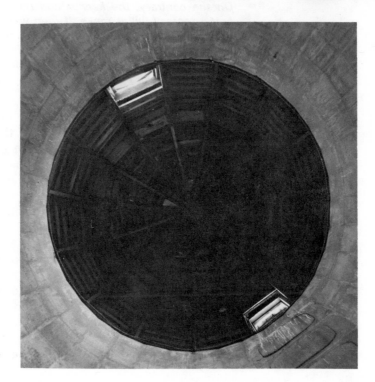

PICTURE E

211

Past bad experiences will, of course, undermine our confidence in our ability to grow. Growth and attainment in the meditative method can therefore increase a person's growth and confidence to grow and reach out beyond himself. It is a strengthening for further action.

With very anxious persons I make a point of introducing into the mountain or house sequence a familiar and comforting person. This has the effect of increasing one's feeling of confidence and self-worth in his own goodness and potential.

IMAGINATION, FANTASY, AND PLAY

When I speak of fantasy in this book, I am referring to creative fantasy and that part of the imagination which does not find itself dominated by symbols of anxiety and fear. I am not speaking so much of the nightmare, but rather of creative fantasy, whether it be while I am dreaming or in my thoughts and daydreams during my conscious hours. Tolkien has the following to say about it:

> "To many, fantasy, this sub-creative art which plays strange tricks with the world and all that is in it, combining nouns and redistributing adjectives, has seemed suspect if not illegitimate; to some it has seemed at least a childish folly, a thing only for people or for persons in their youth.
>
> "Fantasy is a natural human activity. It certainly does not destroy or even insult reason; and it does not either blunt the appetite for, nor obscure the perception of, scientific verity. On the contrary, the keener and the clearer is the reason, the better fantasy will it make. If men were ever in a state in which they did not want to know or could not perceive truth (facts or evidence), then fantasy would languish until they were cured. If they ever get into that state (it would not seem at all impossible), fantasy will perish and become morbid delusion" (The Tolkien Reader, pp. 53-55).

Tolkien goes on to say that creative fantasy is founded upon the recognition of the reality of things in the world. He says that fantasy is based on fact. As an example, he speaks of the work of Lewis Carroll, the point being that stories like *Alice through the Looking Glass,* or *Alice in Wonderland* with its fantasies about mice and rabbits and so on, could not have existed if the imagination were not able to distinguish between such entities.

To Tolkien, then, fantasy as a natural human activity enhances and develops the creative growth of man and is as such essential to his creative existence. For Tolkien whose fairy stories like *The Hobbit* have done so much to enhance the imagination of the reader, joy is an essential ingredient of the creative fantasy. For him the person who fantasizes is a sub-creator. In other words, fantasy is an active part of the creative process of the human being. As such, fantasy must be based on reality.

Fantasy then relates to the whole question of festivity and celebration that we talked about in our chapter on past and memory. Why? Because fantasy must be deeply rooted in the whole area of limitations, not only of the human being, but of creation itself. We only see the potential of creation, the potential of the human being in relation to its limits.

Fantasy then must have an "inner consistency of reality." That is to say, all fantasy must partake in reality. The kind of uncontrolled imagination that overcomes a human being and radically distorts reality is described by Tolkien as well as by many others in the psychological field as psychotic and a hallucination. The difference between creative fantasy and this psychotic experience is in the feeling of joy. He speaks of it in the following way:

> "The peculiar quality of the 'joy' in successful fantasy can thus be explained as a sudden glimpse of the underlying reality or truth. It is not only a 'consolation' for the sorrow of this world, but a satisfaction, and an answer to the question 'Is it true?' The answer to this question that I gave at first was (quite rightly): 'If you have built your little world well, yes, it is true in that world.' That is enough for the artist (or the artist part of the artist)" (The Tolkien Reader, pp. 70-71).

I would offer the following passage as an example of the relationship of anxiety and fear to the hope and joy of something beyond those images as represented in Tolkien's fantasy, *The Lord of the Rings*. This passage is taken from *The Return of the King*, which is the last book of the trilogy, and is the final scene between the Black Rider and Meriadoc Brandybuck who kills him. In this scene the Black Rider, who appeared in the middle of a battle on the back of a terrible monster called the Nazgul, kills King Theoden. As he does so, he is defended by a woman by the name of Eowyn, who kills the monster with a sword, at which point the Black Lord rises from the ground and begins to attack the Lady Eowyn.

> "Out of the wreck rose the Black Rider, tall and threatening, towering above her. With a cry of hatred that stung the very ears like venom he let forth his mace. Her shield was slivered in many pieces and her arm was broken; she stumbled to her knees. He bent over her like a cloud, and his eyes glittered; he raised his mace to kill.
>
> "But suddenly he too stumbled forward with a cry of bitter pain, and his stroke went wide, driving into the ground. Merry's sword had stabbed him from behind, shearing through the black mantle, and, passing up beneath the hauberk, pierced the sinew behind his mighty knee.
>
> "'Eowyn! Eowyn!' cried Merry. Then tottering, struggling up, with her last strength she drove her sword between crown and mantle, as the great shoulders bowed before her. The sword broke sparkling into many shards. The crown rolled away with a clang. Eowyn fell forward upon her fallen foe. But lo! The mantle and hauberk were empty. Shapeless they lay now on the ground, torn and tumbled; and a cry went out into

the shuddering air, and faded to a shrill wailing, passing with the wind; a voice bodiless and thin had died and it was swallowed up and it was never heard again in that age of this world.

"And there stood Meriadoc the Hobbit in the midst of the slaying, blinking like an owl in the daylight, for tears blinded him; and through a mist he looked at Eowyn's fair head, as she lay and did not move; and he looked on the face of the king, fallen in the midst of his glory. For Snowmane in his agony had rolled away from him again; yet he was the bane of his master.

"Then Mary stooped and lifted his hand to kiss it, and lo! Theoden opened his eyes and they were clear, and he spoke in a quiet voice though laboured.

" 'Farewell, Master Halbitla!' he said. 'My body is broken. I go to my fathers. And even in their mighty company I shall not now be ashamed. I felled the black serpent. A grim morn, and a glad day, and a golden sunset' " (The Return of the King, pp. 142-143).

For the most part I think this beautiful passage speaks for itself. This is a fairy story of elves and goblins and such things. In the first paragraph the Black Rider, a faceless horror, is a symbol of anxiety and fear. One could write a great deal on faceless people as they appear in dreams. C. G. Jung has said a great deal about this. The author captures the idea of anxiety and hopelessness in the symbol of power, so powerful that he shatters the shield of his adversary.

The battle takes place. The horror is overcome. Then, as Meriadoc the Hobbit turns, he sees death around him. He feels deep grief for his king. And yet through the darkness and the death, the king finds a satisfaction and even a glimpse of joy in the midst of it all. He finds a golden sunset. That is to say, even in the midst of death, there are alternatives which man can find and discover. A simple fairy story? Deeply seated in reality, I think. The fantasy here is not one that fails to depend on the reality of life, but rather sees it and seeks to make sense out of it in its deepest perspective.

An interesting film made a few years ago, probably in most public libraries in large cities anyway, is the film *Occurrence at Owl Creek Bridge.* In this film, we see a person being hanged by Confederate soldiers during the Civil War. The total film is about the fantasy and the imagination of the man as he falls before the rope jerks and kills him. He sees life around him come alive. He becomes sensitized to the trees and the insects. He looks back to the past memories of his wife and his children. One is captured by the hope of this film. This person had an imagination that presented him the hope of multiple alternatives even in death.

Man's future is dependent on his capacity to use his imagination. But as I fantasize on the future, I must be able to deal with the alternatives that I am confronted with. Therefore, reflection and training on the use of the imagination are essential. That is to say, young people in school need to know how to use their imagination and to understand it as an essential and good part of their lives.

Harvey Cox through Fretigny and Virel raises the question: Why do we need imagination?

> *"We need it because the substance of the universe of thought is just too changing and too complex to be appropriated in a merely rational manner. Therefore, it is the job of the imagination to operate a dialectic of the real and the possible. [Without it] discursive thought would become incurably crippled in a closed and ossified system"* (The Feast of Fools, p. 66).

Where Imagination Develops

Development of the imagination then is essential. It would seem to me that the most opportune place for this to happen is in the classroom. There are various ways in which imagination can be expanded, and I think this depends a great deal on the person involved. But an essential part of this expansion is in the area of study. For example, the study of history is very important as we see the alternatives and the use of the creative imagination of people in our tradition or in other traditions.

Another place where imagination can be developed so well is in the history of art. Kenneth Clark points to the Gothic world, the world of chivalry, courtesy and romance as a world, at least for the courtier, where life was treated with a sense of play. It was in this period that architecture became very extravagant. Huge and beautiful cathedrals rose out of the poverty of Europe, illustrating in their stance an incredible optimism about the potential of man in his relationship to the divine. The architecture and Gothic art were fantastic in the true sense of becoming a fantasy.

It was in this period that persons like Dante emerged and Francis of Assisi. We see pictures of the Virgin Mary with unicorns and lions. It was in this period that love became idealized and women—some women, at least—adored. Such fantasy is in sharp contrast to the eighteenth century and the advent of the Industrial Revolution which has made our society so function- and reason-orientated, often pushing imagination not only to the side but even condemning it as bad.

Kenneth Clark points to a book written in 1667, *Sprat's History of the Royal Society.* It is in this book, he says, that poetry is seen as the "parent of superstition" and that anything related to the imagination is seen as being dangerous and deceiving.

The point, then, is that in the study of art we see the evolution of man, his history, and its effect as he struggles with life. Through literature such as the *The Tolkien Reader* or *Alice in Wonderland,* we can enter the world of fantasy merely by the effort of reading. Through meditative techniques the imagination can be developed as one person perhaps seeks particular growth. Other examples of possibilities of development are in the area of personal history and the development of the imagination through the examination of one's own personal dreams, as in the previous chapter on guilt. It is at this point that we need to be reminded that celebration and the development of fantasy are very closely related.

Play

Before we end this chapter, we should have a look at

Play Forms

play. Fantasy and play are very closely related and are often the same thing, especially with young children. It is in the form of play that I make my imagination, my fantasies, become real by using my total body. In the suggestions above, the emphasis has been much more on the use of the active imagination and the use of the intellect and feelings as a means of stimulating fantasy. Play is, of course, another essential and very important part of fantasy.

Harold Greenwald, in a book called *Ways of Growth,* notes that, in working with executives in industry as a consultant, those who manage to maintain their humor and are able to treat work more like play were more productive, more creative, and generally more efficient. He says that it is unfortunate that too many people only recognize the "hard worker." He also notes that play is more than a useful tool; it is also a way of coping with the absurdities of the human condition.

To cope with the absurdities of the human condition, of course, is to say: How do I deal with those kinds of things that make me anxious—the fact that tomorrow I could die or lose my job or whatever. It seems to me that we need to see the humor in our reality, to see the joy in our fantasy and to play with the alternatives.

Herbert Otto has listed various forms of play as utilized by the adult. This comes in the same article by Greenwald. He lists seven forms, as follows:

1. *Spontaneous play.* This is when the adult plays in a childlike manner and engages in various forms of play, just from impulse, without planning or premeditation. It is the kind of activity characterized by abrupt changes from one activity to another and has elements of joy as part of its character.

2. *Play with children.* This is the kind of play where an adult gets completely involved with children and plays with them at their level. The point of this kind of play is that it is not mechanical.

3. *Play with animals.* He notes that animals often invite adults to play with them. He also notes that this kind of play with animals can be used as a form of destruction to keep a person from engaging in other types of play, in which case it is not very helpful.

4. *Nature play.* Here the adult feels a high degree of oneness with nature. He cites rolling in the grass, smelling and touching flowers, and so on. The emphasis is on the bodily contact with nature.

5. *Primitive play.* This is close to play with nature and he includes here building sand castles, damming up brooks, and so on.

6. *Thrill play.* Here there is an element of danger. Examples include riding motorcycles up steep hills or skydiving.

7. *Mastery play.* This kind of play includes acquiring skills such as playing tennis or golf. He warns that this kind of play can become so competitive that it diminishes all the real potential of play and becomes something else.

Greenwald goes on to say this about play:

"In essence play is more an attitude than an activity. It is approaching life's experiences, looking for the lighter side. With the buoyance of a happy, playful spirit, solutions and inspirations can 'float in on the tide' of expectancy. Thus, the recreative aspect of play is to have a playful spirit in the process of daily living—in the encounters with peoples and problems—meeting them with a perspective through which they can be happily resolved" (Play and Self-Development in Ways of Growth, p. 24).

Play then is very close to the idea of festivity. It can often be an action which is opposite to other actions and as such takes me away from myself and helps me to become free from expectancy in my environment. As such my imagination is free and I am able to act out my fantasies and in so doing maybe even become myself.

IMAGINATION AND FUTURE ENVIRONMENT

Morton Kelsey in a book called *Dreams: The Dark Speech of the Spirit,* tells the story of a conversation between Einstein and Jung. Jung asked the question of Einstein as to how much discipline in the area of mental concentration it took for him to work toward his conclusions. Einstein is reported to have replied, "Oh, no. I meditate and the numbers dance before me." The point that Kelsey wants to make is that many of the great thinkers and persons who have formed so much of the direction of our society have done so only by the help of a creative and active imagination. I suppose one of the most common examples of this is when we think of the conceptualization of the atomic theory, of atoms, and electrons, and so on. These constructs, of course, are imaginative ones, but as such have been profoundly real in their practical application in the development of modern chemistry and physics. These are symbolic ways of thinking.

Bernard Shaw once raised the question, "Why is it that so many people must suffer for the lack of imagination of others?" That is to say, as we look at the tragedy and poverty of the world, as we see the grim spectacle of Hitler's Third Reich or the tragedy in Vietnam, it would appear that what we see, more than anything else, is in reality the nightmare and the darkness of anxiety.

Anxiety then confronts a person with values and priorities he fears to lose. Imagination places a person within a new vista of alternatives, so that he can form new priorities and choose new values, and thus create a new life for himself.

BEYOND HOPE

As we have seen above in the experiences, and through examples such as Joe and Helen, one dynamic cause of increased anxiety is the inability to reach out and value others as being important as myself. The exploration of alternatives then is the exploration of what it is that I value.

An underlying assumption is that persons are of infinite value, and I am of infinite value. However, if I am crippled by exaggerated anxiety, if I am bored with life, I am in reality asserting that others are of little value, and that perhaps I am of little value myself.

The fact is that we live in a value-filled world. If I am to live a healthy life in such a world, I must have some insight into my own values. I cannot grow and discover myself unless I am free to make some choices—unless I have some alternatives to choose from. I cannot create until I am free to create.

In the last section we dealt with fantasy as the beginning of a method to help persons discover their own hope, their own alternatives. But what then? Then we will be free to choose, free to create a better world or destroy it. My personal faith is that once man is really free to choose, he will, for the most part, choose creatively.

Hope leads to creative change. As a counselor I have seen many clients who seemed unable to make choices, who knowingly chose to be uncreative. At the same time, I have met very few who chose to be deliberately destructive. The majority chose creative ways, and it is those who can build a better world.

Millions daily watch television and go to the movies. For many this is the only form of fantasy they deal with, fantasizing their hopes and frustrations. The problem is that they do so only within the limits of the program they are viewing. Through the media they dream, but seldom will they move beyond to decision-making, becoming symbols of hope to others.

It is interesting to observe someone spending an evening watching television. From 7 to 10 he can be comfortable, watching the carefully-scripted actions and pratfalls of imaginary heroes and villains. One observer has dubbed this time "the world as we would like it to be."

Then comes the evening news, "the world as it is." Tension rises; anxiety increases. *We* could be involved in that fire, that war, that riot in the next town. This kind of television-viewing necessitates involvement on the part of the viewer. He has to begin thinking of creative alternatives or fall prey to increased anxiety and hopelessness.

Media like television and motion pictures can often have the effect of deadening the senses and making people less able to make responsible decisions. In my opinion, we should welcome films like *The Hand* and *Z* which leave the viewer with questions rather than answers. Such films provide a process to fantasy, rather than limiting it.

Young people on LSD like to talk about their inner creative experiences. However, in counseling them, I have often found that they are actually losing the ability to choose creatively. All too often they begin to avoid major decisions about school or the war, rather than to face them.

Our churches are full of people who go to fulfill an obligation, but who know little of fantasy and celebration of the hope of resurrection. They have alternatives that will free them, but they

fail to commit themselves to act. All too often they are victims of guilt imposed by a distorted conscience or a manipulative minister, and in turn they express their anger by trying to trap the minister in some way.

It is this kind of poverty—the poverty of alternatives—that we experience as boredom. In the LSD user, the bored churchgoer, the television prisoner, there is the manifestation of a search for hope. If there is search, there is hope. This is the fact that speaks most loudly. Exaggerated anxiety—the enemy of hope—must be converted into the hope of creative alternatives.

One might well ask: What about the type of environment that does not permit choices to be made? What about the poor, the victim of discrimination, the unmarried mother with six kids—what kind of choices do they have? What about pollution or the environment that limits the very air we breathe or the beaches we play on?

The anxiety that all these forces bring, especially the environment of poverty, limits our alternatives. Poverty can be defined as a trapped, limited condition. Poor people will testify that the real hell of poverty is not in being without money, but in the anxiety arising from not knowing where or when they will get some, so that they can even begin thinking in terms of alternatives.

Freeing oppressed people by creating new environments for them, new vistas of alternatives dealing with pollution and allowing creation to create, cannot be done by hopeless people. Hope must touch the inner man to be truly hopeful. Freedom from poverty, the creation of new vistas of alternatives, hope itself in fact, must mean social concern and action.

Therefore this author assumes that the methods delineated here as creating a liberated environment—inner and outer space—are only the beginning of a process, one that must move into choices that reach out to individuals and beyond into social concern.

7.
Search For Meaning and Leisure

> "I remember the parents coming at weekends. And they would say to Neill, 'What can I do, Neill? I don't know what to do.'
> And Neill would say, 'Well, I've got plenty to do. I don't know what you want to get on with.' And they would say, 'I'm bored.'
> And he'd say, 'Well, everyone is bored before they start doing something.' "
>
> Neill and Summerhill: A Man and His Work

DIAGRAM I

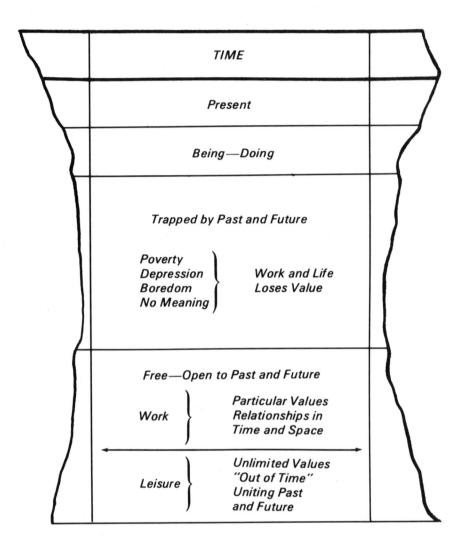

TIME

Present

Being—Doing

Trapped by Past and Future

Poverty
Depression   Work and Life
Boredom   Loses Value
No Meaning

Free—Open to Past and Future

Work   Particular Values
                Relationships in
                Time and Space

Leisure   Unlimited Values
                "Out of Time"
                Uniting Past
                and Future

INTRODUCTION

In relationship to time, this chapter is going to deal with the present. (Please see Diagram I.) The past, as we saw, dealt with memory. The future is seen as imagination. The present, then, has to do with my "being" now, that is to say, who I am in process at this time. It also has to do with what I am "doing" now. In our diagrams, therefore, we talk of past as memory, future as imagination, and the present as self-being and doing. (Please see Diagram II.)

This chapter is going to deal with the present, as the present relates to the past and the future. Obviously, although imagination is seen as a future act, it happens presently as I imagine actively. Of course, the same is true of guilt. The act of which I

222

DIAGRAM II

TIME AS VALUE INDICATOR

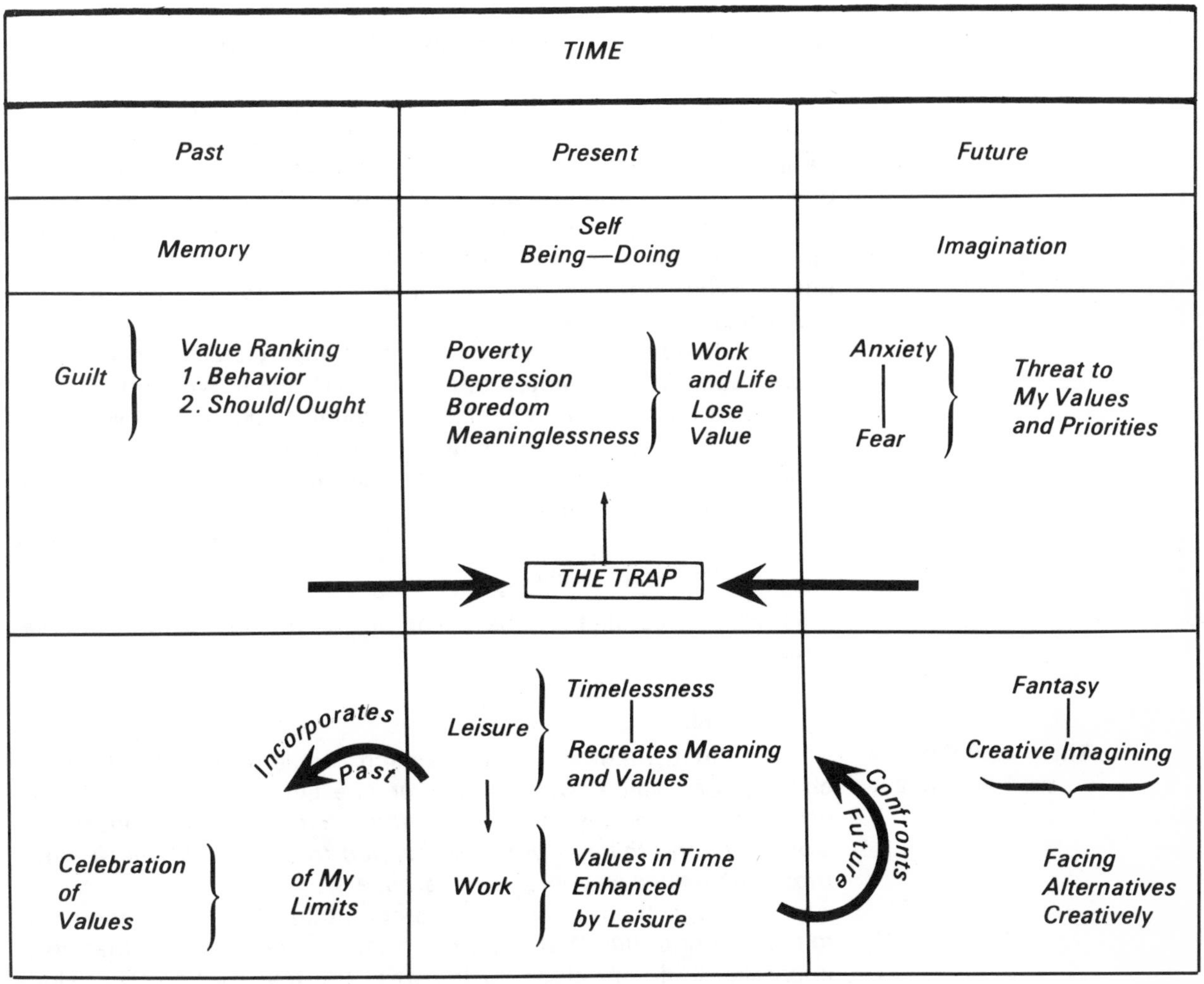

TIME		
Past	Present	Future
Memory	Self Being—Doing	Imagination
Guit } Value Ranking 1. Behavior 2. Should/Ought	Poverty Depression Boredom Meaninglessness } Work and Life Lose Value	Anxiety ─ Fear } Threat to My Values and Priorities
	THE TRAP	
Incorporates Past ↙ Celebration of Values } of My Limits	Leisure } Timelessness Recreates Meaning and Values ↓ Work } Values in Time Enhanced by Leisure	Fantasy ─ Creative Imagining } *Confronts Future* ↖ Facing Alternatives Creatively

feel guilty happened in the past, but as I remember it, I am doing my memory work now in the present. Therefore, this chapter has to deal with the relationship of guilt and anxiety to the present. Anxiety has the particular consequence of rendering people unable to choose in the present. I define this inability to make choices and to act on them as poverty.

Poverty in this chapter is seen as a trapped condition, a condition where choice is a restricted possibility for me due to my personal anxiety and the environment in which I live. The more trapped I am, the more I move toward a condition of meaninglessness. This trapped condition, then, is the relationship of the present to the past as guilt and to the future as anxiety and fear.

The other side of the coin which we will also deal with in the chapter is the relationship of the present to the past as celebration of my limitations, and to the future as creative imagination. The present in this situation is seen as leisure and work.

RELATIONSHIP OF THE PRESENT TO GUILT AND ANXIETY

At this point, then, we are dealing with the present as being dominated for the most part by the negative aspects and in particular by guilt and anxiety. Later we will try to see this in its positive light. First, in regard to anxiety, it is something that exists in the imagination and, as such, is in the future. Guilt, on the other hand, is in the past as memory. The question, then, has to be raised: What is the relationship between the two of them, if there is any relationship at all?

Anxiety is the consequence of and related to every guilt event. Guilt, as we pointed out, was a past event which has inherent within its structure a problem of value ranking. That is to say, a person was confronted with certain priorities which were in conflict—for example, the man who felt guilty about going fishing. The priorities may have been:

Self
Wife and Family

This was in conflict at the point he went fishing, for example, with:

Wife and Family
Self

Time and Guilt and Anxiety

Guilt, then, is a value ranking problem whereby a person chooses one value over another or one set of priorities over another set of priorities. *Anxiety, on the other hand, is the apprehension that something is going to happen to me which will threaten those values necessary to my existence.*

Guilt, then, is when I did something that threatened certain value priorities that were important to me. Anxiety, therefore, is parallel and very close, in that it is the fear that certain values will be eliminated that are necessary to my growth and life-style. The difference between guilt and anxiety is mainly in the time sequence. Guilt is in the memory and, as such, past, whereas anxiety is in the imagination and, as such, future. Guilt, then, directly feeds anxiety, making the subject more and more apprehensive of the possibility (1) of being in a state where his values are annihilated and, therefore, his life rendered meaningless; (2) of being discovered as a person who has broken certain values and, as such, may be rejected by other people in his society. The latter, of course, is the problem of guilt and expectation. The expectation is not only in letting other people down, but also in the fear of being discovered and finally being rejected by others. (See Diagram III.)

Guilt, then, feeds anxiety, and then anxiety, of course, imposes itself upon the person in the present. It is like being judged by one's own guilt. Thomas Oden has the following to say about this:

DIAGRAM III

ANXIETY AND GUILT

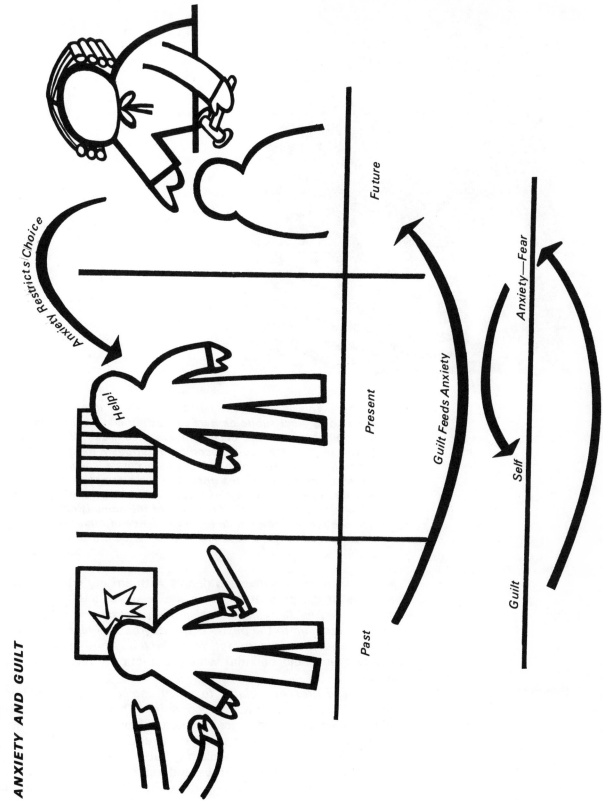

Anxiety Restricts Choice

Help!

Past   Present   Future

Guilt   Self   Anxiety—Fear

Guilt Feeds Anxiety

"This is why guilt tends not only to intensify anxiety, but also to erect subtle barriers toward others. Duplicity toward the neighbor and self-deception are two sides of the same game. In this way, guilt becomes a seriously malignant force separating man from man. All of this occurs allegedly in the interest of the pursuit of the good and the attempt to live a virtuous life. Guilt drives us away from others into loneliness. Like criminals trying to escape the vision of the administrators of justice, we feel uncomfortable in the presence of others who might discover us as value destroyers" (The Structure of Awareness, p. 54).

Guilt then is involved deeply with anxiety which serves to judge us in the present. What is the result of this? *The result is that the degree to which I feel anxiety pressing upon me—and guilt is a problem in the past—is the degree to which my ability to choose, and therefore to act, is restricted.* Another definition of anxiety then could be: that which restricts my present ability to choose.

Poverty: A Trapped Condition

The present inability to make choices is my definition of poverty. Poverty is a "trapped" condition. That is to say, it is a situation in which I find myself where I have restricted ability to make choices and, as a consequence, to act.

What is it that makes me "poor"? My anxiety and my guilt? The answer is "yes," if we understand that both anxiety and guilt have a social dimension and are often the results of our environment. Guilt is a matter of a value ranking problem (which is normally socially influenced) and anxiety, as we have just mentioned, feeds upon guilt and continues to restrict a man in his choices. If a man cannot choose and act, naturally his personal growth and his relationship to others and the whole of society become limited. Therefore, poverty is a social phenomenon resulting from a person's inability to make creative choices in a given situation, and, sometimes at least, that is due to his guilt or anxiety.

Poverty and a trapped condition as social phenomena will be dealt with later in some examples. However, it is possible to see what happens to people as they become more and more trapped and less and less able to make choices. This is not simply a matter of personality and a problem for the counselor, but related very much to the whole social dimension. When we can see symptoms of a trapped condition in the personality and in groups of people, then we can better understand what the problem is. We could, for example, raise the question "What is trapping you?" rather than "Why are you anxious?" What is the difference in the questions? One is social in its origin and one is psychological.

As we proceed, I would like to make it clear that the person who is unable to choose or act in a given situation could be rendered in such a condition through an external environment or an inner environment. In other words, it could be a personal problem, or it could be the problem of his environment, external to himself. In my opinion, it is always a mixture of both. One feeds the other, making problems very complicated. For example, black people who live in low economic conditions are also for the most part people who have difficulties in making personal choices which are created for themselves and others. One could argue that creative choices are impossible because of their environment, or one could argue that their environment has been internalized to themselves and that personal choice therefore is impossible because of internal reasons. The problem of rehabilitation is therefore a complex one that has to be total and social in its dimension.

The Poverty Trap

The *poverty trap* seems to move in the following way with individuals. First of all, a person finds himself or herself in a trapped situation and as a consequence finds it difficult to make choices. The most common trapped situation is knowing that others expect something of me but feeling that I do not have the abilities to come up to their expectations. As a consequence, I feel guilty because I cannot do what I should for them, and I become anxious about what will happen if I try or if I don't try, and as such I feel trapped and unable to choose or do anything. For most people, the first stage of a trapped condition is *frustration and anger*. We all find ourselves caught in two-way streets—for example, discovering that a birthday card was not mailed by someone whom you asked to mail it for you. You do not discover that the card was not mailed until the day after your friend's birthday! There is nothing you can do. You are trapped, disappointed, frustrated, and a little angry.

The second stage is a deeper stage which again most people feel from time to time. It is one where the anger from frustration becomes itself a trap, because I am unable to express it and thus keep it inside. This stage is called *depression.* A common example of this might be the disappointment with fellow workers and the anxiety aroused by the thought that "maybe this is not going to be a good job for me after all." Another example might be a child of mine having difficulty at school. The thought going through my head might be, "Maybe Johnny will have a lot of difficulties in the future." Another might be the consequence of an argument with my wife, and the resulting fear that maybe our marriage will not work out. In many of these situations, I feel frustrated and disappointed, and maybe angry. On the other hand, if I get angry I might really blow it. This kind of trap results in a feeling of depression for most people. Depression is not unusual unless, of course, it becomes something that stays with a person constantly.

Beyond depression we move into the kind of trapped condition which begins to stay and remain with a person, and as a consequence has become more serious. This condition I call *boredom.* Depression is often thought of as being a personal problem, whereas boredom can often be seen as being more social in its content. It can be seen as part of an individual or of a larger group. Boredom, then, is a much more serious state of poverty or being trapped.

A person who is continually bored perhaps has reached a stage in life where choice and action are moving toward the impossible. It is often at this stage that I find that people become much more immoral in their acts. They feel sorry for themselves and perhaps run around with other people's wives and so on. Boredom is an interesting phenomenon and one that I often notice, for example, in church congregations on Sunday morning, or in lectures, or in schoolrooms.

I have often found it very provocative and very helpful just to raise the question with a congregation or with a class, "I have noticed how bored everyone is. To me this means that you are trapped. What do you think is trapping you?" Just to place boredom in these terms has had amazing effects at times. To say I am bored is one thing, but to have it pointed out that this could mean that I am trapped is another. At this point the people can often see that their trapped condition is due to the nature of the lecture or the preacher or the environment or whatever. Not always, but quite often, their problem becomes clarified and as such often motivates people to be able to do something about it.

**Meaninglessness:
Where Values
No Longer Exist**

Beyond boredom is *meaninglessness.* Meaninglessness is the final end-point of the trapped condition. It is at that point that values no longer exist. Why? The trapped condition has come to the point where it is impossible to choose or act. As was pointed out earlier in this book, a value is something that is chosen freely and acted on and that somebody is happy with. Without choice of act, values become impossible. Life has become meaningless. Victor Frankl has said that this is the central trouble of our age:

> "I have said that man should not ask what he may expect from life, but should rather understand that life expects something from him. It may also be put this way: In the last resort, man should not ask, 'What is the meaning of my life?' but should realize that he himself is being questioned. Life is putting its problems to him, and it is up to him to respond to these questions by being responsible: he can only answer to life by answering for his life" (The Doctor and the Soul, p. xv).

A Trapped Family

To illustrate some of the above, I offer the following case experience. Several years ago I worked in Central America as an episcopal priest and counselor. The following occurred in an area called Barrio Cuba which is a very poor part of the city of San Jose in Costa Rica.

The Gonzalez family consisted of a husband and wife, Antonio and Lupe, and seven children. They lived in a small cardboard house approximately ten feet square with one room. They had no bathroom, but used a small area of ground outside the house close to a river, where they also used to wash themselves and their clothing.

Antonio had previously had a problem with alcohol, but apparently had not been troubled for three years. He still drank occasionally and would even get drunk once every couple of months, but this was quite a change from his previous life when he had been drinking heavily every night. Because of the seven children and the fact that he worked in construction, earning about fifteen dollars a week, the problem of pregnancy was uppermost in his wife's mind.

I knew the Gonzalez family quite well, since I had been teaching a class in hygiene in which his wife was a member. Secondly, both the husband and wife were involved in a local community action group concerned with starting a new clinic.

People in the Barrio were extremely poor, and the incidents of various forms of character disorder were phenomenal. The most prevalent problem in the Barrio was the use of drugs and alcohol. There was a very high incidence of the latter, starting with children anywhere from the age of nine years of age up. In this particular area, much of the liquor contained methyl alcohol, causing a great deal of later physical problems. Prostitution started anywhere from ten or eleven years up. Considering the living conditions of the people in the area, none of these things should be considered surprising, especially the prostitution.

Two of the members of our action committee reported to me that there were serious problems in the Gonzalez family and asked if I would inquire. Interestingly enough, they would not say what the problems were, nor had the Gonzalez family indicated any difficulties.

I visited the household several times and was able to talk things through with them enough for them to open up to a degree and tell me that their fear was pregnancy, since they already had seven children and their financial situation was extremely difficult.

The following week I visited the house several times and found Lupe suffering a great deal with severe stomach pains, which I thought could possibly be connected to her anxiety over the fact that their electricity might be cut off, since the bills had not been paid. That week her husband managed to borrow about ten dollars from the fund of the local church, since he would only be paid at the end of his job. In other words, the money was borrowed until his regular check was due, which had been delayed for some reason or another. Owing to the increasing pains of the mother and her increasing anxiety about pregnancy, I arranged for a medical checkup.

The doctor informed me that she was four months pregnant and that in his opinion the anxiety was due to the fact that she was denying her pregnancy. She kept asserting that she was not pregnant. The following Sunday I arrived at the community meeting to find her oldest son in tears. He indicated that there was something wrong at home. On arriving at the house, I discovered Lupe alone in the home, with the electricity cut off, and with blood all over the floor and what appeared to be the fetus of a baby. With the help of a couple of people I got her to the hospital. She had two other babies inside of her, one dead and one alive, and permission had to come immediately from the husband as to whether or not they could remove the babies before Lupe died.

There was an ethical question about such an operation in a Roman Catholic country, so special permission had to be obtained from her husband before any surgery could take place.

However, her husband was not to be found and had reportedly been seen drunk the previous night. I was asked to try to find him. When I got back to the action committee, I discovered that the husband had been there, but when he heard what had happened, he disappeared with a friend. Knowing most of the people in the Barrio, I was able to find him and take him to his wife.

When he got to the hospital, he started shouting at his wife and telling her that she was sick in the head for suggesting that he had not been home the previous night. Naturally, Antonio was confronted. It turned out that his greatest fear would be that, when others discovered how he had behaved, he would be rejected by the action group and not allowed to take part in the project.

Lupe felt considerable guilt over the babies—not because of their death, but rather because of her irresponsibility in allowing them to be born in the first place. She stated that she had been given instruction in contraception through a local clinic and yet had done nothing about it. She went on to say that she had been depressed quite often at the thought that she might get pregnant and that she had been losing interest in the group that we were going to and found herself sitting home with nothing to do continually. Her final statement was, "Life seems quite hopeless and meaningless."

What can we say about this? It is quite obvious that to

simply blame the people and avoid looking at the total environment in which they lived is not the solution. This family was trapped in poverty, and was poor not only in its ability to face and confront issues of choice within the personality, but poor economically, educationally, and materially. First of all, what was the trap?

The Traps

The trap was complicated and could probably be seen as the following:

1. The Gonzalez family lived on fifteen dollars a week in a culture where the cost of living was a little higher than in the United States.

2. The mother and the father received feelings of self-worth, achievement, accomplishment, and meaning through their family, and especially by having children.

3. Having children made life impossible for them financially, and the possibility of having another child threatened their very existence.

4. Their religion, as they personally understood it, forbade the use of contraception to prevent pregnancy.

5. To not have more children took away some of the life, direction, and meaning that was available to this woman. This is to be understood in the context of an environment which offered very little from her point of view.

6. This whole situation confronted the husband with the fact of how little money he earned, plus the fact that the work he was doing was seasonal.

7. The social action committee which also gave meaning to these people consisted of church people and therefore expected a great deal in terms of the responsibility of this family.

As we look over the above list, we can observe several traps making life impossible for a majority of the people of the country. The trap has to do essentially in the areas of meaning. The mother, on the one hand, wanted to have children, but knew this would be irresponsible in terms of their finances. When she did have children, it caused her a great deal of guilt in terms of what this would mean for the future in terms of their finances. The guilt increased her anxiety and not only brought about an inability to choose, but even restricted her ability to face herself, to the extent that she could not bring herself to admit that she was pregnant. This was an example of exaggerated guilt and anxiety. As a consequence, she became depressed and bored. On the other hand, her husband feared failure in terms of not being able to produce the money, and he also feared being turned out of the group for not coming up to their expectations.

The situation shows the multiplicity of trapped situations which come out of the economic poverty situations that control so many lives in our country and elsewhere. It also shows the relationship between the personality and the poverty environment. The point is that we can see here in this exaggerated example the moving from frustration through depression and boredom, and finally into meaninglessness.

It so happens that this family was helped a little. But help was seen for people like this in that particular situation mainly as being a social problem which was attacked partly by the development of a medical clinic that helped people especially in the area of counseling and family life education in the city of San Jose. Central to the problem of this family is the problem that is present with most people, the one that we keep bringing up, namely, the one of expectation. That is to say, most of us are trapped because we fear to confront the expectations of other people. We feel guilty about failing other people. We feel guilty at not being able to accomplish what we promised. We feel anxious at what might happen if we do not come up to what others expect of us, and as such we are rendered silent and unable to speak.

POVERTY AND SPACE

In this section we are going to try to expand the idea of poverty as a trapped condition by relating it to space. (Please see Diagram IV.) By space is understood the relationship of the self—myself—to others and the environment. The categories would be as follows:

1. *Self related to self.* This would be the area of problems of growth confronting a person for which only he could be ultimately responsible. It is the area to which we formerly referred when discussing existential value formers.

2. *Self related to others.* This would be a larger area of space commitment in that I would not only be concerned with myself, my inner world, but I would be communicating verbally and therefore acting in a larger space by relating to people such as my wife, my children, people at work, and so on. This space then takes in the whole area of personal relationships.

3. *Self as related to the world.* By this is understood the idea of space as a person's relating to non-personal objects. This would include not only such things as machinery or animals and creation, but also non-personal things such as income tax forms, government, country, and so on.

4. *Self as related to the cosmos.* This is in itself a religious context. The idea is that certain people do have a sense of design or a sense of the universe apart from the world. This is attested to especially in literature, religious and otherwise.

After expanding these four categories of space, we will attempt to give some examples of how value education can relate to these areas by bringing people to an expanded awareness of the choices and actions available to them. The purpose will be to simply allow you to examine the use of value clarification as a methodology for approaching problems and creatively seeking solutions.

The point of the section then is to relate trapped situations to values. Basically, as we have said, values are non-formable in trapped situations. Therefore, value education should take

DIAGRAM IV

TIME AND SPACE AS VALUE INDICATORS: THE VALUE BOX

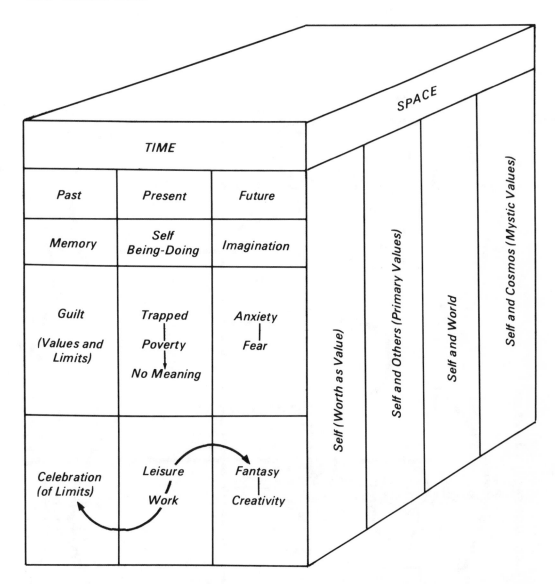

the form of expanding people's alternatives by reducing their anxiety and helping them to confront their guilt. In this way value formation and new choice and action become a possibility. (See Diagrams IV and V.)

Let us first take some examples of trapped situations in relationship to space. Trapped situations are those which permit restricted choice and cause people to become depressed and bored and finally to find life meaningless.

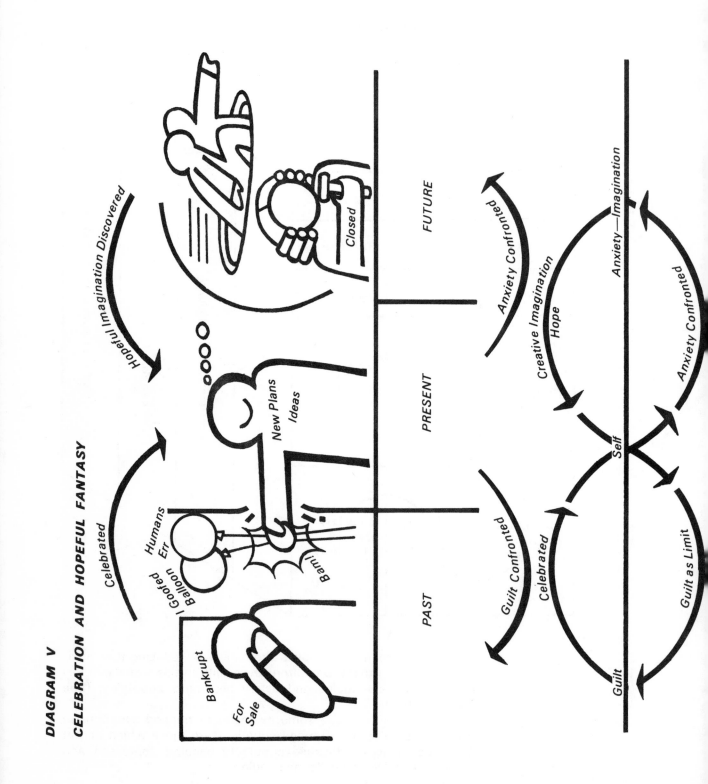

DIAGRAM V

CELEBRATION AND HOPEFUL FANTASY

234

SPACE: SELF AND SELF

One area where all of us are confronted with ourselves and with inevitable trapped situations is that of old age. Why? Because it confronts us all with the probability of death. For many, especially those who have no religious background, death is a trap. The trapped situation is evident from the reality that the old are often unvisited and uncared for in our society. It is a problem for many people. I simply offer this as an example, and as such would ask you to look at the following quotation from Ralph Nader's Study Group Report on Nursing Homes. This appeared in a book called *Old Age: The Last Segregation* written by Claire Townsend, who was the project director.

> " 'A nursing home is a place to go and die, and rot away in the process.' So wrote one of our many correspondents during our study of nursing homes and health care for the aged. Some people may consider such a statement extravagant, born of a reaction to the condition of old age and its peculiar repulsion to most Americans rather than based on an objective as-

sessment of conditions in the nursing homes. Others may write it off as the hysteria of a daughter who cannot bear to see her parents subject to the pain and infirmities that naturally come with old age.

"But the comment is typical. Many others reported similar conclusions about the institutions to which one million elderly Americans are consigned. Their criticisms range from callous and incompetent staff to shocking drug abuses, from lack of rehabilitative programs to neglect of patients by physicians. We were able to observe many examples of inadequate care in nursing homes where we worked or visited. We were able to compare our observations with those of others who had reported similar problems and abuses in newspapers around the country. These examples are not isolated incidents, to be found only in a few substandard nursing homes; it is suggested from the startling fact that 80 percent of the nursing homes that receive public tax dollars do not meet even minimal federal standards" (Old Age: The Last Segregation, p. 80).

The way in which some old people are trapped by their physical condition is made apparent here. The book, incidentally, also makes many recommendations about alternatives that are available to older people. One, for example, is a modern trend toward providing services, both transportation and food services, for older people in their apartments so that they do not have to be relegated to a nursing home. Another alternative is in the whole social process of getting more people, especially young people, concerned about older people in order not only to help the older people but also to help young people confront the issues of aging and death so that they can find alternatives before they find themselves in the same situation.

This has been offered here simply as an example of a trapped situation. It is a fact for any who have visited old people that many have found life meaningless because they are cut off from the outside world, from relationships, from their loved ones, and so on. Others feel life meaningless because their life's meaning was wrapped up in their work, and at the point of retirement they felt themselves trapped by the fact that they could no longer work. In all these situations the trap is always two-edged: (1) what the persons themselves do to discover new alternatives and new choices and values that relate to their personal situation; (2) what society does in trapping them by ignoring such people.

Expanding the "Trapped" Concept

To expand our concept of trapped situations, let us look at the following statement from an article called "What Poverty Does to the Man," by Wilbert Coles:

"The mother of one child I am now studying—he is being bused from a ghetto school to a middle-class one—was recently told by inspectors from her city's welfare department that she seemed upset. 'He said my nerves are bad, and you can tell it by the way I shout at the kids. So I asked him what I was supposed to do. And he told me I shouldn't let the kids make so much noise, and I shouldn't have any more children— because I have too many already. I didn't dare answer him back;

he has the money, and I need the money, or we'd starve. Then my nerves would be even worse' " (Life at the Bottom, p. 117).

Here we have an example of economic poverty and therefore the trapped condition of the individual who has little money or material possessions. This woman is being trapped by a welfare inspector who is imposing his values on her. He is clearly telling her that she should treat her children in such a way that they will be quiet in school. He is also telling her that perhaps a lot of children should not be a value. This value imposition obviously runs contrary to the woman's own values.

She is therefore being trapped by the expectations of another person. Her trap is that if she were to "be herself" she would be against him, and he is the man who has the money for her food. This poor woman is being confronted with values that surround a whole area of survival. Again, we are at the level of choice and alternatives. One could hardly talk about art and music to the woman who needs food for her children. This kind of trap often renders life meaningless, for people then become "bored" with their children because they feel they have little power over them. They can become depressed through their frustration and anger at those authorities who trap them. It is no wonder that so many in such situations become apathetic, or, in other words, find life meaningless.

SPACE: SELF IN RELATIONSHIP TO OTHERS

It becomes clear as we talk about the relationship of self to others and self to self that normally the separation of these two is not in fact very real. Usually, the relationship between myself and other people is always there in some form or other.

There are many sources of the trapped condition in this relationship to self and others. The woman in the last example was trapped by her inner life and expectations of others. In addition, increased anxiety, or being treated as an object rather than as a person by the other, or an increased sense of powerlessness can increase the trapped condition in these relationships.

It is in this relationship that we see many of the things that were evident in the test in the last chapter, where it is so easy for people to categorize students as being this way or that way, or to make statements like "All black people are . . ." "All women are . . ." "Blue collar workers are . . ." This categorizing of other people is placing expectations on them that inevitably trap them.

Women in the Trap
Let's take an example of the problem of the categorization of women. In Robert W. Smuts' book, *Women and Work in America,* it is pointed out that women are, for the most part, discriminated against, particularly in the labor market. Women, for example, are concentrated in occupations which have a low wage structure. Women generally earn less than three-fifths as much as

men, even when the work is equal. Women account for about thirty-seven percent of all workers. In addition to this, most women who work are married and have children. An interesting fact is that the more education a woman has, the more likely she will be in the labor force rather than in the professional force.

With this in mind, the author looks toward some of the history of attitudes toward women and has the following to say:

> "There was wide disagreement, however, about the circumstances that justified a woman's going to work and about the particular jobs a woman might take. At one extreme, a great many Americans believed that no girl or woman should work unless compelled to by the absence of a male breadwinner, and that few jobs were appropriate for women. At the other extreme, a very small minority believed that every woman should be free to follow the career of her choice.
>
> "One may at least be certain, therefore, that changes in woman's work have been profoundly influenced by what people have thought and felt about work and about women" (Women and Work in America, p. 111).

The traps here are self evident. Women are laboring under the expectations of others—expectations which are formulated when a large mass of people, wittingly or unwittingly, assume a specific view of women which encompasses a series of demands that "a woman know her place." It is then that the problem begins.

Why is it a problem? Because people get angry when people do not come up to their expectations. That is another way of saying that people often impose values on women and trap them so that they are not free to work. When they do go to work, of course, they are discriminated against in such a way that they often cannot do what they want to do. The possibility is, then, that a woman, if she does not fit the image of those she has been brought up with or is living with, and is not a strong person who is able to make her own choices, will experience boredom and meaninglessness. That is why the women's liberation movement is important in that it is clarifying the possibility of women to make choices and helping them to see the alternatives that are open to them.

Powerlessness in Society and Personal Hopelessness

The feeling of hopelessness or meaninglessness that so many have in our society and which is on the increase is related, in the mind of many writers, to the increased feeling of powerlessness in our society. Charles C. Reich in *The Greening of America* addresses himself to this. He speaks a great deal about the idea of consumer man and the increased need to organize and make people functionary in our society. This is particularly true of people watching television each night and seeing war and mass disaster all over the world. The medium makes this very present to them and confronts them with many anxiety situations with which they would not be normally faced.

The media, then, have made life more trapping for some people. However, these same media represent a two-edged sword, in that they also make people aware of more options in their life. They reveal to us the variety of new job options, the possibility of mobility in occupation and living conditions, the reality of different life-styles. In every case, as a person sees these options, he may react either with creative choice or with a sense of powerlessness that comes from being overwhelmed by all those choices.

Some Causes of a Sense of Powerlessness

We might reflect for a moment on that sense of powerlessness which seems so widespread in today's society. Some of that sense comes from our inner condition, but some of it is also a result of an increased awareness of social forces which are so gigantic that the individual citizen simply has few resources available to him to counteract these forces.

One such example might be the increased awareness of the political and economic force of the military-industrial complex in modern America. Young people have been especially sensitive to this force in our lives; yet, even President Eisenhower voiced his concern about its influence. Seymour Hersh, in an article about germ warfare, gives some insights into how this force works in our lives:

"Dr. Matthew S. Melsosom, prize-winning Harvard biologist and C.B.W. (chemical biological warfare) expert for the U.S. Arms Control and Disarmament Agency, expressed the view of many prominent scientists when he told the Senate Foreign Relations Committee last April that '. . . the field testing of live biological weapons, and especially the outbreak of

actual biological warfare, would constitute a menace to the entire human species.'

"The Army tends to chalk up such strong sentiments to a kind of irrational, queasy emotionalism about C.B.W. The military is constantly frustrated by otherwise sensible people whose minds are closed on the subject; they just won't give nerve gas and germ warfare a chance. In 1959, the Army Chemical Corps, determined that ignorant prejudice should not stand in the way of progress, hired an outside public relations firm and launched 'Operation Blue Skies,' a program designed to get their side of the C.B.W. story before the American people. Dozens of articles were published in that year, emphasizing either the advances made by Russia or C.B.W. as a 'humane' method of warfare ('War Without Death' was the title of one Army-inspired article). The aim was not to raise the groundswell of bubonic plague, but merely to dull the edge of perfidy so that C.B.W. would no longer be unthinkable. The effort paid off: within the next four years, as the Kennedy Administration moved away from reliance on nuclear weapons to a quite military response, C.B.W. increased by 300 percent" (Divided We Stand, p. 107).

In this article, of course, we are reminded of the larger scene of man's trapped situation in relationship to total society and elements in that society such as government and the military. This relates very much to many people as they feel hopelessly trapped and unable as a consequence to feel that there is much they can do. The very enormousness of our society has this effect on many people.

Now, obviously, the forum for combatting such ideas might be one of the discussion of morality and what certain value priorities might be involved there. Another forum would be in the area of community and social action, political action, and so on. The only point in presenting this as an example is to give another example of the kind of things going on in our society that do make certain people feel hopeless and reduce their ability to feel that they have choices they can make.

In the same light, *Saturday Review* (November 13, 1971) had an article on the front cover by Peter Schrag called "The Ellsberg Affair." Part of the article read as follows:

"It is difficult to fully describe his act, or what it means, or where it will lead. Five months have passed and the ugly secret called the Pentagon Papers is now available in three different versions, one of them published by the government itself. The man who divulged the papers stands indicted for high crimes by the same government, and the war, the militarism and the deceptions go on."

The author goes on to say that Ellsberg fits none of the conventional patterns of dissent. He is not, for example, long-haired or a burner of draft cards, a signer of petitions, or a marcher. He is a man, says Schrag, who took it upon himself to "break the rules of the club." He is, as a result, something of a national hero.

We might conjecture that one of the reasons that Ellsberg is a national hero is that he chose to take a stand. One might easily conjecture that many people who regard their lives as trapped and meaningless would be able to identify with this person as one who had the courage to stand up against the totality of society as government. The same independence is evident as we look at pioneer man and movies such as those featuring James Bond. The identity of people is related closely to the person they see as free and independent compared with their own lives that are so often powerless and without choice.

SPACE: SELF AND WORLD

The Environment

The next two quotations are designed to help us explore a little or look at and reflect on the way an environment itself can be trapping to the human being. That is to say, the environment that man himself builds, the world that he modifies as his work, can in turn modify and trap him. The cruelties of industrialization and inhumanization in many of our large factories in the past and the rise of the unions, of course, are good examples of this. In the modern period, we might look at two quotations, the first from a book called *Cities in a Race with Time*. The following quotation is taken from a chapter called "The Dead Hand of the Past":

> "As almost every American knows, our cities are in serious trouble. More and more the local problems of cities have become the major domestic problems of the nation and a challenge to national policies as well. For an ever greater portion of our rapidly expanding population—nearly three out of every four Americans—and of our economic activities, too, is concentrated in metropolitan regions. Our urban centers must function better if the country is to prosper and our people to live well. In the next two decades, of the expected 50,000,000 more people who will be living in America, four out of five will live in cities. As President John F. Kennedy stated in 1963, in his historic proposal for a cabinet-level urban affairs department, 'We will neglect our cities at our peril, for in neglecting them we neglect the nation.'
>
> "There is not only the visible means we have inherited —vast areas built up in earlier eras—hastily, thoughtlessly, tastelessly, greedily constructed, or, even if once satisfactory, badly maintained over the years. Recently this neglect has been aggravated and urban obsolescence accelerated by enormous technological, social, and economic changes which have taken place at an unimagined pace in industry, on farms and in patterns of living" (Cities in a Race with Time, pp. 3-4).

There are few people living today who are not aware of the growing problem of cities. However, perhaps not too many are aware of the fact that cities are becoming an uncontrollable problem, with telephones breaking down and cars blocking highways, causing pollution, and making parking impossible. There are also increasing difficulties of gigantic growth in industry and business, making many people move out to the suburbs and therefore commuting many hours each week.

The environment itself with the incredible increase of population in the world is becoming more and more difficult to handle. Pollution is hemming people in and becoming so widespread that in many cities in this country people are beginning to develop eye problems and even difficulty in breathing in areas where the pollution is very high. The only point of all this is to state that in modifying his environment man has managed to trap himself with his environment. This is one more element that adds to the question of poverty and being trapped.

This becomes particularly evident and is well pointed out in the following quotation relating to Indian boarding schools.

> "Life at a federal boarding school is regimented and arbitrary. Seen from the air, many of the schools look like military installations. Complexes of one color, one texture buildings sit in the middle of otherwise barren areas. The impression of physical isolation mirrors the cultural isolation in the classroom. The building-complex usually includes dormitories (boys and girls), classroom buildings, and housing for the staff. Many of the buildings are in disrepair. In a number of places (Tuba City, Arizona, for example), condemned buildings are still in use. The Fort Wingate Elementary Boarding School uses old Fort Wingate, once commanded by Douglas MacArthur's father. Forty years ago, the Brookings Institution's Merriam Report declared this site unsuitable.
>
> "Even the new buildings are designed to reinforce the numbing sterility. Long, narrow, lifeless dormitories house row upon row of double-decker iron beds and little else. Windows are sometimes barred. Floors are bare; the vivid personal decorations that are so much a part of so many Indian communities are discouraged. Dress, too, is strictly regulated. The system makes individualizing one's appearance or .environment fairly impossible. Beneath all the regulation is the Bureau's implicit concept of the children: All Indians are alike" (Life at the Bottom, p. 146).

Here then is a vivid example of how man in modifying his environment has trapped himself by trapping others. In this latter example, we see how discrimination against Indians extended to their environment. That is to say, the people were seen as objects much as the buildings were. No consideration was given to the environment because no consideration was given to the persons. In trying to trap and control others in order to gain false security and control the future, man has trapped himself. As the article points out, if the environment is sterile and strict with control, so must the lives of the persons in that environment become sterile.

Environment then teaches us a lot about meaning in life. If the environment does not have within its structure the possibility of alternatives of choosing, then values and choice become impossible for the persons who live within its walls. Such an environment teaches persons that imagination is of little value.

There have been many persons in history and a few in our society whose visionary ability and expanded imagination have enabled them to be conscious of a larger element of space than self, others, and their immediate environment.

This awareness is one that enables a person to see life much more in its totality. It may be through particular creative skills in music or art, such as Van Gogh who saw the world in its totality differently through the use of paint. It might be the figure of a Teilhard de Chardin who saw the significance of the world related to the totality of the universe through the process of evolution. One could also mention St. Francis of Assisi or even, of course, the monumental figures like Guatama Buddha or Christ. These people became revolutionaries because their awareness was expanded beyond that of an average person.

The point here is that such persons often encounter a tremendous feeling of being trapped in their own lives. For example, Teilhard de Chardin had a great deal to say about evolution and its relation to religious life, but was never allowed to publish his works during his lifetime. He was trapped by his own religious denomination. St. Francis of Assisi became the new visionary person and gave new interpretation to the idea of poverty in religious life. As a consequence, he was rejected by his own order.

Why do such things happen? One obvious reason is that to have unusual visionary and creative abilities raises the expectations of people for that person. The more creative a person appears, the more is expected of him. Many creative people have become lonely and distant from society. Van Gogh is a good example of this, since he finally committed suicide. To become a visionary, to become aware of the greater dimensions of life, can trap the human being, since then he is responsible for what he has discovered.

Anxiety Rises With Creative Ability

According to Rollo May, as a person's creative ability increases, his anxiety rises and does not decrease. Why? Because the greater his creativity, the greater his ability to see alternatives, and therefore the greater his ability to fail. The greater the creativity, the greater the responsibility. Therefore, such people with their creativity are often confronting society with alternatives and possibilities that society did not want to act on. Their insight on a particular stance often has made people so guilty that they have turned on the visionary.

As an example in our own society we have Martin Luther King who had a new vision for black people in America. In the area of religions, of course, there is the death and crucifixion of Jesus Christ as the supreme example in the Western culture. Another example of a person who kept confronting people with their limitations and offering alternatives and who died as a direct result is Socrates of Athens. *The Cambridge Ancient History* says the following about Plato and his friend Socrates:

"The great memorial of Socrates is the body of Plato's works; no other man had a more wonderful monument. Having described the last moments of his master, Plato wrote, 'Such was the end of our friend, whom I must truly call the wisest, the most just, and the best of all men I have ever known.' In the study of his imagination, that revered master grew into the ideal figure of a perfect philosopher and as such passed into history. The tragedy changed the course of Plato's own life" (The Cambridge Ancient History, Vol. 5, p. 396).

Plato goes on to say that Socrates was brought into court by certain men who were in power. This was at the time of the fall of Athens to Sparta. They preferred against him a most wicked charge and one which was least applicable to Socrates of all men in the world. They accused him of impiety, and he was condemned and put to death. According to Plato's *Dialogues*, the main problem with Socrates appeared to be the fact that he raised questions about everything from God to justice. His main quest was to discover the truth because he himself had a more comprehensive vision of the totality of life and man's place in it.

It is curious that some four hundred years later in Jerusalem, in quite another culture, another man was also condemned for impiety and revolution. He was also a person who raised questions and had a cosmic vision of things. His name was Jesus of Nazareth.

The reason for this section was simply to point out that, in the whole area of value formation and choice, each area of space, whether it be self to self, to others, to the world, or to the cosmos, there are aspects of poverty and being trapped that all men experience. And even in the last example, where persons of great vision are involved, persons who have formed the values of civilization over the centuries—even they encountered the trapped condition of man.

Profiting from Poverty, Being Trapped and Meaninglessness

Ultimately, then, we might conclude that poverty and a trapped condition and ultimate meaninglessness have something positive to say to all people, namely that in their confrontation with anxiety and man's ability to look at his guilt as his limitation, meaning can be discovered even in the most trapped of conditions, that of the confrontation with death. (See Diagram V.) Therefore, meaning in people is found within. In this sense it is a confrontation with the self of the person. It is only as people find the ability to choose and act from within that they are able to confront society and environment in order that these may be changed to free others to become creative humanizers of the world's environment.

The way in which man modifies the world, the creation, to suit his needs is called work. The subject of work therefore must now be looked at in more detail. In the last section we have seen how work can be a trapped condition. On the other hand, work can also be a liberating experience. At this point, then, we need to look at its history and development and finally at its relationship to leisure.

Riesman, in his book *The Lonely Crowd,* makes a number of interesting comments about our cultural understanding of work. It is really essential that we reflect on that understanding of work if we are to see its place and the corresponding place of leisure in our value system. It is also interesting to note that our culture tells us something different about work than other cultures have.

It is Riesman's view that our cultural understanding of work is filled with ambiguities. It is seen as more important than leisure; yet work that is seen as more "playful" is seen to be more important. Work is seen to be essential in our production/consumer orientated society, yet it is viewed as being against the grain of man's nature. Man is essentially lazy, and work is the remedy to the weakness of his nature.

Because of this ambiguous cultural view of work, all sorts of confused judgments can result. Laziness, which might really be the result of man rejecting the type of work offered to him, is often labeled the result of his nature. Expense accounts and conventions, which are part and parcel of "playful" work, are still seen as work, while the efforts of a housewife are not seen as the efforts of a worker. As a result, she feels guilty about being tired at the end of the day, while her husband, who may have only worked for two hours at his machine, feels entirely justified to put his feet up and watch television every evening.

Linder has pointed out that along with this image which sees man as only being of worth when he is productive, many people feel guilty at recreation, at the idea of leisure. As a consequence, American man is known for the way that he "works at his leisure." He may well see building an addition to his house, fixing up the basement, continually maintaining equipment, washing his car, and so on as relaxation when often in fact they are work. Several people I know who have made additions to their houses are carpenters by profession. The additions are simply an extension of what they do during the week. In order to be successful and productive, the American family will often buy a house in the suburbs and spend two or three hours a day in addition to their work in traveling.

Work as a Struggle for Autonomy and a Productive Life

Work in this society is often related to the idea of the struggle for autonomy and for a productive life—the concept of pioneer man of Charles Reich, the independent Marlboro man, what Riesman calls the "inner-directed man," the person who is generally quiet, often dependent and always fighting for independence. That is to say, independence is the image of what he wants to be. But in reality he finds that productivity has made him a slave to consumer society and its ideal of work. He works for the shorter-hour day. He will often work long hours in travel, rest, or recuperation from his work.

Many people in our society, seeking to be like Riesman's inner man, often find human relationships difficult and tend to see that in terms of objective tasks to be accomplished. The inner-directed man, the pioneer, who had a possibility of being independent earlier in our history, is not very much of a possibility in our present day. This is especially true when his work has definite hours or shifts and has no responsibility beyond the eight-hour day. As a consequence, many of the workers, especially in the large plants, look to the end of the day as the beginning of their life. That is to say, it would appear that leisure is their goal.

The Other-Directed Man

Close to the organization man and to the marketed man of Fromm is what Riesman calls the other-directed man. Originally, and starting especially in the medieval period, the idea of crafts and guilds was utmost as a cultural development. Now, through the development of large organizations, there is more and more pressure in society toward social competence. It is close to what Toffler calls the ad-hocracy as against bureaucracy, the point being that there is an increased restriction on time, and as such there is no time for a long string of bureaucratic decisions. For this reason, people must move toward working together and working out their problems more quickly. The pressure then is toward social competence, with a concurrent playing down of technical competence.

It is also clear, as Rollo May has pointed out, that intimacy is an increasing problem in our society. Therefore, the other-directed life is often a phony one of partial human relationships. There is an increasing emphasis on selling and buying as a subjective rather than objective art.

One of the problems here is with persons who are trained in science. Many people who get degrees in science and engineering are placed in administrative positions because of their qualifications. As such the idea of craft has been taken away and they are often placed in roles where they are expected to have developed abilities in human relations which they simply do not have. As Fromm has pointed out, this is producing an alienated man who often feels continually guilty because of the discrepancy between what is expected of him in the area of productivity and what he feels capable of. As an engineer, he lacks ability in human relationships, yet is expected to be productive in the area of buying and selling of commodities as he relates to other people in the field.

Work as an Image

Work, then, is largely an image of our society as a productive necessity and a part of what man should be doing. It is often at the same time a burden and something that traps people by its intrinsic nature. This is a far cry from the artisan of the medieval period of which Erich Fromm speaks. That man was proud of his work and was a real creator. The historical development of the concept of identifying work and worth came about through the Industrial Revolution. Walter Kerr, in his book *The Decline of Pleasure*, points out that men like John Stuart Mill had a great deal to do with helping man to see his own value in terms of his own utility. As a matter of fact, men like Mill prepared people for the industrialization and organization of a society oriented toward productivity.

In addition to this, there was the pressure of the Protestant ethic where work was seen to be a part of the intrinsic nature of man. To be productive was a part of man's goodness and worth before God. However, at the time that this ethic developed near the end of the eighteenth century, people were still, to a very large degree, working on the land with their hands. There was still a feeling of working with creation. However, with the rapid movement of industrial society and the separation of man from the land, work came to be seen as duty and obligation.

Ultimate Conquest of the Machine

Beyond the idea of work and duty and obligation, we move historically into the ultimate conquest of the machine. We see this prefigured in literature in such stories as *Frankenstein* where a mindless machine monster controlled and destroyed man. In a recent television play, which was the adaptation of a story in *Playboy* magazine, Dennis Weaver played the part of a car driver in a story called "Duel." In the story, the hero, Weaver, is driving along the highway when he suddenly is threatened by a large truck which appears behind him. As the story proceeds, the truck driver forces him to drive his car at an increasing rate of speed and tries to kill him by driving him off the road. Finally our hero, in one last desperate attempt to save his life, drives his car toward the truck whose driver is trying to kill him. As the truck strikes his car, he jumps, at which time the car bursts into flames.

The truck driver does not try to escape from the truck but continues to drive the hero's car as well as the truck over a precipice, in a final act of destruction.

As the film surveys the wreckage, there is no sign of any driver in the truck. The story is one of machines. The duel has been between two machines. The power is in the machines. In the same way, the ultimate dehumanizing concept of work is that man is the one who does the work that the machine cannot do. The final horror of such a story is foreseen and depicted in movies like *2001,* where the machine, the computer Hal, has the possibility of becoming greater than man himself, and there is the further possibility that man will become useless.

Work primarily seen as duty and obligation and work seen as that which man can do and the machine cannot do are both based on the same premise. The concept of work here ultimately is that work is the worth of man; that work is man's primary value. It is this notion which writers like Pieper have taken great pains to challenge. We will be looking at this cultural view as we examine the concept of leisure.

FROM WORK TO LEISURE

Erich Fromm in a book called *The Sane Society* points out that several studies about job satisfaction have pointed out that approximately eighty-five percent of professionals and executives were satisfied with their work. This went down to sixty-four percent in regard to white collar workers and as low as forty-two per-

cent with semi-skilled workers. As we have noted, it would appear that the pre-industrial worker seemingly was more satisfied with his work than the industrial man of today. However, this is not really a fair comparison since, in fact, the pre-industrial worker did not have the opportunity as we do today of coming to grips with his own authority and freedom. He was for the most part under authority, and he accepted that condition. Also, the work which he did was with his hands and was work which he began and was able to complete. He had a real sense of affinity with the creation.

**Pre- and Post-
Industrial Man**

Pre-industrial man then was able to take very seriously the injunction given to him in the Western world, at least through the Church, in Genesis:

> *"Then God said, 'Let us make man in our image, after our likeness; and let him have dominion over the fish of the sea, and over the birds of the air, and over the cattle, and over all the earth, and over every creeping thing that creeps over the earth"* (Gen. 1:26).

Man: Alienated in an Industrial Society

That is to say, pre-industrial man took seriously the injunction that he was to rule the earth, and he did so by working it with his hands. Post-industrial man became separated from the earth, and through increase of industry and with the advent of the computer, man not only became increasingly involved in work where he only saw a minute of the problem, he often was not involved in the product at all. One such example would be the sales force who deal with a product without having anything to do with its creation.

In terms of man and his relationship to material things, life is increasingly such that man is separated from the machine and has less and less control over it. For example, if a machine breaks down in the house, often it consists of standard transistorized or factory-made parts that have to be replaced by an expert. Even if the house owner should be able to replace the part, he is not involved in understanding the machine. Many automobiles, for example, cannot be maintained without special tools. So it is that man is less and less able to be master of the machines and is as such less and less able to control the creation that he himself has created.

It is interesting that, from the point of view of the early states of Greece and Rome, this would be more than an ideal situation. For there the idea of man was to wander and talk in the market place and be concerned with the affairs of state. Manual labor was for the slave. The idea of that society, as expressed by writers such as Aristotle, was one of leisure.

Erich Fromm, moving close to this conclusion, has said that the problem has to do with the difference between the technical and social aspects of work. Taking first the technical, he has the following to say:

> "Starting with the discussion of the first instance (the technical) we find that there are many men who would, for example, take keen pleasure in being railroad engineers. But although railroad engineering is one of the highest paid and most respected positions in the working class, it is, nevertheless, not a fulfillment of the ambition of those who could 'do better.' No doubt, many a business executive would find more pleasure in being a railroad engineer than in his own work if the social context of the job were different. Let us take another example: that of a waiter in a restaurant. This job could be an exceedingly attractive one for many people, providing that its social prestige were different. It permits of constant interpersonal intercourse, and to people who like food, it gives pleasure to advise others about it, to serve it pleasantly, and so on. Many a man would find much more pleasure in working as a waiter than sitting in an office over meaningless figures, were it not for the low social rating and low income of this job" (The Sane Society, pp. 261-262).

This passage points very much to Fromm's concept of man as alienated in an industrialized society. It points to the problem of dissatisfaction and the struggle of man to "be himself," over against man being something for others. As we shall see a little later, man being himself is one of the integral definitions of leisure and as such can also be a part of work. Therefore, the idea of meaning as satisfaction is connected to the choice of man, and here man is often thwarted in his choice because he is competing with the expectations of other people.

He goes on to give an example of technically monotonous work being interesting—an experiment at the Chicago Hawthorne Works of the Western Electric Company. The work selected was that of assembling telephone cords, a repetitive work carried out by women. Five women workers were placed in a room which was separated by a partition from the main assembly room. There were six people in the room, five working on the bench and one distributing parts to those engaged in the assembly. It was noted that two of the women dropped out of the work at the end of the first year. The experiment lasted for five years. During that time rest periods were adopted in the morning and afternoon, with refreshments offered during these rest periods, and the hours of work in the day were cut by half an hour. As these changes varied, the output of the workers rose considerably. At a later part of the experiment, with the agreement of the workers, they returned to the earlier conditions of work where the rest periods and the refreshment were not present. To make a long story short, the work increased when other variations were introduced.

The startling thing, of course, was that apparently the experimental conditions did not vary or alter the output of the women; rather, the work output actually increased even though they returned to the original conditions. On further reflection it was discovered that the real reason for the increase was what Fromm calls the "social aspect" of work; it was this that had changed. As a result the attitude of the workers had changed. They were informed about the experiment and what was going to happen to them in the experiment, and their suggestions and ideas were listened to. They were allowed to participate. As such, they developed a sense of group participation. In addition, they discovered that sickness and fatigue decreased quite rapidly. In Fromm's terms, as the alienation of the worker decreased and social participation was increased, what he was doing became more meaningful to him.

Again in terms of the other things we have said, meaning then is related to choice, and meaninglessness is related to the lack of choice. It is to be noted, of course, that meaning increases rapidly as social participation is increased. Here, of course, a person's ability to choose and act is rapidly increased and some of his more basic needs are met, such as self-worth and being able to affirm the needs of others. The emphasis in this situation was placed on people "working together" and not on people working in order to gain material ends together, such as money. Ultimately, in this concept outlined above, there had been a shift in the value system from work as the end and means of production to work as participation and, in some sense, community.

Humanizing Values in a Profit-Centered Society

Undoubtedly, then, in many of the factories and large plants in our society there is a great deal of work being done in the area of human relations. Many plants such as the Polaroid Corporation are spending a great deal of money on human relations, trying to treat workers as creative people who would rather do a good day's work than just work meaninglessly with the point of view of obtaining a certain amount of money for given ends.

Paul Nash points out that the attempts to humanize people within the context of large companies fail in part because ultimately the value system of our society is production- and profit-centered. Therefore, ultimately the worker is always placed in a competitive relationship with other people. We are all very much aware of the incredible amount of money and technology that has been spent to convince society of the necessity to increase its material consumption. Therefore, the very basic fabric of society is production-orientated, and, as a result, it moves against the possibility of valuing the human being in a participative manner as Fromm describes. However, there are attempts being made to accomplish this.

More clearly, Reich and Revel point to the revolution in our society of expanded awareness where a great many people now are simply refusing to operate under these conditions anymore. People are becoming aware of the value system being imposed on them, and as a result they are trying to change this. The first step in this is to be able to make one's own choices by clarifying one's values and not to be continually and persistently dependent on the value choices of others and/or the expectations of other people. These struggles for new options that are being seen behaviorally in our society are reflected interestingly by Ron Roberts in a book called *The New Communes*, where he has the following to say:

> "Communalists, insofar as they are able to reject excessive materialism, come to see work as a gain. For that reason, they thrive on work which might be considered degrading to a more sophisticated individual. Hip hog farmers made a beautiful game out of the care and feeding of piglets. It was play. Other communalists raised chickens. They can tell you about Danish Brown Leghorns, Mottled Anconas, Silver Laced Columbians, Rhode Island Reds, or even Green-Sheen Black Langshands. The fact is that in a society of affluence, playing at work can produce enough for survival. The idea of work as a game means that, in a sense, hip communalists have regressed to childhood. Children play at work. In this way, the young communalists have given a new meaning to the biblical dictum that 'whosoever shall not receive the kingdom of God as a little child shall in no way enter therein'" (The New Communes, p. 135).

Now, obviously, such a way of life is not for everyone, but it does indicate a striving in our society for new forms of existence and new options to work and new seeking for meaning. It is a turning upside down of our value systems. The book *The Greening of America* spells this out in more detail in terms of the whole youth revolution which often seeks through rebellion, through the cop-out, or through other more creative methods to deal with the press of society, which would have them see productivity and competition as primary values.

Freedom and Work

An Experience. In speaking of freedom and work, Paul Nash points out that subjectively freedom can be seen as the relationship between an individual's desires and his capacities to fulfill those desires. Put in terms of values, this would be the relationship between what a person wants and his ability to choose and act on the life that he chooses. His incapacity may be related to his inability to face the roles, expectations, disappointments and failures of others, as well as his own anxiety about these things. One thing that value education can do in this area is to show people where their priorities are in fact.

An Exercise in Clarification

I have devised and used one such exercise with various groups, such as school administrators and workers in social agencies. The main point of the exercise is not really to tell anybody anything, but rather to help people clarify and discover where they are in a given situation.

Please look at Sheet 1. In this sheet we are taking as an example persons who see themselves in more than one work role. This originally was devised for school teachers working on a team relationship. The two roles that were seen in their team relationship were their teaching role and the administrative part of that role. We then brainstormed on the various aspects of their work. In the two columns on the sheet, one can see various aspects of the administrator and various aspects of the teacher in that particular job function.

SHEET 1

SELF I (Energy)

AS EDUCATOR	AS ADMINISTRATOR
Discipline Class preparation and paper correction Personal involvement with students Inter-faculty involvement Professional meetings Professional reading Parental involvement Teaching	Inter-faculty involvement Class supervision Liaison with school office Meetings with parents Finance Planning and organization meetings Student involvement Reports Correction and confrontation of unhelpful behavior of other teachers

SELF 2—Rank order EDUCATOR/ADMINISTRATOR and place on wall.

The first thing, then, is for you to make up your own sheet. First choose a word that describes your job role. This could be housewife, engineer, etc. Secondly, try to see whether you have more than one role in your job, for example, the above example of administrator and educator. Or perhaps you have the dual role of minister and educator. The point is that many people have various roles in their work. Once you have picked your job role, whether it be a single job role or two job roles as above, then brainstorm and come up with a list of words that explains all the different things you do in your job. Sheet 1 is an example of this.

Next turn to Sheet 2. If you had more than one job role on your original sheet, pick the one that was most important to you. For example, if you had educator and administrator, choose which was the most important, the educator or the administrator. If you picked the administrator first, then choose four functions from that list and two from the second list, and place them on Sheet 2. If you only had one list, then pick six words from that list and place them on Sheet 2.

SHEET 2

SELF 3

Take four priorities from Category 1.
Take two priorities from Category 2.
Rank order them.

Having done the latter, now rank in order of priority six words in terms of the amount of energy you spend on each word function you have listed. What is meant by the amount of energy is for you to decide.

Remember that this is a kind of a game to help you clarify where you are. Try not to get too anxious about the game, but do it in a spirit of openness, and if there are certain things you think should be included, then add them. At this point, I would like you to consider as a working possibility that your work time is an eight-hour day. Consider, then, that what you have above adds up to an eight-hour day. At this point, I suggest that you simply reflect on your priorities in terms of the way you utilize them energy-wise.

Please now turn to Sheet 3, which is designed to help you to see the extensiveness of work and what it means. On the sheet you will notice several words, like recuperation from work, rest alone, rest with others, and so on. The point I am making is simply that all these activities are really an extension of my work. That is to say, work is not only what I do during that eight-hour period of time.

SHEET 3

SELF (TOTAL LIFE) 4

Given your normal work day as eight hours, or one unit, put down the amount of time relative to your work day that you spend on the following:

THIS TIME IS BEYOND THE EIGHT-HOUR DAY

EXTRA WORK	TIME

1. Other work
2. Recuperation from work
   a. alone
   b. with others
3. Rest from work
4. Worry about work
5. Preparation
6. Liturgical prayer	

On the first word in the column under work, put only the amount of hours that you work per week beyond the eight-hour day. That is to say, if you work at another job or if there are other things that you do in your job so that you end up working more than an eight-hour day, then place those hours per week in that top column.

Next look down the column and delete any of those things that are not applicable to you. Some people simply do not worry about their work, but forget about it. Other people simply do not engage in recreation to get over work or do not need to rest when they get home. Depending on who you are, the emphasis will vary. Therefore, delete anything that is not applicable. In addition to this, there are other forms of work that you do—for example, maintenance of your car, or travel time. Or there may be other things that you do around your house that you really don't like but are required to maintain your house and are not really leisure for you, such as working on the plumbing or whatever. Add to the bottom of the list any additional things that you would consider to be work and not leisure.

Once you have done this listing of what you think are more or less the hours that you spend on each activity, rank the list in order, with the thing with the highest time priority at the top of the list and the thing with the lowest time priority at the bottom of the list. This should say something about where your values are in terms of work.

You might reflect on this or even discuss it with some friends or the class or wherever you are using this exercise. You might like to raise questions from the list in terms of what work

SELF (TOTAL LIFE) 5

Time rank the following:

TOTAL LIFE BEYOND OFFICIAL WORK	TIME
1. Work beyond work (time from Sheet 3) *2. Leisure alone* *3. Meditation* *4. Rest* *5. Time with friends* *6. Recreation* *7. Developmental study and reading* *8. Community obligations* *9. Liturgy*	

**Clarification:
Illuminating the
Pressures of Work**

means to you. Are you satisfied with your work? What is it about work in terms of this list that is disturbing or enlightening to you, a discrepancy between what you would like to do and what the list is telling you that you are doing?

What this clarification should do is help you to see where the pressures in terms of work are on you and where some of the discrepancies might be.

Clarification exercises such as this have raised a number of issues. People who find that they have an excessive worry factor in their work are confronted with the possibility that they are in the wrong type of work and should perhaps consider a change in terms of their life-style and value orientation. Other people who are confronted with this feel that they need to place more emphasis on the type of leisure that takes them away from work and helps them to get away from the expectations of others and relax. High worry often occurs because of a lack of structured or creative leisure life.

Other people who work heavily in manual labor have found that they should rest afterward, instead of watching television, for example. Others have discovered that, because of travel time and maintenance (things they never really had examined), they were often tired, and where they were living was not really well situated in terms of where they were working. For others, nothing in the list would be particularly new.

Human Work. As we have seen, one of the problems in our modern society is man alienating himself from his work and from the machine. Often, it is difficult if not impossible to be able to see alternatives because man is overwhelmed by the trapped condition of the situation. Life becomes meaningless to him. Many people are unable to choose the work that they would want because of education. Others find a type of work impossible to choose because they feel it is not up to certain social standards. This is true especially of professionals. They are unable to choose their own direction, but rather are reliant upon the expectations of others. If we fail to fulfill these expectations, we are again confronted with the issue of anxiety and guilt.

Education in Work

What is apparent is that if work is to become meaningful to people then education in what work means must be a part of the educational system. In this way a person can become a man who is a worker rather than a man who is alienated from himself through his work. In talking about this, Paul Nash points to the fact that the difference between vocational and university education will have to disappear in the future if the lines of discrimination causing the kind of expectation problems that Fromm talks about are to be eliminated. Secondly, he asserts that education in work needs to come to grips with helping people to see what work means in terms of the total life pattern and how the choice of alternatives can be possible with that person's given limitations. Education and the productivity of education in terms of how many degrees I have should not be the sign of a person's worth. Rather, a person's worth should be in terms of who he is, his limits being seen as an enhancing and creative aspect of the personality and not one that causes him problems of expectation and discrimination.

Education in work should also be education in teaching people the ability to choose and act out of their own life-style. It should be education in the possibility of real values being formed in a human being. Therefore, to truly be able to work where work is a humanizing factor means that the person must be human. The degree to which he is human is the degree to which work becomes a possibility in its more creative form. Why? Because as I become human, I am able to make my own choices outside of the limits of the expectations of others. I can discover the kind of work and pattern of life that is meaningful to me. We need more people in society who are willing to do menial tasks because it enhances their human development, even though they may be well-educated. We need people who can turn down the value of productivity and see the value of being themselves as primary and important to their existence.

Education in the meaning of work and its relationship to life is especially pertinent in terms of aging people who are facing retirement. After people whose total life has been orientated to work (as their value) retire, they feel that their life has ended, and they often die much sooner than they need to.

Rehumanization of Work

What we are talking about here is the rehumanization of work, as spoken of by Paul Nash in the following quotation:

"Then on the personal level, the individual worker must be helped to recapture a sense of wholeness and purpose in his work. Education, both in the school and in the factory, can contribute here by consciously striving to show the connection between the individual's work, the total product, the industrial en-

deavor and the whole life of society. The differences in moral and creative energy between purposeful and purposeless activity are immense. Sir Richard Livingstone wrote to Alfred North Whitehead that to him the most significant sentence in Whitehead's Aims of Education *was the one that said that the common man's need is to be convinced of the importance of the work he is doing. There is a vital educational task waiting to be done in helping the worker become aware of what Douglas Steere has called the* **'frame of meaning'** *of his work''* (Authority and Freedom in Education, pp. 37-38).

LEISURE AS ENVIRONMENT

To first put this into context, we must complete our section on work. What then is work? Our first definition might be: Work is man modifying his environment. At this first level we might imagine primitive man standing in a rain forest. He needs to protect himself from the elements and he needs to keep himself warm. He needs to fashion instruments with which he can kill animals to gain food. Man at this point modifies his environment in order to survive. The most primitive level of work then is modification of the environment for the purpose of survival.

Soon man begins to modify the wider aspect of creation. He takes materials and builds a house and so protects himself even more completely by placing fences outside of his house— fences to keep away animals and fences to keep away man. Man is thus protecting himself from himself. At this point work is still a modification of the environment for the purpose of survival.

As we move into the development of civilization, which, incidentally, Kenneth Clark identifies as that process where man becomes human, we discover other elements entering into the environment. The most obvious one is the development of art. It is an exercise of pure leisure which really has no direct practical application, especially in the life of survival. The possible exception to this might be the production of carved images of gods. As man built houses and premises for himself, he began to make himself comfortable within them. As man protected himself from the elements through clothing, he found clothing becoming more and more ornate. We begin to see the toga of Rome, often indicating a person's place in society. We see ornate, embroidered clothing of the eighteenth century. We thus begin to see the idea of primary values emerging, in particular the value of self-worth.

Work now has begun to mean the modification of the environment for the purpose of giving man a sense of self and his own value. The activity of hunting, the Viking long ships as a primitive architecture of survival, the cathedral building and the corresponding sense of security and stability—all of these enabled man to define himself and his worth in unique and different ways. We see the emergence of the idea of woman and the development of the cult of the virgin of the medieval period. Kenneth Clark points to the individual development and recognition of man as an individual in the following way:

> "The dazzling sight of human achievement represented by Michelangelo, Raphael and Leonardo da Vinci lasted for less than twenty years. It was followed (except in Venice) by a term of uneasiness, often ending in disaster. For the first time since the great thaw, civilization's values were questioned and defined, and for some years it looked as if the footholds won by the Renaissance—the discovery of the individual, the belief in human genius, the sense of harmony between man and his surroundings—had been lost. Yet this was an inevitable process, and out of the confusion and brutality of sixteenth-century Europe, man emerged with new faculties and expanded powers of thought and expression" (Civilization, p. 139).

We see then an emergence of values in man as well as an emergence in his awareness. We cannot but help comparing the serenity of the Virgin in many of the medieval paintings with the concurrent development of the stability and founds-rooted cathedrals of Europe. As we move into the Reformation period with all the upheavals and violence in Europe, we see the development of a different sort of art. An example would be Albrecht Durer, who was very famous for his use of woodcuts at the time of the development of printing in Europe. An interesting painting of

Durer is that by Oswald Krell. It is a portrait of uncertainty; it is a painting of a young man whose eyes are filled with anxiety and a sense of discomfort—something quite different from the magnificence and optimism found, for example, in Michelangelo. In our terms, it is man confronting his environment and expanding his awareness.

The Age of Industrialization and Man's New Consciousness

Finally, then, we reach the age of industrialization in the modern period. Working man emerges with a new consciousness and the possibility of choosing his own alternatives, an option now expanded to a larger class of people. At least in the modern period, there are a number of professional people who think they can begin to choose their own life and work direction. University and education is opening up for a great many people.

It was during this period that the idea of work involved religious thought and philosophy, and such people as Mill and Jevons made work move toward the concept of work as duty and obligation. Walter Kerr in a book called *The Decline of Pleasure* points out that Jevons was the man who made the unqualified pronouncement that "value depends entirely upon utility."

Thus it seemed that work again would take over man. As our society became industrialized, the need to consume became evident in order to produce more work. As a result, production and consumption became the obsession of the society, developing such concepts as the organizational man and the alienated marketed man of Fromm. Here, then, we see work as modification of the environment for the enhancement of the worth of man, in terms of duty. This developed a sideline which began to sense work as that which the machine cannot do, the ultimate and dehumanizing factor of work and man.

Work for Self-Enhancement and Creative Growth

Yet in the midst of this movement and the compulsive nature of our society, man has produced a great many things that have little to do with self-worth or survival. There is his art, his philosophy about nature and his existence, his seeking for new worlds, as in space travel. There is development of the human growth movements and talk of spirituality and greater growth. These factors are still the creations of environments. Men are employed in full-time work for the betterment of the human race —the United Nations, the immense role of social work in our society, in the medical profession and so on. Work here is seen as the *modification of man's environment for the purpose of self-enhancement and creative growth*. Finally, then, work is related to the development of man *himself*.

Leisure Determines Work

It is at this point that we are reminded of Fromm's distinction between the technical and social aspects of work. We need then to look at the concept and idea of leisure. My hypothesis at this point is the following: *Leisure determines work in its maximum condition*. The maximum condition here would be work as a concept of modification of the environment not only for the survival of man, but also for giving him a sense of self-worth so that he may enhance the self-worth of others and develop the maximum creative potentiality of man himself.

Leisure. What is leisure? Probably the most well-known work on this is that of Josef Pieper in a book called *Leisure—The Basis of Culture,* in which he points out that in the Western world, especially from the time of Aristotle, leisure has been the basis of culture and not work. The ultimate purpose of work for these early writers was for the purpose of leisure. We see this often in the blue and white collar workers who, though living in a society of compulsive work, also often work for the purpose of 5 o'clock or whatever time it is they finish work. Their work is boring to them, and they often work for the purpose of relaxation afterward.

Leisure: In a Timeless Environment

Leisure, says Pieper, is not so much an activity as it is a mental and spiritual attitude. He points out that it is not simply the result of external environment: "It is not the inevitable result of spare time, a holiday, a weekend, or a vacation. It is, in the first place, an attitude of mind, a condition of the soul, and, as such, utterly contrary to the ideal of the 'work'."

The idea here is that when work is seen in terms of activity, leisure becomes an attitude of non-activity, of inner calm or silence. From my point of view the difference between working and leisure at this point is that leisure is in a timeless environment. Work, on the other hand, is something that we usually do within the given limits of certain time and goals. Work has a particular goal normatively, done within a given work span. Even if I am working for myself, I am expected to accomplish so much in a certain amount of time if I am to stay in business.

Leisure, on the other hand, is an attitude of mind which is out of time and, as such, removes itself from the expectations of others. A leisure activity, then, is one where a person is not expected to do anything in that given period of time, but rather can be himself. We now then have two aspects of leisure: (1) an activity which takes place out of time; (2) an activity where I can be myself, and am not restricted by time, specific goals, or the expectations of others.

Another element of leisure that Pieper points to is the element of happiness. He asserts that this happiness is concerned with a growing awareness of the mysteriousness of the universe and a recognition of our incapacity to understand it. He goes on to say that it also is concerned with a confidence and a trust in things.

There are several things implied in what Pieper is saying. The first is that leisure concerns an activity with which we are happy and which confronts us with our limitations. Yet we have trust and confidence to accept that. Secondly, there is the implicit affirmation of the reality of choice and alternatives in leisure. Leisure then, for Peiper, is very close to the idea of the process of valuing. Therefore, leisure has to do with a growth process toward authentic human life.

We then have two elements that define the nature of leisure: (1) it is something that I am happy with and which confronts me with my limitations (in other words, leisure becomes a celebration of my limits); (2) it has the implicit notion of my choosing from alternatives.

An Attitude of Celebration

Leisure also involves an attitude of celebration. Pieper calls it "an attitude of contemplative celebration." Next he points out that leisure is different from work as a social function. This is another way of saying that it takes one away from time and from expectation, as we have already noted. (See Diagram VI.)

Harvey Cox, in *The Feast of Fools,* speaks extensively of the need of fantasy in our lives as an integral part of leisure. At this point, we see leisure as related to the future as a part of the creative imagination. It is also at this point that leisure relates to

DIAGRAM VI

WORK AND LEISURE COMPARED

	Being	Relationship to Time	Consequences
L E I S U R E	To "Be" Relaxed Creating Fantasizing Celebrating Relating In a freeing Environment	Relating "Out of time" Timeless Environment Goals are Process- Orientated, **not** Production-Orientated	Loving being Hoping Dreaming Caring Freeing Non-Manipulative life-style (Max.)
	↓	↓	↓
	*Leisure determines work in its maximum condition*		
W O R K	To "Be" and To "Do" In a particular Environment	Relating: "In specific time" Specific goals Productive	Limited Action Modifying Creating ⟩ World Producing Freeing Environment

the idea of the possibility of man choosing a multiplicity of alternatives after considering the consequences. The bad consequences would be related to the idea of fearful things in the imagination. (See Diagram II.) We then see in Diagram II how leisure relates in time to the future through imagination. It relates, through proposed alternatives, to the development of an imagination which offers freedom and options to a person.

Freedom To Be Oneself

Next, leisure is the freedom to be oneself. It is something that seems increasingly difficult to achieve but is also more and more necessary in a mechanistic society such as ours. Here we see leisure as again related to time through the past. Why? Because in order to be oneself, a person must face his values and priorities and in particular his limitations.

In facing one's limits, one is not trapped by the guilt-anxiety cycle that we spoke of. As people are trapped by their own guilt, their anxiety increases and they are trapped by expectations of others and so on. An integral part of leisure, as being oneself, then, is the freedom to be able to choose in a celebrated environment that itself militates against the possibility of meaninglessness. When I can face my limits, be myself, and live in a world of creative imagining, meaning becomes evident to me. Sunday supplements for years have trumpeted the growing awareness of leisure arising from the shorter work week. Usually, however, leisure is there defined in terms of having things to do and places to escape to.

Leisure lies properly not in the context of escaping (although this can be necessary at times for anyone), but rather in the idea of being an authentic person in whatever you are doing, whether this be work or recreation. Leisure denotes a stance toward life in which the person is able to live freely in the context of his own values.

It is immediately apparent that to adopt an artificial world is both anti-leisure and anxiety-provoking. To play a role is to play into the expectations of others. At that point, we are not self-directed, but directed by others, causing exaggerated anxiety and feelings of guilt.

It is evident as we proceed that as we remind ourselves of the definition of a value:

1. it must have been chosen freely;
2. it must have been chosen from alternatives;
3. it must have been chosen after careful consideration of the consequences of each of the alternatives;
4. the person choosing must be happy with the choice and be willing to affirm it publicly;
5. the choice is celebrated by confronting the limitations that confront the human being;
6. it must have been acted upon;
7. it must be acted on repeatedly and become a pattern of life.

The above, as we have noted before, is not only a definition of what a value is but is more properly a definition of how one goes about choosing priorities in a person's value ranking. This has to do directly with the whole question of growth and identity. The first three, concerned with choice, relate to the future and imagination. The second two relate to the past and the idea of celebration. The last has to do with acting in the present.

What this means is that the attitude of a person evolving from that person being conscious of the valuing process is directly related to what we call leisure. It is a stance toward life that considers my choice, my value, and the value of others as being of primary importance, because if I believe in the valuing process for myself, then naturally I am going to believe in it for others. This would mean creating a freeing environment whereby others could also form their own values, make their own choices, and discover their own priorities.

Leisure as an Environment

Leisure then is an attitude or a stance toward life in which values can be chosen. That is to say, leisure is an environment. At this point, then, let us try to define leisure and describe that environment.

1. TO BE ONESELF. Leisure is an attitude toward life. It is the experience of self that is free, at least for a fleeting moment. It is a non-activity complete in itself, not to produce anything or to fulfill one's needs. It is a serenity where I know my limitations and my worth simultaneously. It is then a situation where I can say what I want, swear as much as I wish, express my thoughts, shout and scream, love my friends, laugh and cry, express my anxieties, hopes, aspirations, without feeling the pressure and fears of anxiety and failure either within myself or from the expectations of others. Being oneself, then, is being in an environment where expectancy does not press upon me.

Related very closely to this concept of being oneself is the question of intimacy. Intimacy is defined as *"the ability to express my deepest aspirations, hopes, fears, anxiety, and guilts to another significant person repeatedly."* This definition of intimacy is of course related to the valuing process. As such it should be chosen freely and one should be happy with it. Does everyone need this kind of intimacy all the time? The answer is: No, not necessarily, but most people do sometimes. If I have received enough intimacy in my life, then I probably do not need that much intimacy presently. I may have become a self-sufficient person in the sense of knowing my worth and being able to affirm the worth of others without that kind of support.

The freeing environment of being able to express those things that I need to express can only be done with persons whom I trust deeply. Social parties that have a business emphasis, therefore, are not acts of leisure because of the problem of expectation. Acts of leisure, fiestas, and parties that are leisurely have to be ones where free expression of myself can be possible.

264

It is here that Cox points out juxtaposition as a part of the ingredients of festivity. It is that act so opposite that it tears me away from the expectation of others and allows me to become who I am.

To extend the idea of intimacy, the question has often been raised: Do I need to be intimate with everyone? Many, especially those who are striving for love and affection in the world as an ideal, find this a difficult question. I often find that priests and religious feel that they should love and be honest with all people. It is at this point that I offer a working definition of what I call social intimacy—the kind of intimacy that is freeing to myself, but is within the limits of a social context, where to "spill my guts"—to use a sensitivity expression—is both naive and unreal, as well as damaging.

Social Intimacy

In such a situation, social intimacy can be described as *the ability to express my feelings, hopes and aspirations and difficulties just a little more deeply than the person with whom I am in conversation.* The point here is that I am willing to open myself for the cause of authenticity, growth, and freedom a little more for the next person. If that next person is unable to reciprocate because of his limitations, because of where he is, I do not impose this attitude as a value upon him, but I rather allow him to be free within the situation in which he finds himself. The idea of expressing myself a little more with the other person means just that. It means simply to share myself to a degree which is acceptable to the other person.

The main point of being oneself within the context of a society In which we are and in which we live is the one of being able to turn away from the impositions and expectations of media, people with whom I work, people who look up to me and see me as a need in themselves, and so on. This being oneself is a necessity because it is of itself a recreative act that rejuvenates and allows me therefore to do my maximum in my work environment. In this sense, we say that leisure maximizes the possibility of work.

We might finish this section by using the following quotation on recreation from Walter Kerr:

> "Armed attack will get us nowhere, which is why the party that everyone tries to make 'go' is the party that will leave everyone's nerves shattered and why a determined evening of quiet with a rewarding book will so often undermine its rewards and make the quiet intolerable in direct proportion to the vigor of its determination. We cannot ourselves create what recreates us. We can only lay ourselves open to friendly invasion, aware that we are subject to the most extraordinary impressions of pleasure and equally aware that the visitation comes from without, touching the within of its own volition" (The Decline of Pleasure, p. 230).

The latter concept of recreation and the concept of being oneself lead us into the second portion of the definition necessary for the understanding of leisure.

2. LEISURE AS A TIMELESS ACTIVITY. Obviously, anything we do is within the scope of time, so that by timeless we are speaking more of the unawareness of its presence during the leisure activity. This is in direct contrast to work, which is normatively something that we do with a great deal of consciousness of time. For example, we may be very conscious of what product we will produce in a given period of time, what time I punch in at work and what time I leave, what time the lunch breaks are, and so on. In leisure, a person forgets the time element, even if it is only for a fleeting moment. This might be illustrated by a dream that I had several years ago.

In the dream I was a prisoner of a dark race of people. It seemed that I was in some South American country and that it was very hot. The buildings were stone buildings, made of sandstone and only one story high. It was a small village that I was in, and at one end of the village there was a sandy, rocky area with a treepost in the middle of it. I was taken by several men into a hut and chained to the wall. A man with a kind face came in, stood before me and said, "I'm sorry but you are going to be shot. Your crime does not permit us any other alternative but that you be taken to the end of the village and placed before a firing squad."

I was taken out and dragged to the end of the village. I was of course full of fear. Finally two men tied me to the post, and as I looked up straight ahead of me I saw six men with rifles. My life was about to end, and nothing more could be accomplished. I was defeated.

Suddenly the air became alive. I became conscious of a breeze in my face even in that awful heat. The sky seemed a brighter blue. The clouds suddenly took on interesting shapes and forms. I was aware of the perspiration on my head, but now instead of being annoying it became interesting—even its taste. In the distance, but vaguely, I heard a sound, "Attention! Get ready!" I was asked if I wanted to be blindfolded, and I said no. I looked around and then at the ground. The small grains of sand became interesting variations of crystal formations. In the middle of the grains of sand a white pebble, suddenly magnificent, became beauty in itself. Strange that I had never noticed these things. And then as if a new world had been introduced, a centipede moved, meticulously searching among the sand. Like a perfect machine each leg moved in harmony and perfect sequence, enhancing the creation around it.

In the dream the firing squad never did shoot, but laid down their arms and went away. The incredible thing about the dream was that in my normal day-to-day life I suddenly became more sensitive to things I had seen in my dream—new life around me, the details and so on.

In the dream the person in front of the firing squad only had a second or two but became aware of the danger and entered into a timeless world. That is to say, he entered into the realm where a great deal was seen and heard, but the person was not aware of the time that was in fact pressing upon him. It is in this sense that we say that leisure is timeless.

The idea of the timelessness of leisure relates directly to the idea of expectation. It is in this that the person lives without the pressure of expectancy of others upon him or her. The person is torn away and is free for the moment at least.

Thus intimacy would relate very much to this and to being oneself, because to be oneself one has to be torn away from the expectancy of another and be in an atmosphere of acceptance rather than expectation.

Leisure: Time Passing as a Fleeting Second

Leisure then is the kind of festival or party where I am so involved in the environment which is freeing to me that the time passes as a fleeting second. I am not aware of it. This is why so often television cannot be a leisure experience, because it is often destroyed by the emphasis on time, broken up by advertisements and the expectancy within those advertisements that you buy this or that, or do this or that, or be this or that image. Related to this timeless element is the attitude of being with another totally at a given moment. How often can we be with another person in a way where time and expectations are foreigners intruding? It is a rare event for most people.

The leisurely person is one who can be present to others with more of his total being than is normatively possible because he is aware of the need to be separate from others' expectations and to forget time occasionally.

Anyone who has children knows how often it is not the amount of time that we spend with them that is so important but the quality of the relationship. Frequently, parents who cannot control or have a decent relationship with their children will tell me they spend a great deal of time with them, that they cuddle them, play with them and so on. Such relationships often are superficial because the person is not in a timeless relationship, so he can give himself totally without worrying about outside expectations. Children who are very sensitive naturally realize this from the start.

3. TO CREATE A FREEING ENVIRONMENT. This part of the definition of leisure follows naturally from the first two parts. For the person who can be himself and let go of time and expectation can free others to be themselves by his or her very attitude. As Pieper points out, leisure is an attitude. Therapeutically it would be an attitude of acceptance. In the wider dimension it is the attitude that creates the freeing environment.

The Proper Environment

It is the attitude of mind that permits other people to be themselves. It is the place where I know that I can say or do anything and no one will be shocked. The environment could be one of silence or one of prayer or one of being with my children. We must remember that many live in impossible environments, such as war areas, prisons and hospitals, or in low economic conditions. We need to help people by creating new environments, both an environment of inner space which is one of freeing attitude, and also one of outer space which militates against trapping conditions of poverty. In contrast to that, we mentioned earlier in this chapter how people in Indian schools were dehumanized and restricted by the very architecture and nature of the buildings in which they lived. They had none of their own cultural amenities present, which meant that they were trapped not only by the buildings but within another culture.

Edward T. Hall speaks about the relationship of buildings to the person in an interesting article called "The Anthropology of Space":

"Fixed-feature space is one of the basic ways of organizing the activities of individuals and groups. It includes material manifestations as well as the hidden, internalized designs that govern behavior as man moves about on this earth. Buildings are one expression of a fixed-feature pattern, but buildings are also grouped together in characteristic ways internally according to culturally determined designs. The layout of villages, towns, cities, and the intervening countryside is not haphazard but follows a plan which changes time and culture.

"Even the inside of the Western house is organized spatially. Not only are there special rooms for special functions— food preparation, eating, entertaining and socializing, rest, recuperation, and procreation—but for sanitation as well.

"Actually the present internal layout of the house, which Americans and Europeans take for granted, is quite recent. As Philippe Aries points out in Centuries of Childhood, *rooms had no fixed functions in European houses until about the eighteenth century. Members of the family had no privacy as we know it today. There were no spaces that were sacred or specialized. Strangers came and went at will, while beds and tables were set up and taken down according to the moods and appetites of the occupants. Children were dressed and treated like small adults. It is no wonder that the concept of childhood and its associated concept, the nuclear family, had to wait until the specialization of rooms according to function and the separation of rooms from each other. In the eighteenth century, the house altered its form. In France **chambre** was distinguished from **salle**. In English, the function of a room was indicated by*

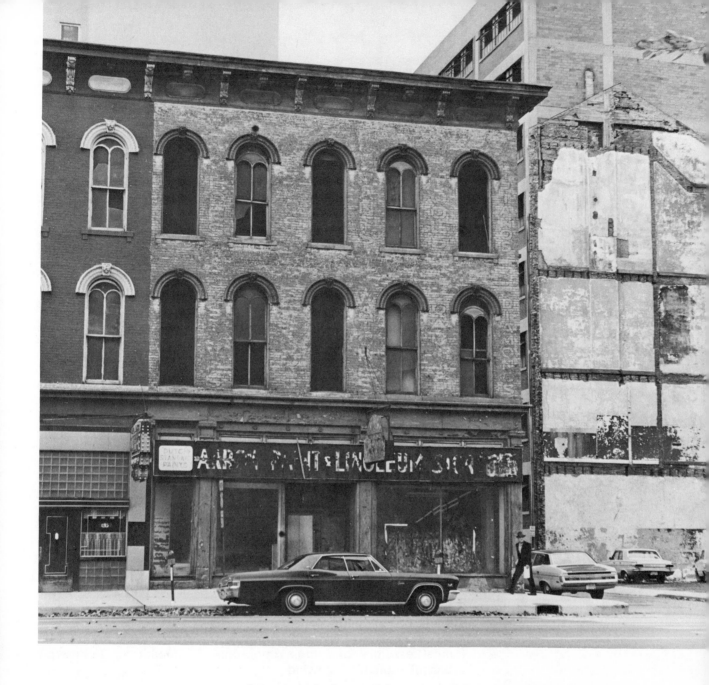

its name—bedroom, living room, dining room. Rooms were arranged to open into a corridor or hall, like houses into a street. No longer did the occupants pass through one room into another. Relieved of the Grand Central Station atmosphere and protected by new spaces, the family pattern began to stabilize and be expressed further in the form of the house" (Environmental Psychology, pp. 16-17).

Hall goes on to mention that the fact that most business-men in this day and age do not have businesses in their houses is not simply a matter of convention but rather of the need to stabilize life, work, and leisure. It is an effort to keep home and office separate. The same efforts can be seen in the design and use of a kitchen. If space is interfered with in the kitchen, it can often cause a great deal of difficulty in homes. Therefore, the size of the kitchen is often very important to the housewife.

Cities: Creators of Strangers

Hall then asserts that uniform patterns within cities often make people within cities strangers to one another. Another excellent example of this is as we move from the house into the school and see the difference manifested by the so-called open school plan of some of the more modern schools, where partitions can be moved, where various classes are held in a large space within which there are multiple movable walls and furniture, and where the child actively participates. This can be compared to the classroom arrangement where the desks are all in a row and the teacher stands at the front and hands out information to the child.

Obviously different values are operating in those varied environments. The point of all this is that the external environment, even as basic as the building itself, can be freeing or trapping to an individual. This is evident, of course, to people who have worked in the dreadful slums of the world, whether in New York, Latin America, or India. The nature of the buildings, with small, cramped rooms possessing few if any facilities, little or no private life, and so on, can be depriving and dehumanizing for the persons living there.

Discovering New Environments

On the social level, we need to discover new environments that will help people to be liberated from themselves. The basic idea would be that the external environment would discover and help the person seek new alternatives in an environment which would permit experimentation with the alternatives that he would have. Of course, the other side of this has to be the need to also be able to discover internal environments. The discovery of a new internal environment which is freeing needs the development of the imagination which we spoke of earlier and which will come as the next definition in our look at leisure. However freeing, environments of the internal sort have also been attempted by man as he works with other people. The most basic way, of course, is the therapeutic model—the idea of counseling and group therapy in many of our group settings in clinics and hospitals. This is also being attempted in varying degrees in our schools, where it is most essential and most important. A student at Summerhill School wrote the following:

> "It is different from other schools. I came from a secondary modern, and it's just like coming out of the dark into the light.
>
> "The whole idea of the thing is different. The lessons are different. Summerhill isn't based on trying to make you learn, trying to make you learn your mathematics. . . .
>
> "It's trying to make you learn about life, a community. You learn from the community, you learn from the meetings, you go through your own little experiences . . . which work out. The whole idea is to be yourself but not to interfere with other people's ideas and what they're learning about and doing. You can be yourself as long as you don't annoy other people" (Neill and Summerhill, p. 4).

Wish good fortune for your children and the children of Mercy Hospital

Rub his Nose—
Drop a Coin

4. TO DREAM AND FANTASIZE. The next two aspects of leisure that we shall be talking about, namely dreaming and fantasy, are the past and future in our schema being brought into the present as a definition of leisure. To dream and to fantasize—by this we mean the active use of the imagination in its creative form rather than in its restrictive form, as an anxiety and fear. This kind of imagining is freeing rather than trapping. It is the reverse of the poverty that we spoke of.

If we are to create a freeing environment for other people, within a social dimension as well as in the narrow confines of our own world, then the most basic ingredient required is that of imagination—the ability to see alternatives, think them out, and choose from them creatively.

Developing the Inner World of Imagination

It is important, then, that in order to be able to be in a state of leisure, the inner world of imagination and fantasy be developed as a part of the educational process. This educational effort will train people to choose their own values, and this training will enable people to see that choice is a possibility in their lives, that there are varied alternatives open to them, that each alternative has its own consequences. In such a way, every child will become able to choose intelligently. This type of training should form a major part of the educational experience for children from the age of one through twelve. In the development of the educational process that will permit people to choose their own values, the development of the idea of choice as a possibility, of the presence of alternatives and their consequences, and the ability to choose from those alternatives and act on them should be a major part of the educational experience from the age of one through twelve. By the time a child gets to the age of twelve, this part of his development should be in an advanced stage.

It is a sad fact that many people in our society are unable to choose or even to see the possibility of choices in their lives. As an example of this, I was conducting a workshop with some sixty teachers on value clarification techniques. Three pictures were placed upon the walls. One picture consisted of a circle of squares, each square representing a student. The circle of squares then represented a small group. In the next picture the squares were lined up with another square representing the teacher at the front. In other words, the picture represented the common classroom situation. In the third picture, the squares were in groups and scattered. This is to say, it looked more like a picture of a crowd of people engaged in conversation in different directions, and not what the common idea of a regimented classroom might look like.

The teachers in the training institute were then asked to look at the three pictures and to put four words down that came to their minds when they saw each one of the pictures. We found that twenty of the sixty people in the room could not think of any words at all for one or two of the pictures. Ten people in the room said they could not think of any words to put down. A larger number of people could think of words, but couldn't think of many words for each picture.

As we began to analyze this, it became evident that many of the people in the room were frightened to put anything down because they were · wondering what their peers would say of them. Others were afraid that some administrator might see what they put down. The reality was that many of the teachers were so trapped that they could see no alternatives in the situation.

The point here is not to make a social commentary on some of the teachers in the school system, but rather to point out that the idea of choice and of seeing alternatives is new to a lot of people, depending on the environment they have come from. Such a situation would not permit the formation of values and should therefore be dealt with extensively as a part of the educational system.

Imagination and the Ability To See Alternatives

The development of the imagination and the ability to see alternatives can come about in a number of ways. In the home, it should come about through flexible parents who do not make rigid decisions for their children but rather offer a variable amount of alternatives, for example, in the disciplinary situation. This is not to say that a parent should go overboard; there are certain limits imposed on everyone. For example, it would not be very practical for a mother to offer variation in food at meals. But it would be possible to ask the children what they would like next time.

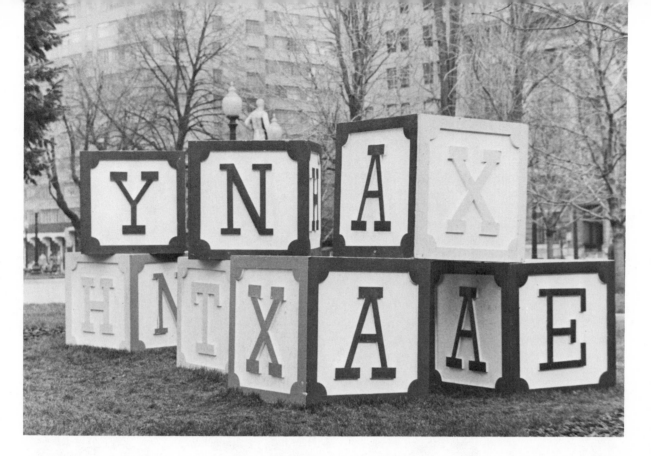

The development of creative environments and creative choice situations in school is, of course, essential to this kind of development. Science, in teaching a child the multiplicity of alternatives present in given situations as a very part of nature, is very important. This is the same, of course, in the area of mathematics. To see the variations of possibilities and possible occurrences in a given historical situation can be very enlightening to a lot of people. To role-play historical situations or to role-play geography through cultural patterns represented through different countries can expand the mind in the area of imagination on the one hand and make clear the application of alternatives of choice on the other.

Apart from the dream and fantasy world of the human being is of course the world of play. We should not forget before we conclude this section on dreaming and fantasy that the way in which men act out their imagination is the spirit of play. We might look at the aspects of play as outlined in the last chapter. Schiller has said that man is only entirely a man when he does play. It is that aspect of a person that takes him back to his childhood. It is timeless in its nature; it is where a person can be himself and do what he wants to do in the moment of acting out his imagination and fantasies through his whole body. And so it is that people watching the sports programs on a Saturday afternoon imagine themselves as heroes in the form of hockey or football players. Play then is something that needs to be studied more and something that is an integral part of dreaming and fantasy.

5. TO CELEBRATE. The final aspect of the definition of leisure that is so important is the one called celebration. It serves to complete the attitude of what leisure is. In our earlier description, celebration was seen as initially being rooted in a past activity, while leisure, with dream and fantasy, was more centered in the present. To celebrate what? To celebrate myself. Celebration is festivity and the awareness of something beyond myself. It is a man's awareness of himself as a limited being in history before the awe of creation. It is a worship experience. To be aware of the limitations in history means to realize that I am limited and that I am so in a community of limited persons. As a man or woman, I am free to choose, to create, and to fantasize within the scope of my limitations. Celebration, therefore, is a festive event which is a value assertion of man's worth.

Celebration: An Awareness of History

Birthday parties, church services, get-togethers, and barbecues are not leisure unless these elements are present. The freedom to be yourself, to be able to relax in a timeless environment, to wear what you like, to swear when you like, to fantasize a little, to be in an environment in which you can be free, if only for a limited time, and finally to be in an attitude of celebration. This is leisure. Celebration is being aware of history.

This relationship to history is very important and one which perhaps should take up another book. Where does history enter into this? Man is an historical person with a memory and a past which colors his every reflection. In addition, what I celebrate are my limits—my limits within a society of limited people. This puts me immediately into the social dimension which has its history of social limitation. It is the inability of man to confront his limits that causes all the poverty and meaninglessness that we have as men. As a result, man is trapped by his own anxiety and fears of failure. To celebrate my limitations therefore is an essential ingredient of my life-style, an essential ingredient of leisure.

Historically, if I can see myself as a person who has come through history and who therefore has to face the limits of my life in terms of death, then perhaps this will help me to see my total life in a more sane perspective. Then I am able to raise the questions of why I am here, what I am doing, and whether what I am doing is really worth it in the context of my total life. Within the context of total history of man's development a person can become more relaxed and less concerned about time.

History offers an expansive time that is incomprehensible to most of us. If I can see myself as a moment within the total history of man, then I will not take what is happening around me (who is going to succeed in the agency that I work for or in the school that I am in) so seriously. As I look, for example, at the conservative and liberal war that goes on in so many of our institutions, if this could be seen within the context of history and the evolutionary development of man, it would seem less important and be placed into a truer perspective. History can make me humble and really help me to come to grips with the reality of leisure.

At various points in this book we have referred to the civilization of man through art, especially with reference to the works of Kenneth Clark. In art we have seen and noted the development of the individual as coming about basically through the Renaissance, and as such something that has come relatively late in the development of man. The same was true of the development of woman as liberated.

To the extent that I can understand man's historical progression, I will have the ability to work for further progress without becoming overly anxious about the present state of affairs. It does not mean that I will do nothing; it means that my working for progress will be with perspective and my life in general will be more relaxed.

This is not to say that we want to take away the urgency of man, but simply to say that history places man in his limited environment and confronts him with his limitations. When he can see more clearly what the reality is, his dreams can become dreams that start from his limits and move to become unlimited. The risk of not considering limits is that we begin with an unreal situation and have unreal dreams. The latter of course is destructive, since the person doing this starts not from where he is, but from some other place, and as such is doomed to failure. In this respect it is interesting to see what Teilhard de Chardin says in his book *The Divine Milieu.* He was a person who was very much aware of man in relationship to his whole evolutionary process moving toward some given end:

Man's Collective Awakening

"The enrichment and firming of religious thought in our time has undoubtedly been caused by the revolution of the size and unity all around us and within us. All around us the physical sciences are endlessly extending the abysses of time and space, and ceaselessly discerning new relationships between the elements of the universe. Within us a whole world of affinities and interrelated sympathies, as old as the human soul, is being awakened by the stimulus of these great discoveries, and what has hitherto been dreamed rather than experienced is at last taking shape and consistency. Scholarly and discriminating among serious thinkers, simple or didactic, among the half-educated, the aspirations toward a vaster and more organic one, and the premonitions of unknown forces and their application in new fields, are the same and are emerging simultaneously on all sides. It is almost a commonplace today to find men who, quite naturally and unaffectively, live in the explicit consciousness of being an atom or a citizen of the universe.

"This collective awakening, similar to that which, at some given moment, makes each individual realize the true dimensions of his own life, must inevitably have a profound religious reaction on the mass of mankind—either to cast down or to exhort" (The Divine Milieu, p. 45).

Finally, to end this I would remind the reader of Cervantes' *Don Quixote.* The following is the last statement in the book and is written as his epitaph.

"Here lies the noble fearless knight,
Whose valor rose to such a height;
When death at last had struck him down,
His was the victory and renown.
He reck'd the world of little prize,
And was a bugbear in men's eyes;
But had the fortune in his age
To live a fool and die a sage."

The whole story of Don Quixote is of the man whose imagination led him to do all sorts of things that continually made him look the fool and be laughed at. Miguel de Unamuno has written a very interesting book called *The Tragic Sense of Life* in which he constantly refers to this figure as being in part an answer to man's environment. He says:

"The greatest thing about him was his having been mocked and vanquished, for it was in being overcome that he overcame; he overcame the world by giving the world cause to laugh at him" (The Tragic Sense of Life, p. 325).

Unamuno says that Don Quixote fought all his life with desperation. However, he fought his way out of despair. He goes on to say that Don Quixote in dying realized his own comic quality and, realizing it, superimposed himself upon it and triumphed over it. That is to say, as a tragic figure he never did surrender to life; he was not a pessimist but always fought on.

"The world must be as Don Quixote wishes it to be, and inns must be castles, and he will fight with it, and will, to all appearances, be vanquished, and he will try it by making himself the object of his own laughter" (The Tragic Sense of Life, p. 327).

This of course is another way of saying that even life with all its tragedies and oppressions is where man is, and that the way out of this is to recognize our limits, to laugh and celebrate, realizing that even in the most tragic circumstances, the imaginative mind, the mind of dream and fantasy, can see the hope that is always present.

LEISURE AND WORK—A CONCLUSION

In the last section we saw how leisure is also intricately connected to the value process, and not simply because it ties in all the value indicators that we spoke of such as the future, and the past and its relationship to guilt, anxiety, imagination and so on. No, it has a greater dimension. Leisure is the environment in which values can be formed. Why? The reason is because the freeing environment permits choice. In addition to this, leisure is the activation of the creative imagination, and is as such the development of alternatives and choices, with the consideration of the consequences of those alternatives for the educated person, or, I should say, the person being educated.

The development of the imagination is a part of the value formation. Celebration is the confrontation of a person with existential value formers, that is, his limits. It is the confronting of man with the reality of who he is so that he may reflect and start to develop the kinds of values that will enable him to free himself and others in a world that desperately seeks freedom and authenticity.

The Relationship between Work and Leisure

What then is the relationship between leisure and work? It could be argued at this point that leisure has been described in this section as a value itself. I state that as a bias because I feel that it is really the natural conclusion to the kind of environment which would maximize the formation of values.

In relationship to work we have stated earlier that leisure determines work in its maximum condition. Any person needs a certain amount of leisure in order to be the best kind of worker. However, another part of this is that leisure as an activity does not need to be separated completely from work. It is simply that work restricts by its very nature the maximum kind of environment that leisure can be in. For example, work is related in time and space to particular goals, whereas leisure is not necessarily limited that way. This does not mean that work therefore is a completely separate activity. It simply means that it is more limited in terms of leisure. Yet, work in its own right has a specific purpose which should fit in as a necessary part of an individual's existence. Work and leisure therefore make up the totality of man's life and should be seen as a creative unity and not as two different things, one being better or more purposeful than the other. They both are important and relate in their importance to each other.

In the Western tradition, especially as related to Aristotle, leisure has been regarded as that area of life in which the highest measure of freedom is obtainable. It was Aristotle who told us that we work in order that we might have leisure. In addition to this, in the Western world we have been told time and time again that the workday week is being reduced and that therefore people will have more time for leisure. As we have pointed out in other chapters, this is not necessarily so, since, as Linder has pointed out, the more time available often means that people work more in a consumer society where they buy more things than they need to maintain and work with.

Another aspect of this is that David Riesman in *The Lonely Crowd* talks about the forced personalization of work, pointing out how work often has such a large emotional demand on people that it has caused an alienation of man from man. This kind of thing we referred to earlier in this chapter with Eric Fromm, and we also pointed to some of the new humanization techniques that are going on in industry to try to combat this type of thing. Riesman sees leisure as the area in which man becomes himself or becomes an individual over against the increasing demand or expectancies of the social sphere in which he lives. This approach to leisure of course is the same thing as saying that part of leisure is meant for man to become or be himself. The idea of intimacy would be very important at this point.

Work: A Need To Become Meaningful

It is Paul Nash who has pointed out that work itself needs to become increasingly meaningful to people. If there is an increased separation between work and leisure so that leisure is a part of a person's life that makes him live and gives him meaning, then the more leisure he has outside of his work, the less meaningful his work becomes. This then makes his work become more and more boring and difficult for him. The point is that work must become more meaningful to people and not become separated totally from leisure as an activity. The purpose of the exercise we did earlier where we tried to see what was meant by work was also meant to help us to see that often rest and recuperation and travel are not leisure but an extension or a part of work. The importance of this is to understand the relationship of leisure and work so that leisure can become a possibility. Nash states:

> "We all need to rest. But in order to understand the kind of rest an organism needs, we must study the nature of the organism. After running to catch a train, our lungs are overworked and need to rest. The way in which they rest, however, is by gradually reverting to the normal rhythm of breathing, not by stopping. This is because they are built for action. Similarly, everything intended to act, from muscles to minds, can find rest in natural action as well as in inertia. 'To act in obedience to the hidden precepts of nature, that is rest,' said Maria Montessori; 'and in this special case, since man is meant to be an intelligent creature, the more intelligent his acts are, the more he finds repose in them.' Leisure should be regarded not as an opportunity to collapse, but as an opportunity to seek out ways of acting that are suitable to our nature, but are not encouraged or permitted by our working conditions" (Authority and Freedom in Education, pp. 46-47).

What is being pointed to here is that leisure as an activity needs to have the quality which Cox called juxtaposition. It must be something that is totally opposite from our work in order to possess full creativity. Similarly, Nash points out that play only takes place when man is fully himself and is in a state of freedom. Play then is one of the natural consequences and a part of leisure. It was A. S. Neill in his development of *Summerhill* who took play particularly seriously, pointing out that it was a necessary part of human development and that if a person did not have enough play, then this undermined his ability to apply himself to work later on in his life.

Therefore, the aspects of leisure that we have mentioned, and the clarification of what is understood by work, enable a person to choose the kind of work that he wants and the kind of life direction that he wants. Once this happens, aspects of leisure can be a part of our educational system. We need, as Nash has said, an education for leisure. By developing certain aspects of leisure about the dream, the imagination, play, the being of oneself, we maximize the person's possibility to be able to choose the kind of life direction, the kind of work that he wants to do in his life.

New Concept of Education Needed To Enhance Freedom Through Leisure

> "Above all we need a new concept of liberal education to help the majority of young people to enhance their freedom through leisure. Havinghurst has suggested that for most people, who are in society maintaining their rather ego-involving jobs, and who find their main self-fulfillment through leisure, the educational system should attempt to find some sort of ego-involving socially constructive activity apart from work. The research of Dubin and Orzack, showing that professionals tend to be work-oriented and factory workers to be leisure-oriented leads one to speculate that perhaps we should reverse the customary emphasis in which future professionals receive more "liberal" education and future factory workers more "vocational" education. For the future leisure-oriented society-maintainers, there is a need not so much of liberal education as a dif-

ferent kind of liberal education. It will be an education that is liberating because it helps these young people to explore areas of leisure activity that are a potential source of serious commitments—deliberate decision-making and reflective behavior. In a word, it will help them to bring a spirit of vocation to some aspects or aspect of the leisure sector of life" (Authority and Freedom in Education. pp. 49-50).

A strange irony that we educate the factory worker in more vocational trades when what he needs is the greater understanding of leisure in order to maximize his work ability. On the other hand, we do a great deal to improve the efficiency of the professional worker when perhaps he should be involved, for the purpose of the development of his leisure life, in more manual types of work. We are reminded at this point of the kind of education that a professional worker gets in China. Every Chinese professional is required to work with his hands in a factory. It would seem to me that there is a great deal of sense in this, since working with the hands could be very much a form of leisure for the professional, and working with the mind could be very much the idea of leisure for the factory worker.

A New and Different Look at Education

We need then to view education in the future in an entirely different way. It should be an education for leisure and not one that obtains all its values from a society which educates people to be more efficient in the area of their own profession. Such an attitude to education would be revolutionary and would turn our present educational system upside down. It would stand as a great threat to the majority of professionals who find working with their hands degrading.

We are fortunate, however, to be living in a society where many people have been able to find work of their choice and in which leisure is a possibility within its own context. Many people do find work pleasurable. However, there is a need for such people and for all people in our society to be very careful that such work does not become the only value in their lives.

In the classroom, teachers should become more aware of who a student is and where he is going so that certain aspects of his personality may be developed. For example, a student moving toward a professional career might be asked to place more emphasis on vocational courses. A student who is moving toward a trade skill might be asked to spend more time in athletics or in some other intellectual activity which may not be so readily available to him in the work situation for which he is preparing. One might accurately say that this is not very practical. But it would be an education that could be truly liberating for a person in his total life development. We simply need to move toward clarifying early in a student's life what his life direction is so that the educational system can be truly educational in guiding a person no longer toward obtaining certain information and qualifications to do a job but rather in obtaining information which will be able to create in that person a total life-style that puts into perspective and balance the factors of work and leisure in order to maximize his human potential.

Work and Play

When play is given a meaning and a purpose in the educational context, it becomes an increased source of freedom. In the same way, work becomes freeing when people are able to reflect on it as an activity that has an end in itself. A great deal could be done in helping workers in tedious jobs to see how their work relates to the orientation of the final product. In addition to this, they may be educated in seeing how the product relates to a positive end in society itself. Even in the long run, such education and such a reflective process as a part of the total educational scene could change the nature of products because it would change the underlying value system that demands such products.

What is work and what is play then becomes a complicated matter. What is important however is the development of the internal spirit of man as he moves toward the completion and meaning of his own life. What is important is that people find meaning in their own lives. This is another way of saying that persons are able to find and discover their own values and life direction. This can only be done as work and leisure are seen as part of our total life-style and are clarified as to what they mean in relationship to the individual.

Leisure is an attitude. So also can a developed sense of work be in the spirit of a leisurely attitude. The main difference between work and leisure is that work is more goal-oriented and within the limits of a certain time span.

Work places certain expectations on us that leisure does not. More attention in work should be placed on the activity of the moment and not so much on the end product. The end product is important in the total context of its meaning. But if that product is very far from the worker and so distant from him that he cannot understand it within the context of his own situation, then life becomes more meaningless as emphasis is placed on the product over against the present activity. The individual needs to be able to see himself specifically in relationship to his work as a person who is growing and making his own value choices in life.

A school that envisages both work and play as vehicles of freedom will give attention to both ends and means in the pedagogical process. According to Nash, "It will try to make work a reflected activity through the development of purpose and commitment in the student and, at the same time, help him to lose himself playfully in the work task of the moment" *(Authority and Freedom in Education, p. 53)*.

Finally, then, leisure is a freeing environment that, as an attitude, can enter into and maximize work. The principle of leisure as an attitude is the expansion of the imagination into realistic dreaming and a coming to grips with one's limits in a spirit of celebration. As such, a person begins to determine and choose his own life. Through making his own choices, he actually combats the hoplessness of anxiety that traps people into feelings of hopelessness, boredom, and finally despair and meaninglessness. Meaning is found in man's ability to choose his own life direction.

Conclusion:
Advice From A Caterpillar

> "The Caterpillar and Alice looked at each other for some time in silence. At last the Caterpillar took the hook out of its mouth, and addressed her in a languid, sleepy voice. 'Who are you?' said the Caterpillar."
>
> Lewis Carroll, Alice in Wonderland

I was recently talking to a distraught father of a twenty-year-old son. He asked "Who am I? Is anything I do worthwhile? Is my history or my tradition worth anything?" I asked him what he was upset about. He replied that his son didn't seem to have any of the values that his family had. He was not so concerned about working, only playing around.

John described his background and the fact that he had held down two jobs for the last ten years and in addition to this his wife had been working. He noted that they had worked very hard so that their son could go to college, yet all he was doing was hitchhiking around the countryside. As we talked to him further, he related how difficult it was for him in the depression years with his father away from home so much of the time looking for work, while his mother would worry about the children. He also noted that when he got married he gave his children a lot of love and care. He was sure that they had all the security and material needs provided for them—they did not have to suffer as he did. He was of course very angry. I casually asked whether the three values of security, home and family were very important to him. He became very enthusiastic and said "You bet they are."

I then asked him how he supposed that security had become such a high value in his life. He replied that he'd already told me that—the depression years had such an effect on him. I asked him: "Do you feel then that the experience of the depression and those hard days and your reaction to them helped you to see the necessity of security and home life?" "Of course!" he said.

As we talked on I began to ask him what he felt the experience of his son was. He began to see that his son had had a totally different experience. His son had been brought up in a family where his parents had come through the depression and made sure that he did not suffer from all the insecurities that they had in those years. Consequently he had not experienced the need for security in his life that his father had. Security as a value had been provided for him. With the father, security as a value had been a reaction to the insecurity of his own history. I remember that he finally said to me: "You know, he could never see the need for security as we have because I made sure that he never experienced it." He then went on to say: "You know, I don't know that I'd really want it any other way."

That particular father went on to talk to his son about these matters and the result was that the son began to see significance and meaning in his parents' own history. He began to understand why they put so much emphasis on the need for security. It does not mean that the son changed but rather that he understood, and there thus was a real place for conversation and renewal of life in that family between son and father. In the interaction the father was able to understand the environment he had provided. He understood why his son was able to do things without worrying so much about the consequences of such things as life goals and work. True, one could argue that this was not good for the boy, but at least this father and son were able to come closer together by struggling with the meaning of their own history. After this was done they were then able to move on to choose new values and make new decisions in their lives and in their relationships to one another.

The Real Place and Significance of Education

What does this mean? Does it mean that we should institute programs of counseling for parents? No indeed! In the example we see the real place and significance of education. Education must go beyond the content of secondary sources and help people to make sense and meaning out of their own experience as a primary source. This kind of education of necessity must have within its structure the ethic of balance. That is to say, if people saw education as being totally concerned with the reflection of my own personal experience, it would become narcissistic and consequently stunting to the growth of the individual.

Education must have a balance of the cognitive and the affective, of such things as skills in reading and writing as well as the development of the understanding of history and space in the individual's life. What I am saying is that as I understand history, for example, I must also understand my own history and make sense out of it. As I find meaning in my history, I will also understand the meaning of world history.

When we find meaning in our own lives, we grow in our own personality and expand relationships with others. The alternatives expand, and the possibility for meaning not only in terms of myself and history but also in the cosmic sense emerges. That is to say, when I see meaning through the total creation, so the religious as an activity becomes a renewed dimension for me.

Survival of the . . . ?

Related to the need to find meaning is also the problem of survival. We live in a society which is moving rapidly in terms of knowledge and communication explosions, and these in turn are causing all sorts of changes in our culture. So rapid are the changes that often the environment itself impinges on a person and brings about the necessity of clarification in order that we can deal with strange and new alternatives.

As an example of the latter I was speaking recently to a consultant in public education. Jim gave me two examples of expanded alternatives as a problem for teachers who are not ready to deal with those same alternatives. He told me that he had recently been to a school district in the midwest which had just constructed a multi-million-dollar building on the outskirts of a small town. Previously the school had been in the city and had had no playgrounds. In addition to this the old school had separate entrances for black children and white children. That is to say, the school was segregated. Since the school had no playground when classes were cancelled or there was a break such as the mid-day meal, students had to leave the building and go home, walk on the streets, or visit the corner drug store.

Then, said Jim, they built a new school on the outskirts of town. The new school was progressive and non-graded, with large open classrooms which would allow for a multiplicity of activities and even various grades in the same learning area. The new school had no separate entrances, and black and white students came and left by the same doors and mixed with one another freely inside the school. There was a large playground, so that the students did not have to leave during the break periods. Consequently, black and white students met each other, fought each other and discovered new problems and relationships.

The consultant whom I was talking to noted that the people who had the most difficulty were not the students but the teachers. Suddenly they were faced with a large new range of alternatives that up to this point they'd only read about in the newspapers or seen on television. Now they had racial problems at their own school with conflicts between students; now they had the students on their hands during break periods; and now they had students mixing in grades and coming to grips with one another not only after school but during school.

The new situation was one where the central concern was with the teachers who felt insecure and inadequate in the situation. He noted that there was a great deal of state money to build new schools very progressive in nature, and a great deal of federal money to provide means for integration in school systems, but there was almost no local or federal money available to help teachers understand the complexities of human relationships so that they could deal with their new alternatives.

Jim had visited another very progressive school, also new, also with open learning area structures. He said that in the new school there were four teachers to each learning area. The principal of the school showed him around the school but did so with a great deal of anxiety. Jim noted that the principal did not seem at all pleased with his new multi-million-dollar building, since it was causing him more problems than he previously had conceived as being possible.

They went into one classroom and found that the teachers, rather than utilizing the learning area, had barricaded themselves off with filing cabinets and book shelves. That is to say, they had placed their book shelves and filing cabinets in the corners of the room with their desks behind them, simulating as it were the kind of small office they'd had known in their previous experience.

Briefly the teachers had been introduced into new realms of creative experience for which they simply had not been trained, either in their own personality development or academically as teachers. A tragedy? Yes indeed. What is needed then is new skills for the teacher in understanding and making sense out of new alternatives that press upon her.

Value Clarification as a Methodology

What will happen to a student who experiences a new environment on the one hand, and a teacher who he sees cannot deal with it on the other? Value clarification then, more than a theory, is a methodology which helps people who are professionals in the area of human relations, such as teachers, ministers and social workers, to clarify where they are and to help other people to do the same. As educators they help persons to discover meaning in the world in which they live. It is a science and methodology that will help people to deal with a society which is changing rapidly due to an increased pace of life. Ivan Illich speaks of it in the following way:

> "To the primitive the world was governed by fate, fact, and necessity. By stealing fire from the gods, Prometheus turned facts into problems, called necessity into question, and defied fate. Classical man framed a civilized context for human perspective. He was aware that he could defy fate-nature-environment, but only at his own risk. Contemporary man goes further; he attempts to create the world in his image, to build a totally man-made environment, and then discovers that he can do so only on the condition of constantly remaking himself to fit it. We must now face the fact that man himself is at stake" (Deschooling Society, p. 107).

As man modified his environment so totally, so his primary value became work. It is as if he worked so hard to find the environment within which he can work securely that he became the work itself.

Balancing Our Lives

We need balance in our lives. We need balance between work and leisure. We need to clarify what work means to us and to discover meaning in it. We need to do the same thing with leisure. When work becomes predominant in our lives, then it becomes our value, and we find that our worth is our work. We become products of a consumer society, compulsively trying to find meaning by stressing achievement for ourselves and our families. When leisure gets out of perspective and man struggles to avoid work and to see his life in terms of pleasure, then he becomes alienated from the creation which he was given responsibility to modify for the creative development of man. Alienated from the environment rather than trying to enhance his growth through it, he abuses it, and so becomes alienated from himself in the process.

When man tries to become God he always alienates himself in the discovery of himself as failure. But as man seeks to recognize his limitations, he can discover his potential and become a hope in the world by creating a new society whose environment will free man to truly accept his inheritance. As responsible for the creation in himself, he will become a resurrected being. With the emergence of a new society, a new strain or man may also emerge, whose potential and creativity will reflect him as an image of God not only as a theological construct but as manifested through his behavior. A dream is possible and can begin now as man examines his limits and sees his potential in relationship to others in perspective, so that he can become a responsible person, not only making choices for his own emancipation but also creating environments which will free the race to become itself.

Sources Consulted

Assagioli, Roberto, M.D. *Psychosynthesis*. New York: Hobbs, Dorman and Company, Inc., 1965.

Binswanger, Ludwig. *Being in the World*. Translated by Jacob Needleman. New York: Harper and Row, 1963.

Brown, Charles R. Quoted in the *International Dictionary of Thoughts*. Edited by John P. Bradley, *et al.* Chicago: J. G. Ferguson Publishing Company, 1969.

Bury, J. B., *et al*, eds. *The Cambridge Ancient History*, Vol. V. London: Cambridge University Press, 1969.

Cervantes, Miguel. *Don Quixote*. New York: The New American Library, 1957.

Clark, Kenneth. *Civilisation*. New York: Harper and Row, 1969.

Coles, Wilbert. "What Poverty Does to Man." *Life at the Bottom*. Edited by Gregory Armstrong. New York: Bantam Books, Inc., 1971.

De Chardin, Pierre Teilhard. *The Divine Milieu*. New York: Harper and Brothers, 1960.
———. *The Future of Man*. New York: Harper and Row, 1964.

De Grazia, Sebastian. *Of Time, Work, and Leisure*. Garden City, N.Y.: Anchor Books, 1964.

De Unamuno, Miguel. *The Tragic Sense of Life*. New York: Dover Publications, Inc., 1954.

Ellul, Jacques. *The Technological Society*. Translated by John Wilkinson. New York: Vintage Books, 1964.

Erikson, Erik H. *Childhood and Society*. New York: W. W. Norton and Company, Inc., 1950.

Evans, Richard I. *Dialogue with Erich Fromm*. New York: Harper and Row, 1968.

Fitch, James M. *Environmental Psychology*. New York: Holt, Rinehart and Winston, Inc., 1970.

Frankl, Viktor. *The Doctor and the Soul*. New York: Alfred A. Knopf, 1966.
———. *Psychotherapy and Existentialism*. New York: Simon and Schuster, 1967.

Fromm, Erich. *The Sane Society*. New York: Rinehart, 1955.

Glasser, William. *Reality Therapy: A New Approach to Psychiatry*. New York: Harper and Row, 1965.

Greenwald, Harold. "Play and Self Development." *Ways of Growth*. Edited by Herbert A. Otto and John Mann. New York: Pocket Books, 1971.

Hall, Edward T. *The Hidden Dimension*. New York: Doubleday and Company, 1966.

Henninger, David, and Esposito, Mary. "Indian Boarding Schools/Indian Jails." *Life at the Bottom*. Edited by Gregory Armstrong. New York: Bantam Books, Inc., 1971.

Illich, Ivan D. *Celebration of Awareness: A Call for Institutional Revolution*. New York: Doubleday and Company, 1969.
———. *Deschooling of Society*. New York: Harper and Row, 1971.

Kelsey, Morton. *Dreams: The Dark Speech of the Spirit*. Garden City, N.Y.: Doubleday and Company, 1968.

Kerr, Walter. *The Decline of Pleasure*. New York: Simon and Schuster, 1962.

Linder, Staffen. *The Harried Leisure Class*. New York: Columbia University Press, 1970.

Lowe, Jeanne R. *Cities in a Race with Time*. New York: Abingdon Press, 1968.

May, Rollo. *The Meaning of Anxiety*. New York: The Ronald Press Company, 1950.

Nash, Paul. *Authority and Freedom in Education*. New York: John Wiley and Sons, Inc., 1966.

Oden, Thomas C. *The Structures of Awareness*. New York: Abingdon Press, 1969.

Piaget, Jean. *Six Psychological Studies*. New York: Random House, 1967.

Pieper, Josef. *Leisure: The Basis of Culture*. New York: The New American Library, 1961.

Ramparts, The Editors of. *Divided We Stand*. New York: Harper and Row, 1970.

Reich, Charles A. *The Greening of America*. New York: Random House, 1970.

Revel, Jean-Francois. *Without Marx or Jesus: The New American Revolution Has Begun*. Garden City, N.Y.: Doubleday and Company, 1971.

Riesman, David. *The Lonely Crowd*. New Haven: Yale University Press, 1969.

Roberts, Ron. *The New Communes*. Englewood Cliffs, N.J.: Prentice-Hall, Inc., 1971.

Rogers, Carl R. *Freedom To Learn*. Columbus, Ohio: Charles E. Merrill Publishing Company, 1969.

Sartre, Jean Paul. *Being and Nothingness*. New York: Harper and Row, 1961.

Shirer, William. *The Rise and Fall of the Third Reich*. New York: Fawcett World Library, 1969.

Silberman, Charles E. *Crisis in the Classroom*. New York: Random House, 1970.

Smuts, Robert W. *Women and Work in America*. New York: Schocken Books, 1971.

Theobald, Robert. *An Alternative Future for America II*. Chicago: The Swallow Press, Inc., 1968.

Toffler, Alvin. *Future Shock*. New York: Random House, 1970.

Tolkein, J. R. R. *The Return of the King*. New York: Ballantine Books, 1968.

————. *The Tolkein Reader*. New York: Ballantine Books, 1971.

Tournier, Paul. *Guilt and Grace. New York: Harper and Row, 1958.*

Townsend, Claire. *Old Age: The Last Segregation.* New York: Bantam Books, 1971.

Townsend, Robert. *Up the Organization*. New York: Alfred Knopf, 1970.

Van der Poel, Cornelius J. *The Search for Human Values*. New York: Newman Press, 1971.

Walmsley, John. *Neill and Summerhill: A Man and His Work*. Baltimore, Md.: Penguin Books, Inc., 1969.

Research Bibliography

Ackerman, Nathan W., M.D. *The Psychodynamics of Family Life*. New York: Basic Books, Inc., 1958.

Adorno, F. W. *The Authoritarian Personality*. New York: Harper and Row, 1950.

Aiden, Henry D. "Good and Evil: A Study of Some Relations Between Faith and Morals," *Ethics*, 68 (1958) 77-97.

Albert, Ethel M., Clyde Kluckhohn, *et al. A Selected Bibliography on Values, Ethics, and Aesthetics.* Glencoe, Illinois: Free Press, 1959.

Allison, C. Fitzsimons. *Guilt, Anger, and God: The Patterns of Our Discontents*. New York: The Seabury Press, 1972.

Allport, Gordon W. "Attitudes." *Handbook of Social Psychology*, ed. Carl Murchinson. Worcester, Massachusetts: Clark University Press, 1935, 798-844.

————. *Becoming: Basic Considerations for a Psychology of Personality*. New Haven and London: Yale University Press, 1955.

————. *Pattern and Growth in Personality*. New York: Holt, Rinehart and Winston, 1961.

Allport, Gordon W., Philip E. Vernon, and Gardner Lindzey. *Study of Values*. (3rd ed.) Boston: Houghton Mifflin Company, 1960.

Anderson, R. G. "Subjective Ranking Versus Score Ranking on Interest Values," *Personnel Psychology*, (1948), 349-55.

Anerbach, J. G. "Value Changes in Therapy," *Personality*, 1 (1950), 63-67.

Archambault, R. D. "Criteria for Success in Moral Instruction," *Harvard Educational Review*, 33 (Fall, 1963), 472-83.

Armstrong, Gregory, ed. *Life at the Bottom*. New York: Bantam Books, 1971.

Arnstine, D. G. "Some Problems in Teaching Values," *Educational Theory*, 11 (July, 1961), 158-67.

————. "Value Models and Education: Content in the Popular Arts," *Journal of Educational Sociology*, 35 (September, 1961), 41-48.

Arrow, Kenneth. *Social Choices and Individual Values*. New York: Wiley, 1951.

Ayres, C. D. "The Value Economy." *Value: A Cooperative Inquiry*, ed. Ray Lepley. New York: Columbia University Press, 1949, 43-63.

Bach, George R. *Intensive Group Psychotherapy*. New York: Ronald Press, 1954.

Bagolini, Luigi. "Value Judgements in Ethics and Law," *Philosophical Quarterly*, 1 (1951), 423-32.

Bales, Robert. "Bales Value Profile," Unpublished form, Harvard University, Department of Social Relations.

Ballou, Richard Boyd. "Religious Values in Public Education," *Religious Education*, 49 (September, 1954), 317-24.

Bandura, Albert, and Frederick J. MacDonald. "Influence of Social Reinforcement and the Behavior of Models in Shaping Children's Moral Judgement," *Journal of Abnormal Psychology*, 67, No. 3 (1963), 274-81.

Barbour, Ian G. *Issues in Science and Religion*. Englewood Cliffs: Prentice-Hall, 1966.

Battrick, Delmar H. "How Can We Use Our School Program to Contribute to a Better Understanding, Appreciation, and Acceptance of Moral and Spiritual Values," *National Association of School Principals Bulletin*, 38 (April, 1954), 79-81.

Bennett, John C., Howard R. Bowen, William A. Brown, Jr., and G. Bromley Oxnam. *Christian Values and Economic Life*. New York: Harper and Brothers, 1954.

Berger, Peter L. *The Noise of Solemn Assemblies*. Garden City, New York: Doubleday and Company, Inc., 1961.

————. *The Sacred Canopy*. Garden City, New York: Doubleday and Company, Inc., 1967.

Berkowitz, Leonard. *The Development of Motives and Values in the Child*. New York: Basic Books, 1964.

Bertalanffy, Ludwig von. "Human Values in a Changing World," *New Knowledge in Human Values*, ed. Abraham H. Maslow. New York: Harper and Row, 1959, pp. 65-74.

Bidney, David. "The Concept of Value in Modern Anthropology," *Anthropology Today*, ed. A. L. Kroeber. Chicago: University of Chicago Press, 1953.

Bills, R. E. "A Comparison for Scores on the Index of Adjustment and Values with Behavior in Level of Aspiration Tasks," *Journal of Consulting Psychology*, 17 (1953), 206-12.

Bills, R. E., Edgar Vance, and Arison S. McLean. "An Index of Adjustment and Values," *Journal of Consulting Psychology*, 15 (1951), 257-61.

Bion, W. R. *Experiences in Groups*. New York: Basic Books, 1961.

Birnabaum, Max. "Whose Values Should Be Taught?" *Saturday Review*, 47 (June 20, 1964), 60-62.

Bloom, Benjamin. *Stability and Chance in Human Characteristics*. New York: John Wiley and Son, Inc., 1964.

Bloom, Martin. "Mechanisms of Value Transmission: A Social Psychological Study," *Dissertation Abstracts*, 24, No. 3 (1963).

Boehm, L. "Development of Conscience: A Comparison of American Children of Different Mental and Socio-Economic Levels," *Child Development*, 33 (September, 1962, 575-90. See also pp. 591-602, 565-74.

Baleratz, J. M. "Learning by Discovering: An Experimental Study to Measure Its Effectiveness for Teaching Value Concepts," *Journal of Experimental Education*, 36 (Winter, 1967), 13-21.

Boovstin, Daniel J. *The Image: A Guide to Pseudo-Events in America*. New York: Harper and Row, 1961.

Bougle, C. C. A. *The Evolution of Values*, trans. by Helen Sellars. New York: Henry Holt Co., 1926.

Bousfield, W. A., and G. Samborski. "The Relationship Between Strength of Values and the Meaningfulness of Value Words," *Journal of Personality*, 23 (1955), 375-80.

Bower, William C. *Moral and Spiritual Values in Education*. Lexington: University of Kentucky Press, 1952.

———. "A Program of Moral and Spiritual Values in Education," *Educational Leadership*, 8 (May, 1951), 471-74.

Boyd, Malcolm. *Are You Running With Me, Jesus?* New York: Avon Books, 1965.

Bracey, John H. Jr., August Meier, and Elliott Rudwick, eds. *Black Nationalism in America*. Indianapolis, Indiana: Bobbs-Merrill Company, Inc., 1970.

Bradford, Leland P., Jack R. Gibb, and Kenneth D. Benne, eds. *T-Group Theory and Laboratory Method*. New York: John Wiley and Sons, Inc., 1964.

Brameld, Theodore. "Inductive Approach to Intercultural Values," *Journal of Educational Sociology*, 21 (September, 1947), 4-11.

Brameld, Theodore, and Stanley Elam, eds. *Values in American Education*. Bloomington, Indiana: Phi Delta Kappa, Inc., 1964.

Brandt, Richard B. "Some Puzzles for Attitude Theories of Value," *The Language of Value*, ed. Ray Lepley. New York: Columbia University Press, 1957, pp. 153-77.

———. *Value and Obligation*. Burlingame, New York: Harcourt Brace & World, Inc., 1961.

Bravo, Francisco. "Teilhard de Chardin and Pastoral Renewal," *CIF Report*. Mexico City: Center of Intercultural Documentation, V: 2, 10.

Brightman, T. *Nature and Values*. New York: Abingdon-Cokesbury Press, 1945.

———. "Values, Ideals, Norms, and Existence," *Philosophy and Phenomenological Research*, 4 (1943), 219-24.

Broaten, Carl E. *Toward a Theology of Hope in New Theology*. New York: Macmillan, 1968.

Brogden, Hubert E. *The Primary Personal Values Measured by Allport-Vernon Test: A Study of Values*. "Psychological Monographs," Vol. 66, Part 16, No. 348. Washington, D.C.: American Psychological Association, 1952.

Bronowski, Jacob. *Science and Human Values*. New York: Harper and Row, 1965.

———. "The Values of Science." *New Knowledge in Human Values*, ed. Abraham H. Maslow. New York: Harper and Row, 1959, pp. 3-12.

Brown, L. B., and D. J. Pallant. "Religious Belief and Social Pressure," *Psychological Reports*, 10 (1962), 813-14.

Brubalder, D. L. "Normative Value Judgements and Analysis," *Social Education*, 32 (May, 1968), 489-92

Bruner, Jerome S., and Cecile C. Goodman. "Value and Need as Organizing Factors in Perception," *Journal of Abnormal and Social Psychology*, 42 (1947), 33-44.

Bruner, Jerome, and Leo Postman. "Symbolic Values as an Organizing Factor in Perception," *Journal of Social Psychology*, 27 (1948), 203-08.

Bugental, James F. T. "Commitment and the Psychotherapist." *Existential Psychiatry*, VI, 23 (1968), 291ff.

———. "Investigations into the Self-Concept III. Instructions for the W-A-Y Method," *Psychological Reports*, XV (1964), 643-50.

———. *The Search for Authenticity*. New York: Holt, Rinehart and Winston, 1960.

———, and Evelyn C. Gunning. "Investigations into the Self-Concept II, Stability of Reported Identifications," *Journal of Clinical Psychology*, XI, 1 (1955) 41-46.

———, and Seymour L. Zelan, "Investigations into the Self-Concept I, the W-A-Y Techniques," *Journal of Personality*, XVIII (1950), 483-98.

Buhler, Charlotte. *Values in Psychotherapy*. New York: Free Press of Glencoe, 1962.

Callahan, Robert J. "Value Orientation and Psychotherapy," *American Psychologist*, 15 (1960), 269-70.

Cantril, Hadley. "The Qualities of Being Human," *American Quarterly*, 6 (1954), 3-18.

Carter, Harold J., ed. *Intellectual Foundations of American Education*. New York: Pitman Publishing Corp., 1965.

Catton, William R., Jr. "A Theory of Value," *American Sociological Review*, 24 (1959), 310-17.

Cerf, Walter. "Value Decisions," *Philosophy of Science*, 18 (1951), 26-34.

Chaffee, S. H. "Salience and Pertinence as Sources of Value Change," *Journal of Communications*, 17 (March, 1967), 25-38.

Child, I. L. "Socialization," *Handbook of Social Psychology*, ed. G. Lindzey. Cambridge, Massachusetts: Addison Wesley, Inc., 1954.

Clark, Walter Houston. "Psychology of Religious Values," *Personality*, Symposium #1 (1950), 45-62.

Clarke, Mary Evelyn. *A Study in the Logic of Value*. London: University of London Press, 1929.

Clebsch, William A., and Charles R. Jaekle. *Pastoral Care in Historical Perspective*. New York: Harper and Row, 1967.

Clinebell, Howard J. and Charlotte H. *The Intimate Marriage*. New York: Harper and Row, 1970.

Coe, G. *Motives of Men*. New York: Charles Scribner's Sons, 1928.

————. "My Search for What Is Most Worthwhile," *Religious Education*, 46 (March, 1951), 67-73.

Coleburt, Russell. *The Search for Values*. New York: Sheed and Ward, 1960.

Commager, Henry Steele. *The American Mind*. New Haven: Yale University Press, 1950.

Cook, T. E. "Influence of Client-Counselor Value Similarity on Change in Meaning During Brief Counseling," *Journal of Counseling Psychology*, 13 (Spring, 1966), 77-81.

Cooper, John Charles. *The New Mentality*. Philadelphia: The Westminister Press, 1969.

Corkey, R. "Basic Intrinsic Ethical Values," *Philosophy*, 29 (1954), 321-31.

Cox, David Franklin. "Karl Marx's Philosophy of Values." Unpublished Ph.D. dissertation, Boston University, 1953.

Cox, Harvey. *Ernst Bloch and the Pull of the Future in New Theology*. New York: Macmillan, 1968.

Cully, Kensig Brubaker, ed. *The Episcopal Church and Education*. New York: Morehouse-Barlow Company, 1966.

Curran, Charles A. *Counseling and Psychotherapy*. New York: Sheed and Ward, 1968.

Currie, Robert J. "Value Orientations of Parents of Academically Successful and Unsuccessful Children," *Dissertation Abstracts*, 27, No. 7-A (1967), 2064.

Dahlke, H. *Values in Culture and Classroom*. New York: Harper, 1958.

Davison, Donald, J. C. C. McKinsey, and Patrick Suppes. "Outlines of a Formal Theory of Value," *Philosophy of Science*, 22 (1955), 140-60.

DeCamp, L. Sprague. *The Tritonian Ring*. New York: Paperback Library, 1968.

Dechanet, J. M., O.S.B. *Christian Yoga*. Translated by Roland Hindmarsh. New York: Harper and Brothers, 1960.

de Chardin, Teilhard Pierre. *Le Milieu Divin*. London: Collins, 1957.

———— *The Phenomenon of Man*. New York: Harper & Brothers, 1959.

————. *The Appearance of Man*. New York: Harper and Row, 1965.

————. *The Future of Man*. New York: Harper and Row, 1964.

————. *The Vision of the Past*. New York: Harper and Row, 1957.

DeLaszlo, Violet S., ed. *The Basic Writings of C. G. Jung*. New York: The Modern Library, 1959.

Desoille, Robert. *The Directed Daydream*. New York: Psychosynthesis Research Foundation, 1966.

Dewey, John. *Experience and Education*. London: Collier Books, 1963.

————. "Some Questions About Value," *Journal of Philosophy*, 41 (1944), 449-55.

————. "The Field of Value," *Value: A Cooperative Inquiry*, ed. Ray Lepley. New York: Columbia University Press, 1949, pp. 64-77.

————. "Theory of Valuation," *International Encyclopedia of United Science*, 2, No. 4, Chicago: University of Chicago Press, 1939.

————. "Valuation Judgements and Immediate Quality," *Journal of Philosophy*, 40 (1943), 309-17.

Dinkmeyer, Donald C. *Child Development: The Emerging Self*. Englewood Cliffs, New Jersey: Prentice-Hall, Inc., 1965.

Dobzhansky, Theodosius. "Human Nature as a Product of Evolution," *New Knowledge in Human Values*, ed. Abraham H. Maslow. New York: Harper and Row, 1959, pp. 75-85.

Dorfman, Joseph. *The Economic Mind in American Civilization*. 5 Vols. New York: The Viking Press, 1959.

Driekhurs, Rudolph. *Character Education and Spiritual Values in an Anxious Age*. Boston: Beacon Press, 1952.

Drucker, Peter F. *The Effective Executive*. New York: Harper and Row, 1966.

Dunnam, Maxie D., Gary J. Herbertson, and Everett L. Shastrom. *The Manipulator and the Church*. Nashville, Tenn.: Abingdon Press, 1968.

Durkin, Helen E. *The Group in Depth*. New York: International Universities Press, Inc., 1964.

Egan, Gerard. *Encounter: Group Processes for Interpersonal Growth*. Belmont, Calif.: Brooks/Cole Publishing Company, 1970.

Eliade, Mircea. *Myths, Dreams and Mysteries*. Translated by Philip Mairet. New York: Harper and Row, 1960.

Elkino, David, and John H. Flavell, eds. *Studies in Cognitive Development: Essays in Honor of Jean Piaget*. New York: Oxford University Press, 1969.

Erikson, Erik H. "Identity and the Life Cycle," *Psychological Issues*, I, 1 (1959), 18-171.

Fast, Julius. *Body Language*. New York: Pocket Books, 1970.

Fernsterheim, Hebert, and Margaret E. Tresselt. "The Influence of Value Systems on the Perception of People," *Journal of Abnormal and Social Psychology*, 48 (1953), 98-98.

Festinger, Leon. *A Theory of Cognitive Dissonance*. Evanston and White Plains: Row, Peterson, and Co., 1957.

Findlay, John N. *Values and Intentions*. New York: The Macmillan Co., 1961.

Fletcher, Joseph. *Moral Responsibility: Situation Ethics at Work*. Philadelphia: The Westminster Press, 1967.

————. *Situation Ethics: The New Morality*. Philadelphia: The Westminster Press, 1966.

Frankel, Viktor E. *The Doctor of the Soul*. New York: Knopf, 1962.

————. *Man's Search for Meaning*. New York: Washington Square Press, 1966.

Freire, Paulo. *Pedagogy of the Oppressed*. Translated by Myra Bergman Ramos. New York: Herder and Herder, 1970.

Freud, Sigmund. *Group Psychology and the Analysis of the Ego*. New York: Bantam Books, 1960.

————. *The Ego and the Id*. New York: W. W. Norton and Co., Inc., 1927.

Friedenberg, Edgar Z. *Coming of Age in America: Growth and Acquiescence*. New York, New York: Vintage Books, 1967.

Fromm, Erich. *Man for Himself*. New York: Holt, Rinehart, and Winston, 1961. Originally published, 1947.

————. *The Art of Loving*. New York: Bantam Books, 1956.

————. *The Sane Society*. New York: Fawcett, 1965.

————. "Value, Psychology and Human Existence," *New Knowledge in Human Values*, ed. Abraham H. Maslow. New York: Harper and Row, 1959, pp. 151-64.

Frondizi, Risieri. *What Is Value?* trans. Solomon Lipp. LaSalle, Illinois: Open Court, 1963.

Fuller, R. Buckminster. *Operating Manual for Spaceship Earth*. New York: Pocket Books, 1970.

Fuller, R. Buckminster, Eric A. Walker, and James K. Killiman, Jr. *Approaching the Benign Environment*. New York: Collier Books, 1970.

Furter, Pierre. *L'imagination Creatrice LaViolence et le Changement Social; une Interpretation*. Cidoc Cuaderno (C-14) Cuernavaca, Mexico, 1968.

Gabriel, Ralph H. *Traditional Values in American Life*. New York: Harcourt, Brace and World, 1963.

Gardner, Eric F. "Can Values Really Be Measured?" *Catholic Psychological Record*, 1, No. 2 (1963), 23-31.

Garnett, Campbell A. "Intrinsic Good: Its Definition and Referent," *Value: A Cooperative Inquiry*, ed. Ray Lepley. New York: Columbia University Press, 1949, pp. 79-92.

Gellerman, Saul W. *Motivation and Productivity*. New York: American Management Association, Inc., 1963.

Gerard, Robert. *Psychosynthesis: A Psychotherapy for the Whole Man*. New York: Psychosynthesis Research Foundation, 1961.

Gerth, Hans, and C. Wright Mills. *Character and Social Structure*. New York: Harcourt, Brace, & World, Inc., 1964.

Ginott, Haim G. *Between Parent and Child*. New York: Avon Books, 1965.

Glasser, William. *Mental Health or Mental Illness?* New York: Harper and Row, 1960.

————. *Reality Therapy: A New Approach to Psychiatry*. New York: Harper and Row, 1965.

Goldman, Ronald. *Readiness for Religion*. New York: The Seabury Press, 1965.

Goode, William J. *The Family*. Englewood Cliffs, N.J.: Prentice-Hall, Inc., 1964.

Gootschalk, Louis. *Understanding History*. 2nd ed. New York: Alfred A. Knopf, 1969.

Greenacre, Phyllis. *Emotional Growth*. Vols. I and II. New York: International Universities Press, Inc., 1971.

Gregson, R. A. "The Psychology of Value," *British Journal of Statistical Psychology*, 15, No. 2 (1962), 163-65.

Greenblatt, Milton. "Altruism in the Psychotherapeutic Relationship," *Explorations in Altruistic Love and Behavior*, ed. Pitirim Sorokin. Boston: The Beacon Press, 1950, pp. 188-93.

Gunther, Bernard. *Sense Relaxation Below Your Mind*. New York: Collier Books, 1968.

Hahn, Lewis E. "A Contextualist Looks at Values," *Value: A Cooperative Inquiry*, ed. Ray Lepley. New York: Columbia University Press, 1949, pp. 112-24.

Hall, Roy M. "Religious Beliefs and Social Values," Unpublished Ph.D. dissertation, Syracuse University, 1950.

Hall, W. E. *What Is Value?* London: Routledge and Kegan Paul, Ltd., 1952.

Hare, R. M. *The Language of Morals*. Oxford: Claredon Press, 1952.

Harmin, M., and Sidney B. Simon. "Values and Teaching: A Humane Process," *Educational Leadership*, 24 (March, 1967), 517+.

Harris, Robin S. *Quiet Evolution: A Study of the Educational System of Ontario*. Toronto: University of Toronto Press, 1967.

Hartman, Robert S. "Value Propositions," *The Language of Value*, ed. Ray Lepley. New York: Columbia University Press, 1967.

Havighurst, Robert J. "Psychological Roots of Moral Development: Discussion," *The Catholic Psychological Record*, 1, No. 1 (1963), 35-44.

————. *Human Development and Education*. New York: David McKay, 1965.

————, and B. L. Neugarten. *Society and Education*. Boston: Allyn and Bacon, Inc., 1958.

Hein, Piet. *Grooks*. Cambridge, Mass.: The M.I.T. Press, 1966.

Herndon, James. *How To Survive in Your Native Land*. New York: Simon and Schuster, 1971.

Hill, Winfred F. *Learning: A Survey of Psychological Interpretations*. Scranton: Chandler Publishing Company, 1971.

————. "Learning Theory and the Acquisition of Values," *Psychological Review*, 67 (1960), 317-31.

Hilliard, A. L. *The Forms of Value*. New York: Columbia University Press, 1950.

Hillman, James. *Insearch: Psychology and Religion*. New York: Charles Scribner's Sons, 1967.

Hiltner, Seward. *Self-Understanding*. New York: Abingdon Press, 1951.

Hora, Thomas. "Ontic Perspectives in Psychoanalysis," *American Journal of Psychoanalysis*, XIX: 2 (1959), 134ff.

Hovda, Robert W., and Gabe Huck. *There's No Place Like People*. Chicago: Argus Communications, 1971.

Jacob, Phillip E., and James J. Flink. "Values and Their Function in Decision-Making," *The American Behavioral Scientist*, 5, No. 9 (May, 1962) (Supplement).

Jacobi, Jolande. *The Psychology of C. G. Jung*. London: Routledge and Kegan Paul, Ltd., 1962.

Jacobson, E., et al. "Communication and Information," *International Social Science Journal*, 14, No. 2 (1962), 251-348.

Jahoda, Marie, and Neil Warren, eds. *Attitudes*. Baltimore: Penguin Books, 1966.

Jarolimek, Jr. "Social Studies Education: The Elementary School; Focus on Values," *Social Education*, 31 (January, 1967), 33-48.

Jeffreys, Montagu V.C. *Personal Values in the Modern World*. Baltimore, Maryland, Penguin Books, 1962.

Jessup, Bertram E. "On Value," *Value: A Cooperative Inquiry*, ed. Ray Lepley. New York: Columbia University 1949, pp. 125-46.

Johnson, Prescott J. "The Axiological Theism of Wilbur Marshall Urban," *Internation Philosophical Quarterly*, 5, No. 3 (1965), 335-60.

———. "The Fact-Value Question in Early Modern Value Theory," *The Journal of Value Inquiry*, 50, No. 1 (1967), 64-70.

———. "What Is Value?" *Monmouth College Faculty Forum*, 1, No. 1 (July, 1963), 7-14.

Johnson, Ronald C. "Early Studies of Children's Moral Judgements," *Child Development*, 33, No. 3 (1962), 603-05.

———. "Study of Children's Moral Judgements," *Child Development*, 33 (June, 1962), 327-54.

Jones, Alfred Winslow. *Life, Liberty, and Property*. Philadelphia: Lippincott, 1941.

Jones, Ernest. *The Life and Work of Sigmund Freud*. New York: Basic Books, Inc., 1961.

Jones, Lyle W., and Charles W. Morris. "Relations of Temperament to the Choice of Values," *Journal of Abnormal and Social Psychology*, 53 (1956), 345-49.

Jones, Richard M. *Fantasy and Feeling in Education*. New York: New York University Press, 1968.

Jourard, Sidney M. *The Transparent Self*. New York: Van Nostrand Reinhold Company, 1971.

Junell, J. S. "Intelligence Without Morality," *Phi Delta Kappan*, 49 (September, 1967), 42.

Jung, C. G. *Analytical Psychology: Its Theory and Practice*. New York: Pantheon Books, 1968.

———. *Memories, Dreams, Reflections*. Edited by Aniela Jaffe. Translated by Richard and Clara Winston. New York: Pantheon Books, 1961.

———. *Modern Man in Search of a Soul*. Translated by W. S. Dell and Cary F. Baynes. New York: Harcourt, Brace and World, Inc., 1933.

———. *Psychology and Religion*. New Haven, Conn.: Yale University Press, 1938.

Kagan, Jerome, ed. *Creativity and Learning*. Boston: Beacon Press, 1967.

Kahl, Joseph A. *The American Class Structure*. New York: Rinehart and Co., Inc., 1957.

Kaiser, Hellmuth. *Effective Psychotherapy*. New York: Free Press, 1965.

Kallen, David J. "Inner Direction, Other Direction, and Social Integration Setting," *Human Relations*, 16, No. 1 (1963), 75-87.

Katz, Martin. *Decisions and Values; A Rationale for Secondary School Guidance*. New York: College Entrance Examination Board, 1963.

Kecskemeti, Paul. *Meaning, Communication and Value*. Chicago: University of Chicago Press, 1952.

Kelsey, Morton T. *Dreams, The Dark Speech of the Spirit*. Garden City: Doubleday, 1968.

Kemp, C. G. "Changes in Patterns of Personal Values," *Religious Education*, 56 (January, 1961), 63-64.

Kew, Clifton. "Psychological Factors Involved in Spiritual Therapy," *Pastoral Counselor*, V: 1 (Spring 1967), 12ff.

Kinnane, John, and Joseph Gaubinger. "Life Values and Work Values," *Journal of Counseling Psychology*, 10, No. 4 (1963), 362-72.

Kintner, William R. "Power and Values in the Nuclear Age," *The Intercollegiate Review*, 2, No. 5 (March-April, 1966), 300-04.

Klevan, Albert. "Clarifying as a Teaching Process," *Educational Leadership*, 25 (February, 1968), 454-57.

Kluckhohn, Clyde. (Title of Article Unknown). *Values in America*, ed. D. Barrett. Notre Dame, Indiana: University of Notre Dame Press, 1961, pages unknown.

———, and O. H. Mowrer. "Culture and Personality: A Conceptual Scheme," *Intellectual Foundations of American Education*, ed. Harold J. Carter. New York: Pitman Publishing Corporation, 1965, pp. 393-412.

———. "Has There Been a Discernible Shift in American Values During the Past Generation?" *The American Style*, ed. E. E. Morrison, New York: Harper and Row, 1958.

———. "Implicit and Explicit Values in the Social Science Related to Human Growth and Development," *Merrill-Palmer Quarterly*, 1 (1955), 131-40.

———, et al. "Value and Value-Orientations in the Theory of Action," *Toward a General Theory of Action*, eds. Talcott Parsons and Edward A. Shills. Cambridge, Massachusetts: Harvard University Press, 1951, pp. 388-433.

Kluckhohn, Florence and Fred L. Strodtbeck. *Variations in Value Orientations*. Evanston, Illinois and Eimsford, New York: Row, Petterson & Co., 1961.

Koffka, K. *Principles of Gestalt Psychology*. New York: Harcourt, Brace & World, 1963.

Kohl, Herbert R. *The Open Classroom*. New York: The New York Review, 1969.

Kohlberg, L. "The Development of Children's Orientations Toward a Moral Order: I. Sequence in the Development of Moral Thought," *Vita Humana*, 6 (1963), 11-33.

———. "The Development of Children's Orientations Toward a Moral Order: II Social Experience, Social Conduct, and the Development of Moral Thought," *Vita Humana*, 9 (1966).

———. "The Development of Modes of Moral Thinking and Choice in the Years Ten to Sixteen," Ph.D. dissertation, University of Chicago, 1958.

———. "Moral Development and Identification," *Child Psychology*, ed. H. W. Stevenson, et. al., Sixty-second Yearbook, Part I, National Society for the Study of Education. Chicago: University of Chicago Press, 1963.

———. "Moral Education in the Schools: A Developmental View," *School Review*, 74, No. 1 (1966), 1-30.

Kohler, Wolfgang. *The Place of Value in a World of Facts*. New York: Liveright Co., 1938.

Kohn, Melvin L. "Social Class and Parental Values,"

Readings in Child Development and Personality, ed. Mussen, *et al.* New York: Harper and Row, 1962, pp. 345-74. Also: *American Journal of Sociology*, 64 (1959), 337-51.

Kozol, Jonathan. *Death at an Early Age*. Boston: Houghton Mifflin Co., 1967.

Kroeber, A. L. *The Nature of Culture*. Chicago: University of Chicago Press, 1952.

Kunkel, Fritz. *Del yo al nosotros*. Barcelona: Editorial Luis Miracle, S. A., 1966.

Kurtz, P. W. "Human Nature, Homeostasis, and Value," *Philosophy and Phenomenological Research*, 17 (1956), 36-55.

Laird, John. *The Idea of Value*. Cambridge: Harvard University Press, 1929.

Lake, Frank. *Clinical Theology*. London: Darton, Longman and Todd, 1966.

Larkin, Oliver. *Art and Life in America*. New York: Holt, Rinehart, and Winston, Inc., 1949.

Lazersfeld, Paul F., and Wagner Thielens. *The Academic Mind*. Glencoe, Illinois: The Free Press of Glencoe, Inc., 1958.

Lecky, Prescott. Self-Consistency. Harndon, Connecticut: Shoe-String Press, 1961.

Lee, Harold N. "The Meaning of 'Intrinsic Value.'" *The Language of Value*, ed. Ray Lepley. New York: Columbia University Press, 1957, pp. 178-96.

―――. "Methodology of Value Theory," *Value: A Cooperative Inquiry*, ed. Ray Lepley. New York: Columbia University Press, 1957, pp. 178-96.

Lepley, Ray. "The Dawn of Value Theory," *Journal of Philosophy*, 34 (July 8, 1937), 365-73.

―――, ed. *The Language of Value*. New York: Columbia University Press, 1957.

―――, ed. *Value: A Cooperative Inquiry*. New York: Columbia University Press, 1949.

Lessor, L. Richard. *Love and Marriage and Trading Stamps*. Chicago: Argus Communications, 1971.

Levy, Jerome. *Modified Study of Values*. Boston: Houghton-Mifflin Company, 1958.

Lewis, C. I. *An Analysis of Knowledge and Valuation*. LaSalle, Illinois: The Open Court Publishing Co., 1946.

Link, Mark, S. J. *He Is the Still Point of the Turning World*. Chicago: Argus Communications, 1971.

Lins, L. J. *Basis for Decision*. Madison, Wisconsin: Dembar Education, 42 (September, 1947), 284-90.

Little, Lawrence C. *Toward Better Education in Moral and Spiritual Values*. Pittsburgh, Pennsylvania: Department of Religious Education, University of Pittsburgh, 1953.

Lowe, Marshall. "Value Orientation—and Ethical Dilemma," *American Psychologist* 14 (1959), 687-93. Also in *Human Values and Abnormal Behavior*, ed. Walter D. Nunakava. Chicago: Scott Foresman and Co., 1965, pp. 2-9.

Luthe, Wolfgang, M.D., ed. *Autogenic Training*. International ed. New York: Grune and Stratton, 1965.

Lynd; Robert S. *Education for What?* Princeton: Princeton University Press, 1939.

McDowell, Ruth, ed. *So You're Having an Adolescent*. Chicago: Peacock Books, 1970.

McGiffert, R. *The Character of Americans*. Homewood, Illinois: Dorsey, 1964.

McLuhan, Marshall. *The Gutenberg Galaxy: The Making of Typographic Man*. New York: New American Library, Inc., 1962.

―――. *Verbi-Voco-Visual Explorations*. New York: Something Else Press, Inc., 1967.

Mace, David and Vera. *Marriage East and West*. Garden City, New York: Dolphin Books, 1959.

Madden, Ward E. *Religious Values in Education*. New York: Harpers, 1951.

Margolin, E. "Do We Really Prize Creativity?" *Elementary School Journal*, 64 (December, 1963), 177-21.

Marcuse, Herbert. *One-Dimensional Man*. Boston: Beacon Press, 1964.

Maslow, Abraham H. "Higher and Lower Needs," *Journal of Psychology*, 25 (1948), 443-36.

―――. "Higher Needs and Personality," *Dialectica*, 5 (1951), 257-65.

―――. *Motivation and Personality*. New York: Harper and Brothers, 1954.

―――, ed. *New Knowledge in Human Values*. New York: Harper and Row, 1954.

―――, and Bela Mittleman. *Principles of Abnormal Psychology*. New York: Harper and Brothers, 1941.

―――. "Psychological Data and Value Theory," *New Knowledge in Human Values*, ed. Abraham H. Maslow. New York: Harper and Row, 1959, pp. 119-36.

Mason, Aopheus T., and Richard H. Leach. *In Quest of Freedom: American Political Thought and Practice*. Englewood Cliffs, New Jersey, 1959.

Mason, Robert E. *Moral Values and Secular Education*. New York: Columbia University Press, 1950.

Masters, William H., M.D., and Virginia E. Johnson. *Human Sexual Response*. Boston: Little, Brown and Company, 1966.

May, Rollo. *Love and Will*. New York: W. W. Norton and Company, Inc., 1969.

―――, *The Meaning of Anxiety*. New York: The Ronald Press Co. 1950.

―――, Ernest Angel and Henri F. Ellenberger. *Existence*. New York: Simon and Schuster, 1967.

Menninger, Karl, M.D. *The Vital Balance*. New York: Viking Press, 1963.

Metraux, R. "Values in Education and Teaching," *Education and Culture*, ed. G. D. Spindler. New York: Holt, Rinehart, and Winston, 1963, pp. 121-31.

Metz, Johannes Baptist. *Poverty of Spirit*. Translated by John Drury. Glen Rock, N.J.: Newman Press, 1968.

Mielke, Keith W. "Evaluation of Television as a Function of Self-Beliefs," *Dissertation Abstracts*, 26, No. 2 (1966), 4105.

Miller, C. H. "Occupational Choice and Values," *Journal of Colorado and Wyoming Academy of Science*, 4 (1956), 55. (Abstract)

Miller, Randolph Crump. *Education for Christian Living*. Englewood Cliffs, N.J.: Prentice-Hall, Inc., 1956.

Mitchell, E. T. "Values, Valuing, and Evaluation," *Value: A Cooperative Inquiry*, ed. Ray Lepley. New York: Columbia University Press, 1949, pp. 190-210.

Moore, G. E. *Principia Ethica*. Cambridge: At the University Press, 1903.

―――. *Philosophical Studies*. London: Kegan Paul,

Trench, Trubner and Co., Ltd., 1922.

Morris, Charles W. "Axiology as the Science of Preferential Behavior," *Value: A Cooperative Inquiry*, ed. Ray Lepley, New York: Columbia University Press, 1949, pp. 211-22.

―――. *Varieties of Human Value*. Chicago: University of Chicago Press, 1956.

Moore, Willis. "The Language of Values," *The Language of Value*, ed. Ray Lepley. New York: Columbia University Press, 1957, pp. 9-28.

―――. "The Teaching of Values," *Educational Record* 28 (October, 1949), 412-19.

Morris, Van Cleve. *Existentialism in Education*. New York: Harper and Row, 1966.

Montessori, Maria. *Dr. Montessori's Own Handbook*. New York: Schockon Books, 1965.

Moustakas, Clarke E. "Moral and Ethical Value," *Collected Papers of the Inter-Institutional Seminar in Child Development*, 1964, Dearborn, Michigan: Henry Ford Museum, 1965.

―――. *The Self*. New York: Harper and Row, 1956.

Mowrer, O. H. *Learning Theory and Personality Dynamics*. New York: Ronald Press, 1950.

Mowry, I. J. "Teaching Values Through Today's News," *Instructor*, 77 (March, 1968), 62+.

Munroe, Ruth L. *Schools of Psychoanalytic Thought*. New York: Holt, Rinehart and Winston, 1955.

Murray, H. A. and Clyde Kluckhohn, *Personality in Nature, Society and Culture*, second ed. Henry Murray & Clyde Kluckhohn, eds. New York: Alfred Knopf, 1953.

Munsterberg, Hugo. *The Eternal Values*. Boston: Houghton Mifflin Co., 1909.

Mussen, Paul Henry, John Janewar Conger, and Jerome Kagan. *Child Development and Personality*. New York: Harper and Row, 1963.

Niebuhr, H. Richard. *Christ and Culture*. New York: Harper and Brothers Publishers, 1951.

Norton, William J., Jr. "Towards a Value Theory of Mind," *Philosophy of Science*, 8 (1941), 255-63.

Nowell-Smith, P. H. *Ethics*. Baltimore: Penguin Books, Inc., 1954.

Nunokawa, Walter D. *Readings in Abnormal Psychology: Human Values and Abnormal Behavior*. Chicago: Scott, Foresman and Co., 1965.

Oates, W. J. *Aristotle and the Problem of Value*. Princeton: Princeton University Press, 1963.

Oden, Thomas C. *Contemporary Theology and Psychotherapy*. Philadelphia: The Westminster Press, 1967.

Osborne, H. *Foundations of the Philosophy of Value*. Cambridge: At the University Press, 1933.

Osgood, C. E. "The Nature and Measurement of Meaning," *Psychological Bulletin*, 49 (1952), 197-237.

Otto, Herbert A., and John Mann. *Ways of Growth*. New York: Pocket Books, 1971.

Otto, M. C. *Things and Ideals*. New York: Henry Holt and Co., 1924.

Paschal, B. J. "Values as Basic in Education," *School and Society*, 96 (February 3, 1968), 77-78.

Parker, Dewitt H. *The Philosophy of Value*. Ann Arbor, Michigan: University of Michigan Press, 1957.

Patka, Frederick. *Value and Existence*. New York: Philosophical Library, 1964.

Patterson, C. H. "The Place of Values in Counseling and Psychotherapy," *Human Values and Abnormal Behavior*, ed. Walter P. Nunokawa. Chicago: Scott, Foresman, and Co., 1965, pp. 94-101.

Peake, Mervyn. *Gormenghast*. New York: Ballantine Books, 1967.

―――. *Titus Alone*. New York: Ballantine Books, 1967.

―――. *Titus Groan*. New York: Ballantine Books, 1967.

Peck, Robert F., and Robert J. Havighurst. *The Psychology of Character Development*. New York: John Wiley, 1960.

Pepper, Stephen C. *A Digest of Purposive Values*. Berkeley: University of California Press, 1947.

―――. *The Sources of Values*. Berkeley: University of California Press, 1958.

Perry, Ralph Barton. *A General Theory of Value*. Cambridge, Massachusetts: Harvard University Press, 1926.

―――. *Realms of Value*. Cambridge, Massachusetts: Harvard University Press, 1954.

Persons, Stow. *American Minds*. New York: Holt, Rinehart and Winston, 1958.

Phillips, John L., Jr. *The Origins of Intellect: Piaget's Theory*. San Francisco: W. H. Freeman and Company, 1969.

Piaget, Jean. *The Moral Judgement of the Child*. New York: The Free Press, 1966.

―――. "Will and Action (Values and Will)," *Bulletin of Menninger Clinic*, 26, No. 3 (1962), 138-45.

Postman, Neil, and Charles Weingartner. *Teaching as a Subversive Activity*. New York: Delacorte Press, 1969.

Pound, Roscoe. *Law and Morals*, 2nd ed. Chapel Hill: University of North Carolina Press, 1923.

Prall, D. W. *A Study in the Theory of Value*. Berkeley: University of California Press, 1921.

Preston, Charles Franklin. "The Development of Moral Judgement in Young People," *Dissertation Abstracts*, 27, No. 4 (1964), 3001-2.

Prior, A. N. *Logic and the Basis of Ethics*. Oxford: The Claredon Press, 1949.

Progoff, Ira. *The Symbolic and The Real*. New York: Julian Press, Inc., 1963.

Rainwater, Lee, Richard P. Coleman, and Gerald Handel. *Workingman's Wife: Her Personality, World and Life Style*. New York: Oceana Publications, Inc., 1959.

Raths, J. "Clarifying Children's Values," *National Elementary Principal*, 42 (November, 1962), 35-39.

―――. "Values and Valuing," *Educational Leadership*, 21 (May, 1964), 543-46.

Raths, Louis. "Appraising Changes in Values of College Students," *Journal of Educational Research*, 35 (1941-42), 557-64.

―――. "Approaches to the Measurement of Values," *Educational Research Bulletin*, 19 (1940), 275-82.

―――, *et al.* "Helping Children To Clarify Values," *N.E.A. Journal*, 56 (October, 1967), 12-15.

———. "Values Are Fundamental," *Childhood Education* 35 (February, 1959), 246-47.

———, Merrill Harmin, and Sidney B. Simon. *Values and Teaching: Working with Values in the Classroom.* Columbus, Ohio: E. E. Merrill Books, 1966.

Rasmussen, Margaret, ed. *Implications of Basic Human Values for Education.* Washington, D.C.: Association for Childhood Education International, 1964.

Rasmussen, G., and A. Zander. "Group Membership and Self-Evaluation," *Human Relations*, 7 (1954), 239-51.

Report to the President: White House Conference on Children, 1970. Washington, D.C.: Government Printing Office, 1971. "Crisis in Values: Report of Forum 3," 61-72.

Rettig, S., and B. Rasamanick. "Moral Value Structure and Social Class," *Sociometry*, 24 (1961), 21-35.

Robinson, Edward Schouten. "The Languages of Sign Theory and Value Theory," *The Language of Value*, ed. Ray Lepley, New York: Columbia University Press, 1957, pp. 29-57.

Rodman, Hyman. "The Lower Class Value Stretch," *Social Forces*, 42, No. 2 (December, 1963), 205-15.

Rogers, Carl R. *On Becoming A Person.* Boston: Houghton Mifflin Company, 1961.

Rogers, Carl R. "Toward a Modern Approach to Values: The Valuing Process in the Mature Person," *Journal of Abnormal and Social Psychology*, 68, No. 2 (1964), 160-67.

———, and B. F. Skinner. "Some Issues Concerning the Control of Human Behavior," *Science*, 124, Part II, No. 3231 (1956), 1057-66.

Rokeach, Milton. *The Open and Closed Mind.* New York: Basic Books, Inc., 1960.

Romero, Fred E. "Anglo and Spanish American Culture Value Concepts and Their Significance in Secondary Education," *Dissertation Abstracts*, 27, No. 6-A (1966), 1559-60.

Romine, S. "Education Is a Value Process," *Phi Delta Kappan*, 31 (November, 1949), 153-54.

Rood, Wayne R. *Understanding Christian Education.* Nashville, Tenn.: Abingdon Press, 1970.

Rosen, Bernard C. "Family Structure and Value Transmission," *Merrill-Palmer Quarterly*, 10, No. 1 (1964), 59-76.

Rosenberg, M. J. *Occupations and Values.* Glencoe, Illinois: The Free Press, 1957.

Rosenthal, David. "Changes in Some Moral Values Following Psychotherapy," *Journal of Consulting Psychology*, 19 (1955), 431-36.

———. "The Selection of Stimulus Words for Value: Duration Threshold Experiments," *Journal of Abnormal and Social Psychology*, 50 (1955), 403-04.

Ross, Sir David. "The Nature of Goodness," *Readings in Ethical Theory*, Wilfred Sellars and John Hospers, eds. New York: Appleton-Century-Crofts, Inc., 1952, 310-31.

Ross, W. D. *The Right and the Good.* Oxford: The Claredon Press, 1939.

Roszak, Theodore. *The Making of a Counter Culture.* Garden City, N.Y.: Archer Books, 1969.

Rowland, M. K. and P. Del Campo. "Values of the Educationally Disadvantaged: How Different Are They?" *Journal of Negro Education*, 27 (1936), 292-98.

Rubins, Jack L. "Notes on the Organization of the Self," *American Journal of Psychoanalysis*, XVIII: 2 (1958), 171.

Rundell, W., Jr. "Communication of Values in Teaching History," *Social Studies*, 54 (December, 1963), 243-47.

Russell, B. *Religion and Science.* New York: Oxford University Press, 1935.

Sanders, Ed. *The Family: The Story of Charles Manson's Dune Buggy Attack Battalion.* New York: E. P. Dutton and Company, Inc., 1971.

Sanford, John A. *Dreams, God's Forgotten Language.* New York: Lippincott, 1968.

———. *The Kingdom Within.* Philadelphia: J. B. Lippincott Company, 1970.

Sanford, Nevitt. *The American College.* New York: John Wiley and Sons, Inc., 1962.

Santayana, George. *The Life of Reason: Reason in Common Sense.* New York: Charles Scribner's Sons, 1905.

Schleirmacher, Friedrich. *On Religion.* Translated by John Oman. New York: Harper and Brothers, 1958.

Schlesser, George F. *Personal Values Inventory.* Colgate University, 1952.

Schlick, Moritz. *Problems of Ethics.* trans. David Rynin. New York: Prentice-Hall, Inc., 1939.

Schneiderman, L. "Value Orientation Preferences of Chronic Relief Recipients," *Journal of Social Work*, 9, No. 3 (1964), 13-19.

Schrickel, H. G. "On the Objectivity of Aesthetic Values," *Psychological Review*, 50 (1943), 622-31.

Schultz, William C. *Joy: Expanding Human Awareness.* New York: Grove Press, 1967.

———. *Firo. A Three Dimensional Theory of Inter-Personal Behavior.* New York: Rinehart, 1958.

Schultz, Johannes H., and Wolfgang Luthe. *Autogenic Training: A Psychological Approach to Psychotherapy.* New York: Gruen and Stratton, 1959.

Schwartzberg, Herbert, and Sheldon Stoff. *The Human Encounter: Readings in Education.* New York: Harper and Row, 1969.

Schwarzweller, H. K. "Values and Occupational Choice," *Social Forces:* 30 (1960), 126-35.

Scott, William A. "Empirical Assessment of Values and Ideologies," *American Sociological Review*, 24, No. 3 (June, 1959), 299-310.

Scroggs, Schiller. "Problem of Value in the Age of Science," *Association of American Colleges Bulletin*, 35 (December, 1949), 519-27.

Sears, R. R., E. E. Macohy, and H. Levin. *Patterns of Child Rearing.* Evanston: Row, Peterson and Co., 1957.

Sellars, Wilfred S., and John Hospers. *Readings in Ethical Theory.* New York: Appleton-Century-Crofts, 1952.

Seward, Georgene H. "Learning Theory and Identification V: Some Cultural Aspects of Identification," *Journal of Genetic Psychology*, 84, (1954), 229-36.

Shane, Harold G. "Educational Values as Guides to Planning with Children," *Childhood Education*, 31 (October, 1964), 56-60.

Shaver, James P. "Reflective Thinking Values, and Social Studies Textbooks," *School Review*, 73, No. 3 (Autumn, 1965), 226-57.

Sherif, Carolyn W., Muzafer Sherif, and Roger E. Nebergall. *Attitude and Attitude Change*. Philadelphia: W. B. Saunders Co., 1965.

Sherif, M., and Carl I. Hovland. *Social Judgement: Assimilation and Contrast Effects in Communication and Attitude Change*. New Haven, Connecticut: Yale University Press, 1961.

Shoben, E. J., Jr. "Moral Behavior and Moral Learning," *Religious Education*, 58 (March, 1963), 137-54.

Shostrom, Everett L. *Man, the Manipulator*. Nashville, Tenn.: Abingdon Press, 1967.

Shubin, John A. *Business Management*. New York: Barnes and Noble, Inc., 1954.

Shuster, W. "Values of Negro and Caucasian Children: Do They Differ?" *Journal of Negro Education*, 37 (Winter, 1968), 90-93.

Simon, Sidney B. "To Study Controversial Issues Is Not Enough," *The Social Studies*, 45, No. 5 (October, 1964), 163-66.

———. "The Subject Matter Controversy Revisited," *Peabody Journal of Education*, 42, No. 4 (January, 1965), 193-205.

———. "Value Development: A High Sense of Individualization," *42nd Yearbook of the Association for Student Teaching* (1963), pp. 111-25.

———. "Values and Student Writing," *Educational Leadership*, 22, No. 6 (March, 1965), 414-21.

———. "Current Events and Values," *Social Education*, 24 No. 8 (December, 1965), 532-33.

Skinner, B. F. *Beyond Freedom and Dignity*. New York: Alfred A. Knopf, 1971.

Smith, H. P. "Do Intercultural Experiences Affect Attitudes?" *Journal of Abnormal and Social Psychology*, 51 (1955), 469-77.

Smith, John E. *Value Convictions and Higher Education*. New Haven, Connecticut: The Edward W. Hazen Foundation, 1958.

Smith, M. Brewster. "Conflicting Values Affecting Behavioral Research with Children," *Children*, 14 (March, 1967), 53-58.

———. "Personal Values as Determinants of Political Attitude, *Journal of Psychology*, 28 (1949), 477-86.

———. "Toward Scientific and Professional Responsibility," *American Psychologist*, 9 (1954), 513-16.

Smith, Nicholas M., Jr. "A Calculus for Ethics: A Theory of the Structure of Value, Part I," *Behavioral Science*, (1956), 111-42.

———. "A Calculus for Ethics: A Theory of the Structure of Value, Part II," *Behavioral Science*, (1956), 186-211.

Snygg, Donald. "The Place of Psychology in the Development of Values," *American Psychologist*, 4 (1949), 212.

———. "The Psychological Basis of Human Values," *Goals of Economic Life*, ed. A. Dudley Ward. New York: Harper and Brothers, 1953, 335-64.

Solomon, Lawrence N., ed. "A Symposium on Human Values," *Journal of Humanistic Psychology*, 2, No. 2 (1962), 89-111.

Sorenson, Roy and Hedley S. Dimock. *Designing Education in Values*. New York: Association Press, 1955.

Sotela, Alfredo Alfaro. *Conceptos Sobre Las Neurosis*. London: Carnauba, 1957.

Spaulding, Irving A. "Of Human Values," *Sociology and Social Research*, 47, No. 2 (1963), 169-78.

Spindler, George D. "Education in a Transforming American Culture," *Intellectual Foundations of American Education*, ed. Harold J. Carter. New York: Pitman Publishing Corp. (1965), 354-62.

Spranger, Edward. *Psychologie des Jugendalters. Achtzehnte auflage*. Leipzig: Quelle and Meyer, 1945.

———. *Types of Men*. trans. Paul J. V. Pigors. Halla (Salle): Max Niemeyer, 1928.

———, *et al. Padagogische Wahreheiten und Halbwahrheitan*. Heidelberg: Quelle und Meyer, 1959.

Stahmer, Harold. "Religion and Moral Values in the Public Schools," *Religious Education*, 61 (January, 1966), 20-26.

Stanley, J. C. "Insight into One's Own Values," *Journal of Educational Psychology*, 42 (1951), 399-408.

Stevenson, Charles L. *Ethics and Language*. New Haven: Yale University Press, 1944.

———, I. Morris, and Benjamin Bloom. *Methods in Personality Assessment*. Glencoe, Illinois: The Free Press, 1956.

Strodtbeck, Fred. "Family Interaction, Values, and Achievement," *Talent and Society*, eds. D. D. McClelland, *et al*. Princeton, New Jersey: Van Nostrand, 1958.

Sullivan, Harry Stack, M.D. *The Interpersonal Theory of Psychiatry*. New York: W. W. Norton and Company, Inc., 1953.

———. *The Psychiatric Interview*. New York: W. W. Norton and Company, Inc., 1954.

Summerhill: For and Against. New York: Hart Publishing Company, Inc., 1970.

Suzuke, D. T., Erich Fromm and Richard De Martino. *Zen Buddhism and Psychoanalysis*. New York: Harper & Brothers, 1960.

Takahashi, Seiki, and Yuji Naito. "Aspects of Value Formation in Primary and Secondary School Children: On the Period They Hope To Be Living in Their Lifetime," *Psychologia: An International Journal of Psychology in the Orient*, 7, No. 3-4 (1964), 185-91.

Taylor, John F. A., ed. *An Introduction to Literature and the Fine Arts*. East Lansing, Michigan: Michigan State University Press, 1950.

———. "Politics and the Human Covenant," *Centennial Review of Arts and Science*, 6, No. 1 (Winter, 1962), 1-18.

———. "The University and the Moral Frontier," *Educational Forum*, 4 (May, 1962), 417-25.

Taylor, Graham C., and Martha Crampton, *Approaches to the Self. The "Who Am I?" Techniques in Psycho-Therapy*. New York Psychosynthesis Foundation, 1968.

Thieliche, Helmut. *The Ethics of Sex*. New York: Harper and Row, 1964.

Thomas, Walter L. *A Comprehensive Bibliography on Personal Values*. Spring Arbor, Michigan: Educational Service Co., 1965.

Thompson, W. R., and R. Nishimera. "Some Determinants of Friendship," *Journal of Social Sociology*, 21 (1927), 384-400.

Thurber, James. *My World, And Welcome to It.* New York: Harcourt Brace and World, Inc., 1965.

————. *The Thurber Carnival.* New York: Dell Publishing Company, Inc., 1964.

Thurian, Max. *Confession.* Translated by Edwin Hudson. London: SCM Press, Ltd., 1958.

Tiryakian, Edward A., ed. *Sociological Theory, Values, and Socio-Cultural Change.* Glencoe, Illinois: The Free Press, 1963.

Titiev, Mischa. "Cultural Adjustment and the Interiorization of Social Values," *Journal of Social Issues*, 5, No. 4 (1949), 44-46.

Tolkein, J. R. R. R. *The Hobbit.* New York: Ballantine Books, 1937.

————. *The Tolkein Reader.* New York: Ballantine Books, 1966.

Trow, William Clark. "A Valuistic Approach to Religious Education," *Religious Education*, 43 (May, 1948), 169-74.

Ullman, Albert D. *Sociocultural Foundations of Personality.* Boston, Houghton Mifflin, 1965.

Underhill, Evelyn. *Mysticism: A Study in the Nature and Development of Man's Spiritual Consciousness.* New York: Meridian Books, 1955.

Urban, Wilbur M. *The Intelligible World.* New York: The Macmillan Co., 1929.

————. *Valuation: Its Nature and Laws.* London: S. Sonnenschein and Co., Ltd., 1909.

————. "Value, Theory of," Encyclopaedia Britannica, Vol. XXII (1957), 962-64.

Veblen, Thorstein. *The Theory of the Leisure Class.* New York: A Mentor Book, 1953.

Vernon, Philip E. and Gordon W. Allport. "A Test for Personal Values," *Journal of Abnormal and Social Psychology*, 26 (1931), 231-48.

Vivas, Eliseo. *The Moral Life and the Ethical Life.* Chicago: The University of Chicago Press, 1950.

Von Mering, Otto. *A Grammar of Human Values.* Pittsburgh: University of Pittsburgh Press, 1961.

Wallace, Anthony F. C. *Culture and Personality.* New York: Random House, 1961.

Warner, W. Lloyd. *American Life.* Chicago: University of Chicago Press, 1953.

————, and Associates. *Democracy in Jonesville.* New York: Harper and Brothers, 1949.

————, and Paul S. Lunt. *The Social Life of a Modern Community.* New Haven, Connecticut: Yale University Press, 1941.

————, Marcia Meeker, and Kenneth Ells. *Social Class in America.* Chicago: Science Research Associates, 1949.

Werner, Wolff. *Values and Personality.* New York: Grune and Stratton, 1950.

White, Ralph K. "Hitler, Roosevelt, and the Nature of War Propaganda," *Journal of Abnormal and Social Psychology*, 44 (1949), 157-74.

————. "Value Analysis: A Quantitative Method for Describing Qualitative Data," *Journal of Social Psychology*, 19 (May, 1944), 351-58.

Whitley, Paul L. "The Constancy of Personal Values," *Journal of Abnormal and Social Psychology*, 33 (1938), 405-08.

Whittaker, J. E. "The Psychology of Value," *British Journal of Statistical Psychology*, 16, No. 1 (1963), 47-50.

Wickes, Frances G. *The Inner World of Choice.* New York: Harper and Row, 1963.

William, Robin M., Jr. *American Society.* New York: Alfred A. Knopf, 1960.

————. "Religion, Value Orientations and Intergroup Conflict," *Journal of Social Issues*, 12 (1956), 12-20.

Williams, E. D. "The Psychology of Value," *British Journal of Statistical Psychology*, 16, No. 1 (1963), 53-58.

Willis, C. L. "Public Education and the Dilemma of Responsibility," *Peabody Journal of Education* 44 (May, 1967), 347-49.

Willner, Dorothy, ed. *Decisions, Value and Groups,* Vol. 1. New York: Pergamon, 1960.

Wilson, S. Dunham, and W. Earl Biddle. "Sub-Rational Obstacles to Effective Pastoral Counseling," *Pastoral Psychology*, XVIII: 178 (November 1967), 22-30.

Winthrop, Henry. "Some Neglected Considerations Concerning the Problem of Value in Psychology," *Journal of Genetic Psychology*, 64 (1961), 37-59.

Wolff, Werner. *Values in Personality Research.* New York: Grune & Stratton, Inc., 1950.

Wolpe, Joseph, Andrew Salter, and L. J. Reyna, eds. *The Conditioning Theories.* New York: Holt, Rinehart and Winston, Inc., 1964.

Woodruff, Asahel D. "The Concept-Value Theory of Human Behavior," *Journal of General Psychology*, 40 (1949), 144-54.

————. "Personal Values and the Direction of Behavior," *School Review*, 50 (January, 1942), 32-42.

————. "Personal Values and Religious Backgrounds," *Journal of Social Psychology*, 22 (1945), 141-47.

————. *Psychology of Teaching.* New York: Longmans, Green and Co., 1951.

————. "The Relationship Between Functional and Verbalized Motives," *Journal of Educational Psychology*, 35 (1944), 101-7.

————. "The Roles of Value in Human Behavior," *Journal of Social Psychology*, 36 (1952), 97-107.

————. "Students' Verbalized Values," *Religious Education* 38; (1943), 645-59.

————, and Francis J. Divesta. "The Relationship Between Values, Concepts and Attitudes," *Educational Psychology Measurement*, 8 (1948), 645-59.

Woods, Frances Jerome. *Cultural Values of American Ethnic Groups.* New York: Harper and Brothers, 1956.

Woods, Richard. *The Media Maze.* Dayton, Ohio: George A. Pflaum, 1969.

————. *The Occult Revolution.* New York: Herder and Herder, 1971.

Worchel, Philip and Donn Byrne, eds. *Personality Change.* New York: John Wiley and Sons, Inc., 1964.

Worsnop, Chris M. *What Do You Think?* Toronto: Copp Clark Company, 1969.

Wyckoff, D. Campbell. *Theory and Design of Christian Education Curriculum.* Philadelphia: The Westminster Press, 1961.

Annotated Bibliography

(Books worth special consideration)

Flynn, Elizabeth W., and John F. LaFaso. *Group Discussion as Learning Process.* New York: Paulist Press, 1972. Combines solid theory and practical application to give assistance to those interested in improving and expanding their abilities for participating in or leading group discussions.

Freire, Paulo. *Pedagogy of the Oppressed.* Translated by Myra Bergman Ramos. New York: Herder and Herder, 1968. Illich calls this work "truly revolutionary" and the ideas in it helped gain the author an "invitation" to leave Brazil, his homeland. The work is a strident statement that everyone, no matter how "illiterate" or "ignorant," is capable of much more than a cursory comment of his world.

Krathwohl, David R., Benjamin S. Bloom, and Vertram B. Masia. *Taxonomy of Educational Objectives; The Classification of Educational Goals.* New York: David McKay Company, Inc., 1964. Definitely not for the casual reader. The work offers a highly technical discussion of values and education.

McLuhan, Marshall. *Understanding Media: The Extensions of Man.* New York: McGraw-Hill Book Company, 1964. Where our eyes and minds have been since Gutenberg and movable type right up to mind-boggling, super-giant-size color television. The medium is the message and it is hot, cold, and even lukewarm. Most of all, it is communications and the effects of communications on the world.

Nash, Paul. *Authority and Freedom in Education: An Introduction of the Philosophy of Education.* New York: John Wiley and Sons, 1966. An introduction designed to show how the theme or problem of authority and freedom in education can be approached through the use of practical dialectic. It has an excellent treatment of work and leisure in education.

Oden, Thomas C. *The Structure of Awareness.* Nashville, Tenn.: Abingdon Press, 1969. Certainly not for those who have "dropped out" of society; more for those seeking deeper awareness, hungering for a more intimate taste of human existence. A "celebration of now." It is a basic book in values.

Parsons, Talcott, and Robert F. Bales. *Family, Socialization and Interaction Process.* New York: The Free Press, 1955. A worthwhile collection of papers discussing the role of differentiation and the functioning of the family and its place in the structure of society.

Pieper, Josef. *Leisure and the Basis of Culture.* Translated by Alexander Dru. New York: Pantheon Books, Inc., 1952. The title almost says it all, but a reading of the stuff between the covers opens to view a reaffirming of the importance of leisure and its value relationship to culture.

Proshansky, Harold M., William H. Ittelson, and Leanne G. Rivlin, eds. *Environmental Psychology: Man and His Physical Setting.* New York: Holt, Rinehart and Winston, Inc., 1970. A thorough presentation of the concepts, approaches, findings, and methodological issues that characterize the still-to-be-defined field of environmental psychology.

Raths, Louis E., Merrill Harmin, and Sidney B. Simon. *Values and Teaching: Working with Values in the Classroom.* Columbus, Ohio: Charles E. Merrill Publishing Company, 1966. Value theory and the teaching strategies associated with it are presented in this book, as well as an outline of a theory of values and a methodology for the clarification of values. It is a classic in values that everyone interested in the subject should have read.

Rogers, Carl E. *Freedom to Learn.* Columbus, Ohio: Charles E. Merrill Publishing Company, 1969. This is for educators and it is, appropriately enough about learning —LEARNING—insatiable curiosity, discovering, drawing in from the outside; not "the lifeless, sterile, futile, quickly forgotten" charade which has been passed off as education for too many years.

Silberman, Charles E. *Crisis in the Classroom: The Remaking of American Education.* New York: Random House, 1970. Not only does the author show that the school systems of contemporary society are a bust, he shows what to do to go about making them halls of learning. Guaranteed to enrage administrators and be disdained by teachers, but unlike some of their own inadequacies, it can't be swept under the rug or sent to the principal's office.

General Index